*Exciting Times in
the Accounts Department*

PAUL VAUGHAN

Exciting Times in the Accounts Department

SINCLAIR-STEVENSON

First published in Great Britain in 1995
by Sinclair-Stevenson
an imprint of Reed Books Ltd
Michelin House, 81 Fulham Road, London SW3 6RB
and Auckland, Melbourne, Singapore and Toronto

A CIP catalogue record for this book
is available at the British Library
ISBN 1 85619 526 0

Typset by Falcon, Wallington
Printed and bound in Great Britain
by Clays Ltd., St Ives plc

D.E.D.
1922–1994
In affectionate memory

See how the Past rustles
Stirring to life again.

Richard Hughes

Contents

Prologue

REACHING A CERTAIN age leaves you no choice but to look back. The past can become a more inviting prospect than the future: for one thing, there's more of it.

For me, time has become foreshortened. I can understand why some old people I have known have given the impression of wanting the clock to move more quickly as they contemplate the end – bringing forward the hour of the next meal and going to bed absurdly early in order to be ready for the next day. You can become preoccupied with time, in apparently pointless and random ways. Frequently I have found myself performing calculations solely to illustrate the brevity of the human time-scale. Fifty years ago I was a soldier – of no merit whatever – in the war against Hitler, and those fifty years seem to have gone at incredible speed: children have been born, grown up, gone to make their livings. The war seems only a short time ago to me. But fifty years before *I* was born, Elgar was the age I was in 1944; the American West was still wild; and there must have been people living who had fought at Waterloo. A man who, in the year of my birth, was the age that I have now reached could have known other men who'd met Beethoven, Schubert, Weber and Berlioz.

And then I wonder too about coincidences and their apparent randomness in one's life: do they really happen at random?

1

their echoes can sound across the generations. Why? Whose fault is it?

A contemporary American novelist* has written, 'We have to resurrect the past constantly, erect monuments to it, and keep it alive in order to remember who we are.' When I wrote about my childhood and upbringing in suburban London, in an earlier book, it was partly in order to identify the patterns that have recurred in my life and in my parents' life – and indeed in the lives of earlier generations of my family.

I hope the book that follows will complete that process of exploration, and erect another monument, however small, to times and places and people whose lives have touched mine.

* James Lee Burke: *The Neon Rain*

One

Menley, James, and Mother Siegel

IT WAS 1950, AND in those days there was a train at thirty-two minutes after eight on weekday mornings, travelling all the way from Wimbledon to Holborn Viaduct, carrying up to the front line yet another force of office workers, who read their newspapers or went to sleep, or gazed from the windows and let the south London landscape play upon their thoughts.

The train was never very full: sometimes you had a compartment all to yourself. The carriages were shabby, ready for replacement. The rail system had not long been nationalised: there was a new organisation called British Railways, which had only just been invented and couldn't afford costly refurbishments or new stock. The separate compartments had pre-war, sepia-tinted photographs of Surrey landmarks screwed to the wall under luggage racks made of string netting; there were leather straps on the doors and you used these to hoist up the windows, impaling them on a brass stud to hold them fast. Only one or two compartments were labelled No Smoking, but in each carriage there was one with a green sticker on the window that said Ladies Only.

The train had its regulars, usually in the same place every day. In one carriage there would be four men, always in exactly the same seats in their sober business suits, and they would spread a cloth over their knees for a daily game of whist, which I suppose they played all the way to the City. If you had to get out on their side, they would frown and sigh and raise their eyes to heaven as they lifted their improvised card-table to let you pass.

My stop was Loughborough Junction. In 1950, the year I began to make this regular daily journey, it had won the Best-Kept Station Competition and there was a framed certificate to that effect displayed on the platform.

Loughborough wasn't a large station: just a single platform on the down side of a bridge over Coldharbour Lane. Downstairs, when you were on the way home, a middle-aged woman in a hat and spectacles with thick lenses sat in the entrance hall and sold the *Star*, *Evening News*, or *Standard*, and to regular customers she always said the same thing as she took your tuppence and handed over your newspaper: ' 'Ere y'are, straight orf the ice.'

Outside, there was a small shopping parade, including a sweet shop. On the too frequent mornings when I'd missed the 8.32 and ran – breakfastless – from our flat for the next train, the eight forty-something, I would sometimes dash in there on the way to the office and buy a bag of toffees or a bar of chocolate. On one of those occasions it was the day sweets had come off the ration. I told the shopkeeper, a plump and superior man, I wanted something to make up for having had nothing to eat that morning. He replied, 'You are now in the fortunate position of being able to equalise your lack of nutriment.' Impressed by this answer, I wrote it down when shortly afterwards I arrived, twenty minutes late, at my desk.

My destination was a hangar-like building further along Cold-harbour Lane, housing the offices of Menley & James Ltd, Pharmaceutical Chemists. A few decades earlier it had been the headquarters of the Edwardian theatre impresario Fred Karno. A tattered photograph reproduced in Charles Chaplin's *My Life in Pictures* shows five of Karno's companies, of which there were more than thirty, setting out simultaneously on tour from outside the building in the year 1907. It's a pity the building itself isn't vis-ible – the photographer was on the wrong side of the street looking at the packed omnibuses and the throng of onlookers on the other side of Coldharbour Lane, outside the solid mid-Victorian houses that were still there fifty years later. A little way along there was a turning called Vaughan Road.

Once, the houses here must have looked almost exactly like Weedon Grossmith's drawings of The Laurels, in Brickfield Terrace, Holloway, in *The Diary of a Nobody*. Now, any traces of Pooter-style gentility have vanished. 'The district from hell' is what one resident called it not long ago: he was the Pakistani keeper of Super Save Food and Wine, quoted in a newspaper article about Coldharbour Lane and the district around it. The fact that John Major lived with his parents in a flat in Coldharbour Lane in 1955 (which I may have passed every day) made the area briefly worthy of comment. Oddly, the Major-Ball family gave up their bungalow in Worcester Park when the family garden gnome business collapsed, and moved *back* to Camberwell: a complete reversal of the usual pattern. Major himself became a pupil at Rutlish School in Wimbledon, which existed in a state of rivalry to my own school in Raynes Park: there may be some pattern in these coincidences which I cannot fathom.

Now, in the 1990s, the district is plagued with crime – theft, stabbings, or worse. In post-Thatcher Britain, Camberwell is an inner-London suburb where the signs of poverty and urban decay stare you in the face. Not so in 1950. Nor in Fred Karno's day. It was still an acceptable address when, in the 1920s, the building became an ice-rink.

Later still, it became the offices of A. J. White & Co. They were the parent company of Menley & James, and when you knew what the building had formerly been, it explained the peculiar internal geography. There was a large open space on the ground floor, some of which had been partitioned off to be used for storage purposes, and above that, a long enclosed corridor running all the way round the interior – offices on one side, blank wall on the other. From this you must once have been able to look down and observe the patrons of the rink, moving gracefully around on their hissing skates to the music of Waldteufel.

Across Coldharbour Lane, down a short roadway, was the factory, where they made the pills, ointments and tonics that made up the Menley & James 'range'. These included some products with peculiar names: Pragmatar, Mandelamine, Ovendosyn. The laboratory was across the road too, and so was the works canteen, and at dinner-time – one o'clock, and not a minute earlier – those of the office staff who didn't make for The Plough, a couple of hundred yards along Coldharbour Lane, trooped over for their meat and two veg., shepherd's pie, or fish and chips.

Most of the 'M&J lines' were manufactured and sold under licence from American proprietors like the Pyridium Corporation (Pyridium was a pill for urinary infections), or – their biggest and most important principal – the Philadelphia firm of Smith Kline & French. At the core of the business, though, was the only genuine Menley & James product, an antiseptic ointment called Iodex.

Iodex's popularity was steadily diminishing, and those with business acumen could see the product had a limited future. Yet, in 1951, it was still a bit of a household name – a means of putting iodine on an open wound that, supposedly, wouldn't sting or dribble all over the place. Iodex, and a kind of sister product which had a local pain-killer mixed in as well, was an evil-looking greenish-black paste, rather like a jar of Bovril. I never had occasion to smear it on a wound but, mixed with blood, it must have been a gruesome sight.

Yet Iodex had made Menley & James's reputation and put their name on the map of the pharmaceutical industry, even though that name was, as a matter of fact, entirely fictitious.

The truth was, there never had been either a Mr Menley, or a Mr James. The title was an invention – a firm created only to sell Iodex, bought from some small-scale and probably ailing company and into the marketing of which they had thrown their considerable commercial skill and experience. Those attributes had been gained in a harsher and more clamorous area. The original company had been A. J. White Ltd, who sold a fabulously popular remedy called Mother Siegel's Syrup, one of those turn-of-the-century nostrums that contained no recognisable treatment for anything but was peddled for pretty well everything. Mother Siegel's Syrup was one of the most successful patent medicines of the day, and it was all because of A. J. White's merchandising methods: hundreds of thousands of leaflets advertising the syrup were dropped through letter-boxes; once, they even organised a competition for syrup-lovers to suggest the best way for the millionaire philanthropist Andrew Carnegie to spend some of his money.

The heyday of this kind of product had been the first decade of this century, but such medicaments could not survive even the beginnings of the age of scientific medicine. The passing-bell was sounded with the appointment in 1912 of a Select Committee on Patent Medicines: to this inquisitorial body, A. J. White & Co's Managing Director, a certain Harrison Ratcliffe, had been summoned to appear, and was mercilessly grilled about Mother Siegel (actually, like Mr Menley and Mr James, there was no such person) and 'her' syrup (a concoction of flavoured but medicinally meaningless herbs). With the encouragement of the *British Medical Journal* and a publication of theirs called *Secret Remedies – What they Cost and What they Contain*, the whole Mother Siegel operation was made to look decidedly fishy, and Ratcliffe must have known the game was up, or soon would be. Eventually, an Act of Parliament was to put a stop to the trade in secret remedies. But by then A. J. White & Co had gone 'legit', and retreated behind the respectable alias of Menley & James Ltd, manufacturers of Iodex Antiseptic Ointment, and in due time agents for a host of products only available on prescription, and therefore advertised to doctors only. In the parlance of the drug trade, that made them 'ethical' products.

Keeping this business afloat was a small force of adminis-trators, secretaries, advertising copywriters, sales reps, chemists, machinists, storemen and other rank-and-file who had somehow welded themselves into a reasonably contented and mutually tolerant unit. There were two Joint Managing Directors, I never understood why. But both of them were given to declaring that Menley & James was 'a family firm'. One of them was Harrison Ratcliffe Jr, son of the man who had come a cropper before the Select Committee forty years back, and the other was a gentlemanly individual called David Taylor Marsh. Both men were in their fifties. Quite a few people in the business were cousins, nephews, or family friends of one or other of them and there were frequent references in company small talk to 'teamwork' and 'pulling together'.

These are the clichés of commerce but there was an atmosphere about the place which encouraged the use of that kind of platitude. There were quite a few long-serving workers. Everyone was very polite in the office. We called each other Mr or Mrs or Miss. When a certain Miss Dick retired from the firm after forty years 'raising' invoices and other such labours, nobody got drunk, as they would now, but there was a celebratory tea with iced cake, presided over in the canteen by Mr Marsh, who made a speech recalling past years when he and Miss Dick had worked in the same office: he spoke nostalgically of the 'exciting times in the Accounts Department' through which they had both lived, and there were murmurs of recognition and reminiscence from the gathering, standing there with teacups raised.

In the factory, relationships were a bit more basic and robust, but still friendly: higher-up office staff were addressed as Sir. A lot of the employees came from round about, walking to work or taking a bus from Camberwell, Brixton or Denmark Hill, and taking an interest in the same local affairs. The firm's communal activities were popular: ping-pong, darts and whist played every dinner-time at one end of the canteen, Saturday Night dances ('Dancing to the Music of Wally Bunyan and his Band') – these all thrived. And when it came to the big, important events – the Christmas Dinner and Dance at the local Function Room, or the annual summer outing – everyone from office cleaner to company director was expected to turn up.

Life was simpler then. In 1952, when Princess Elizabeth married Prince Philip, the entire work-force was allowed an hour off after lunch to see the royal couple drive down Denmark Hill, ten minutes' walk away, as they showed themselves to what were in those days the King's loyal subjects. Their motor car, escorted by another limousine and a few motor-cycle police, had been all round the East End. The Export Department of Menley & James were there to see the small procession pass by – a little quickly by this time – and we waved at the tanned and privileged pair; while the crowd lining the street applauded, as though approving the performance of actors, waved small Union Jacks, or gave voice to a few self-conscious cheers.

Then we strolled back to our offices, past the roads where nowadays it is not uncommon for people to get mugged or even shot.

It was autumn, 1950, a Monday morning, when I took the 8.32 from Wimbledon for the first time and grown-up life began. A few weeks earlier I had been sent a circular from the Oxford University Appointments Committee, who were enthusiastically promoting the fashionable concept of The Arts Graduate in Industry. They had advertised two vacancies at Menley & James, both of them as Assistant Export Manager. Nothing else was in prospect, and I had caused a stir around the family dining table by actually signing on at the local Labour Exchange. My father was indignant that a youth with a university degree should be, as he put it, 'drawing the dole'.

One of the reassuring things on the Appointments Committee's circular was the requirement that candidates send with their applications a thousand-word 'essay' on anything that interested them. As an Oxford English graduate, I thought, this was where I would score. When I discovered that the other dozen or so people who waited in the Board Room for an interview had submitted mini-theses on export procedure or office management, I knew my potted history of the Victorian Toy Theatre must have seemed either ridiculously irrelevant or interestingly eccentric. Luckily for me, the Export Manager was a man with artistic leanings and I suppose he inclined to the latter view.

But before being interviewed we all had to answer a kind of examination paper about exporting matters. The questions probed our knowledge, or in my case utter ignorance, of matters of marine insurance, shipping and Bills of Exchange, and we were asked to define such expressions as CIF and 'ex works'. I sat there wondering if I dared put down something about The Ministry of the Ex Works Museum: but it was no time for levity. I remember writing – demonstrating my grammar school education – 'Out of, or Away from, the works'. The rest of my paper was more or less blank. But it didn't seem to matter. When the whole ordeal was finished, interview and all, I was astonished that I was one of two young men asked to remain behind. With the Export Manager, a man called Ronald Clark, in attendance, Harrison Ratcliffe Jr explained to me, 'We have decided you are the M&J type.' They were offering me one of the posts they'd advertised, but there was no need to decide there and then. I was to let them know within the next three days.

So – this was the great moment that separated you from your youth. I was twenty-five years old – a bit mature to be starting, but I'd spent three years in the army and five, altogether, at Oxford. Now, I was expected to start earning my own living, with a salary, not a government grant, and not the few shillings a week the army had paid me: and no longer having to approach my father and apologetically ask him for a pound or two 'to keep me going'. I didn't dither long: it was slightly flattering to have been made an offer, for one thing. And my father, business-wise after thirty years in the linoleum industry, gave his verdict: 'Everything you do at your age is good experience.' That seemed advice enough: he returned to his evening paper. But he didn't seem displeased that I was following, more or less, the path he'd trodden.

The Export Department is at one end of the building, on the first floor, under the eaves. The largest of the seven rooms has windows on to the inside corridor, and it accommodates the Shipping Clerk, Mr Hicks, and his three women assistants. The two women who have been there longest are Mrs Days and Mrs Hunt, both in their early thirties – Mrs Days slim, blonde and wary, and Mrs Hunt cheery, a bit plump, bright red lipstick, with a flirtatious look behind owlish spectacles. Round the corner are separate small offices for Barnes, me, and our respective secretaries. Then, further along, one each for Clark and his secretary Miss Bowley, a long-standing M&J type who has attained the enviable status of three-week-holiday employee (one extra day per year's service). She is prominent in the firm's social life, goes to the firm's dances and plays ping-pong after lunch in the canteen.

My own tiny office, up against the roof of the building, has one small window which opens on to Coldharbour Lane. In winter it is going to be chilly in spite of the radiators, and in summer, often stifling. Here I am introduced to that taken-for-granted feature in the lives of hundreds of thousands of people: office furniture. I don't have much: a tin desk with large blotting pad, a three-tier filing cabinet, a Tan-Sad Executive chair with a lever for adjusting its height, a visitor's chair and a metal bookcase. On my desk, a large blotting pad and a wonky sort of structure for my In, Out, and Pending Trays.

I haven't got very much to put in the eight steel drawers that run in and out on their ball bearings: Miss Bowley has supplied me with a note-pad and some pencils, and a small 'Iodex' blotter, as she explains, 'for individual blotting'. On the bookcase I place the hefty maroon-coloured Export Manual Clark has given me to read: I have made uncomprehending notes on the first ten or so pages – what is a go-down? what are 'measts'? When I ask Clark he explains that the first is, disappointingly, a word for a warehouse on the docks and the other is an abbreviation for measurements. He purses his lips afterwards, which makes me feel I should have thought of something more important or profound to ask him.

The manual is destined to remain among the Great Unread. Soon, the desk drawers begin to fill up, with samples of the M&J range and specimens of our advertising literature, supplies of M&J writing paper, even some of A. J. White's, with curly letters coloured yellow and green, manila folders for letters I don't know how to answer. Into my In Tray come things to read. My name is typed at the bottom of the circulation list. A daily file of copies of yesterday's letters written by the Home Sales Manager Mr Taylor, who can't spell 'unforeseen': he is forever referring to 'unforseen circumstances'. There is *Office Magazine, Chemists' and Druggists' Weekly, The Pharmaceutical Journal.* The editorial matter means nothing to me but the advertisements can be stimulating: *Sterile Urine is Not Enough!* over a rigmarole puffing some urinary antiseptic, and *He Too Needs a Little Help Sometimes!* over a picture of a child on a tricycle who seems to be a victim of juvenile constipation: it's a laxative ad.

We get Clark's letters too. His epistolary style is old-fashioned, courteous to the point of smarm. 'Dear Rome, as you are kind enough to allow me to call you,' he begins a letter to a certain Mr R. O. M. Edenborough; and he is always on about 'our Smith Kline friends'. He has been to their offices in Philadelphia and is on Christian-name terms with their chief executives. One day, will all this be mine?

At first there doesn't seem to be anything to do. No one comes in, except a motherly woman around 10.30 in the morning who wheels a large, clattering trolley around the offices and offers me tea from a huge urn, and sandwiches or a cheese roll: gratefully accepted. She is back again at half-past three with tea and cakes. No letters arrive – only those dull periodicals.

But people are fond of quoting the epigrammatic Professor Parkinson: 'All work expands to fill the time available for its completion.' In a month or two, my In Tray begins to fill with letters that ask puzzling questions about shipping delays, insurance, Bills of Lading and Bills of Exchange. Clark has scribbled a few notes about what I should say and insists I show him my letters before he lets them go.

Two other new recruits arrived when I did. One was Barnes, an ex-pilot in Coastal Command who seemed to know all about exporting matters. He had taken some professional exam in the subject and had been in the Export Department of Allen & Hanbury, makers of Haliborange, Allenbury's Pastilles and Rusks, Bynotone and other popular remedies. The other was a drily witty man called Peter Creightmore who, like me, had just come down from Oxford, and who was appointed to be a kind of personal assistant to one of the Managing Directors, Mr Marsh. Peter Creightmore was more interested in the law than in pharmaceuticals, and it was agreed that his job at Menley & James should be regarded as a stop-gap until he could take his Bar exams. Meanwhile he was allowed time off for the work this entailed. He and I shared a feeling of displacement: things had gone wrong for both of us. We were a two-man cell of discontent and ribaldry at the *longueurs* of life in Coldharbour Lane as well as the ridiculous details of our situation. The 'M&J range' was a source of curiosity and amusement. When we discovered Iodex was available in suppository form Creightmore gravely told Clark he thought it was a product that should go a long way. We would compete in devising outlandish anagrams for the names of other employees, whom we would privately hold up to ridicule. A particular butt of sarcasm was the Company Secretary, a Mr Phypers, whom Creightmore usually referred to as Phindscreen Phypers, or sometimes plain Phindscreen.

Menley & James had evidently decided to go for graduate recruits in a big way. There was a Miss Hosegood, with a degree in History, and a Mr Sommers, an immensely tall young man, six foot ten or more, and also from Oxford: both of these had arrived a few months earlier. Sommers had taken readily to the commercial life, though he was beginning to feel restless with Menley & James. His area of responsibility was the company's overseas branches, in India and South Africa, where they actually manufactured the goods locally.

Creightmore and I would give vent to our shared feelings in private mirth, inventing mad and insulting biographies for our colleagues and parodies of their laboured epistolary style. In this pastime we were not entirely in tune with our tall colleague Sommers. He was a pleasant but chronically discontented individual. Nowadays it is not at all uncommon to see men as tall as he was: the average height of an adult male in this country has demonstrably increased in the forty years since then. But in the comparatively dwarfish fifties Sommers had to endure the irritation of being called Lofty by people he didn't know, and being asked by other waggish strangers if it was cold up there. I dare say this helped to explain his rather melancholic and resentful turn of mind, which was made worse by what he considered to be the demeaning treatment he received in the firm. His perpetual grumble was that he wasn't given enough responsibility. He would come into my small office in the eaves of the building and give vent to his indignation as he saw me signing the day's pile of customs invoices, or writing in a ledger the number of tubes of Pragmatar, for athlete's foot, they had sold in Malta in the previous month. It was a job I could do, and even quite enjoyed: filling in column after column of sales figures required no business or marketing skill – I wasn't in the least interested in why or how the Lebanese, the Cypriots or the Nigerians had bought more Benzedrine in January than in June. But for Sommers that kind of question was the whole reason for our being there. 'We should be taking decisions on policy matters,' he would rail, striding up and down: three steps were enough to cover the whole room. 'You shouldn't be doing that. That's a clerk's job. And Marsh is treating me like some kind of superior office boy! We're wasted here!'

*

It wasn't a very large business. Small pharmaceutical 'houses' could still thrive then, although Menley & James was in a slightly precarious position as a one-product firm, dangerously dependent on its revenue as agent for companies overseas. True, Mother Siegel's Syrup was still going strong here and there: in Ireland, for instance, where habits changed more slowly and perhaps the tonic-quaffing public was more gullible than the English, there was even a market for vast containers called Winchester Quarts, two and a quarter litres of the stuff.

Ireland was one of the countries to which I was assigned in my position as Assistant Export Manager. I was also 'given' East and West Africa, Egypt and the Middle East, where Menley & James had appointed local merchants as sole agents to import and distribute the range. Some of these personages were picturesque enough. Our man in Alexandria, for instance, was a certain A. N. Valsamis, known (ironically, I believe) as Honest Aristide. Though I found no reason to doubt his probity, I always thought of him as a wily Egyptian merchant in burnous and Forty Thieves hat, smiling and soaping his hands in some bazaar out of a Walter Crane drawing of *The Arabian Nights*. I expect in reality he was more likely to have been seen in a smart business suit. But his letters, ending with his large, flowery signature, did somehow possess a curiously ingratiating yet flamboyant tone. Meanwhile, in Baghdad we were represented by the interestingly named Samy Fetto (surely wearing a fez), and in Tehran by a Dr Bral, something of a big shot – he was a member of the Shah's Parliamentary Assembly. I met him once when he came to London: I called on him at his suite in the Savoy, where he gave me an immense Jaffa orange. I wondered if he had any political objections to eating Jewish fruit, but Bral explained blandly (perhaps reading my thoughts) that they were the best oranges you could buy. Afterwards he took to sending me each Christmas a quantity of red caviare from the Black Sea, or perhaps it was the other way round: so little of it reached my table it is hard to remember. The fact was, the British Customs would not part with this tempting consignment until the intended recipient had paid the excise duty on it, and I had to sell most of the caviare round the office in order to be able to pay for one very small jar.

Apart from Dr Bral, I met few of our numerous representatives. I did spend some time with the M&J agent from Nicosia, a portly, amiable man with little English called Costas Christoforides. In 1954, after I had been working for the firm for nearly four years, he and his wife visited London: I was deputed to show them the places tourists were supposed to visit – Parliament Square, the Abbey, Whitehall, the Tower of London. I can recall little of our day together except for our tour of the Tower Armoury, where we stood in respectful silence before a suit of armour made for Henry VIII: it had an extremely large steel codpiece jutting out at a right angle from its crotch, to accommodate and protect one of the most important penises in sixteenth-century Europe. Later, we dined in a Greek-Cypriot restaurant in Charlotte Street where the proprietor affected to know my guest from Nicosia days, though it was an obvious lie.

We did business with similar establishments: Menley & James's shipping and forwarding agents, for instance, a comfortably settled City firm called Stephenson & Ephgrave. Their man Mr Philo was responsible for finding the ships which would carry consignments of our medicines to the likes of the Malta Wholesale Drug Company, A. D. Fetto and Co, United Africa Co, and Khalil Fattal et Fils, Beirut.

One seldom saw Mr Philo, unless something had gone wrong – a cargo not collected, a Bill of Lading inaccurately made out, and once, dramatically, a vessel on fire in the Indian Ocean – and then he would be round in a flash at Coldharbour Lane with an apology. Otherwise we saw him only at Christmas, when, a few days before the holiday, he would appear in the department, a tall, blue-suited, worried man in his forties, wearing a black Homburg hat, and bearing parcels for me and my colleagues which he would

16

proffer with the Compliments of the Season. After awkwardly presenting each of us with the cigarettes, sherry, chocolates or port he had brought with him, he would linger for a chat, which he obviously found as delicate and difficult a matter as we did: Mr Philo's embarrassment at the slightly servile nature of his errand was rapidly communicated to the recipients of his largesse. Making things worse were Mr Philo's rather odd turns of speech, of interest to anyone who had read Freud's *Psychopathology of Everyday Life*. The conversation would turn to the weather, our home life, our comforts, or lack of them, in winter. 'My wife's a cold morsel,' he said when discussing the problem of electricity bills ('I found you as a morsel Cold upon dead Caesar's platter', I wanted to say), and, 'They fight like tooth and nail,' he said of his two sons, one of whom was 'torn between two schools of thought'. Creightmore and I wanted to snigger at this kind of thing and sometimes had to make an excuse to leave the room for a few moments and give vent to mute hilarity in the corridor or the Gents.

The present was basically a bribe, I suppose, to prevent us from transferring Menley & James's custom to any other shipping agent. I presume Mr Philo didn't realise I would have had little say in such a decision.

That would have been a matter for the Export Manager. His name was Ronald Carlos Clark, a short, very slightly effeminate man with a curiously small mouth and pinched, bee-stung lips, who bustled about the department smoking furiously. He was a prodigious cigarette smoker: forty a day at least and, when he got going, victim of epic coughing fits that thoroughly alarmed onlookers and left him gasping and wiping his eyes. He lived with his sisters and two brothers – all unmarried – in the house in which they had been brought up. Ronald Clark had taken charge of the original job interviews and he was the man who had asked us to demonstrate our M&Jishness by sending in an essay with our applications. He played the piano, and was the organist in his local church in Shirley. Once, he invited me and my wife

17

to dine with him: he announced that, this being a Saturday, we would be eating what they always had on that evening of the week – bacon and eggs. This was before the prolonged gastronomic revolution of the seventies and eighties and there was really nothing particularly odd about the fare Clark and his sister provided. The meal was preceded by a visit to a man near by, a Hungarian who made little figures of coloured blown glass: he would make one on the spot, there and then, for Clark's guests – cute animals, or what Clark called 'dancing ladies' about three inches high perched on coloured balls, heads thrown back in attitudes of ecstatic abandon. When we returned his dinner invitation, we made sure it was conspicuous on the sideboard. I offered him a drink on arrival and he asked for gin *and* sherry – in the same glass, explaining that the quality of wartime sherry had made it a fitting substitute for vermouth. An inexperienced drinker, I had no choice but to accept his story.

Clark was good-humoured and kindly enough, but he could be a fussy sort of man and he was not pleased by my chronic unpunctuality. Once or twice, he did give voice to his annoyance: 'I have had oh-casion to rebuke you before about your late arrival,' he began with a severe look. Usually, he confined himself to frowns and pursed lips, and muttering something when I got married about buying me an alarm clock for a wedding present. His manner towards the ten people in the Export Department – secretaries, shipping clerks, and his two assistant managers – was not entirely easy. An occasion of general discomfiture was the Department's own Christmas party, when we all gathered in the Shipping Office and stood in a half-circle round a bottle of sherry, which stood next to a bottle of mead manufactured at home by Clark himself and labelled Merlin's Mead. Merlin, I believe, was the name of his house. 'Who would lake to tray may mead?' Clark would inquire. 'Heah, Miss Bowley, tray may mead,' and he would pour each of us a small sherry glass of the sweet, honey-coloured liquid. After half an hour or so of polite small talk, the party would break up, and we were all permitted

18

to go home an hour early, at four o'clock. The day after Boxing Day, we were all back at work.

Like Mr Philo, Clark too had a revealing way of scrambling his metaphors. He once told me in front of a visitor that the man would like to 'suck my brains' over exporting drugs to Turkey (little sustenance would he have found there), and that two of our agents were 'running neck and nail' for the same contract. However, he took the M&J life very seriously. My starting salary in 1951 was £500, which even then seemed niggardly, and it was to rise by annual increments of £50 to a maximum of £800 after six years – a prospect which cast me into near-suicidal despair whenever I thought about it. Yet when the annual increment came, I was instructed by Clark to write to the Joint Managing Director, Mr Marsh, and thank him.

Clark was the one who made sure we all attended the firm's major social events. One was the Christmas 'do', a huge affair held at some local pub or hotel, with everyone sitting down to turkey and Christmas pudding, with speeches from the directors, followed by a turn or two from professional entertainers, and then a dance, this time to music from someone closer to the big-time than Wally Bunyan.

Another event, on an even larger scale, was the annual outing. I cannot imagine anything like those outings surviving into the 1990s. Somehow – I think by pleading the demands of a small family – I avoided going on more than one, and it was a remarkable affair. It must have been organised long in advance, with a specially chartered train for the five hundred or so M&J employees, who gathered at Waterloo early one Friday morning. Our destination was Weston-super-Mare. On the train, factory workers sat before an array of fresh bottles of whisky or gin, which they opened and started on before we had left the terminus – first downing pints of milk as a precaution against getting plastered too soon. It was a bleak and windy day, but that didn't prevent them from having a wonderful time, boozing and snoozing and capering along the promenade in their kiss-me-quick headgear. A few sexual promises were redeemed, either in town or in the neighbouring countryside. Cheddar Gorge wasn't far away: secretaries finally yielded, lab assistants succumbed.

But these were the 1950s. This modest bacchanal was far from the unbridled affair it would have been thirty years later.

Two

A Steady Trade

MORE THAN FORTY years later, I sit writing these words in a slack moment in a Soho recording studio. I am waiting for the sound engineer to say what he usually says, 'Ready on a green . . . running forward now.' Then he will touch the green cue light. The detritus of the 'voice-oh' business (as I have heard it called) is all round me in a sound-proof room: trailing cables in the way of my legs, microphone, lectern and TV monitor on the desk, headphones, and a tray of gravel for simulating the sound of marching feet – an 'effects' device seldom seen nowadays in places like these: now all the noises a producer could ever want are available, canned, on effects CDs.

The microphone is now the main tool of my trade, cashing in on a knack I was lucky enough to have been born with but knew nothing about at Menley & James in the early 1950s. My life has changed course in a way I could never have foreseen then: but the England all around me has radically changed too.

Gone now are the optimism and confidence of those days, when the war against Hitler was fresh in everyone's memory. Gone, too, is the shabby, battered, after-the-blitz England with its clearly defined, mostly foolish social distinctions. And much altered, if not gone altogether, are old-fashioned 'family firms' like Menley & James, where the number of people who turned

21

up for work each morning was small enough for the managers to know everyone.

There are few photographs of those years at Menley & James. None of the regular staff would have dreamed of taking a camera into the office. But a later recruit to the Export Department did do so, a roly-poly young man with fair wavy hair and a German accent called Eugene Marx, who was taken on as one of two travelling representatives of the firm. His job was to move about 'my' export areas, encouraging the agents, studying local opportunities for pharmaceutical sales and business conditions in general, and sending reports back to Clark with his observations and conclusions.

Marx feared he might be put at a disadvantage in politically sensitive countries like the Lebanon or Jordan, by the fact that he was Jewish. So he changed his name to Marsh. His reports to us, mailed from Nairobi, Alexandria, Accra or wherever his current tour had taken him, were long, detailed and tedious, and I could only hope his reports about us, to our overseas agents, sparkled a bit more. However, at least he did his best to show them what we looked like: the only photographs I possess of life in Coldharbour Lane were Eugene's none too skilful work, taken with the idea of showing them to the likes of Aristide Valsamis, Samy Fetto and Khalil Fattal. In one, Creightmore, Barnes and I are standing on the pavement in the rain, outside the unprepossessing entrance to Menley & James, all set, as I remember it, to catch the early train home and anxious to get the photo-call over. We are wearing overcoats and gloves. (Eugene, behind the camera and out of sight, was about to fly to Egypt, where the sun was shining.) I am wearing my demob hat and carrying a cheap imitation-leather document case which I expect contains the *News Chronicle* and a book to read on the train to Wimbledon. I wonder what it can have meant to the men who must have scrutinised it thousands of miles away.

Eugene also took a group photograph of the entire Export Department: Clark in the middle, arms folded, proud Captain of the team he has recruited; Sommers at the back, soaring high above everybody else. Barnes and I are on either side of Ronald Clark next to our respective secretaries. Mine is Mrs Harmer, in her grey gabardine two-piece with white nylon blouse, her hair in a tight roll: she is smirking a little in embarrassment and leaning politely away from me, out of respect, I suppose, or to allay suspicions of any deeper liaison. I am in the 'going away' suit I bought for my wedding: a dark outfit with waistcoat. Eugene has taken the picture with a delayed-action shutter and, as swiftly as his generous physique allowed, nipped daintily round to join the back row. This undoubtedly accounts for the suppressed mirth that shows on most of the faces.

Not shown, and probably on a trip at the time, was Eugene's opposite number in Barnes's Far Eastern markets, an interesting individual called Eric Abderhalden, a man in his late forties, well travelled, said to have been born in Switzerland, with a swift, booming way of speaking and an air of energetic amusement, as though determined at all costs to see the comic possibilities of his work. I envied Barnes the Abderhalden reports that came in from Malaysia, Hong Kong and such places: they were racy and entertaining documents, well spiced with gossip, badly typed on Abderhalden's pre-war portable Remington, and they made you feel you had just walked down the main street of the city he was reporting from. I considered him wasted at Menley & James. It didn't surprise me that his daughter became a journalist on a popular paper.

With his tales of pre-war travel in China and the Malay States, Abderhalden brought a hint of exoticism to the Export Department when he reported back to London. It didn't happen often: when it did, Clark greeted him like a long-lost boon companion. Once the simultaneous presence of Abderhalden and Marsh caused Ronald Clark to organise an Evening Out in the West End for everyone, paid for by the firm. We met for dinner in Kettner's, where, Clark explained knowingly, Edward VII had entertained his mistresses, and then proceeded to the Prince of

Wales Theatre to see Norman Wisdom cadging the audience's favour in a revue.

Abderhalden's and Marsh's arrival finally abolished one of the allurements that had been dangled before the dozen young men at that first interview: the probability of foreign travel. After all, the vacancy was in the Export Department, so that seemed quite likely.

In fact the only place I travelled to for Menley & James was Coldharbour Lane – except for one occasion. Sitting at my gun-metal green desk, I had been imagining an assignment in Baghdad, Beirut or Tehran, where I doubt if I should have done the company much good. But it all came down to one brief excursion to Dublin, and furthermore it was in Clark's company. I really cannot say why he wanted me there. At any rate he made it clear I was to take the excursion seriously, and recommended me, as a representative of the firm (those were his words), to obtain a hat for the occasion. Luckily I had my demob hat, the brown city hat I had worn for Marsh's photograph, which I had crushed into a rather implausible-looking pork-pie shape, and this seemed to be more or less acceptable: at any rate, Clark was silent on the matter.

Though far from glamorous, this trip to Dublin had its moments of drama. In a pub in the city centre I was unwise enough to eat for lunch a steak and oyster pie, a peculiar, Dickensian dish only a gastronomic ignoramus would have entertained. I thought it rather typical of Dublin at the time, where I was shocked to see children begging barefoot, and gypsy women in greasy trilbies, selling pots and pans and wild flowers from baskets. As for the oysters, I dare say they had been gathered in Dublin Bay or the Liffey. At any rate, two hours later, when I was sitting in the offices of May Roberts, our Dublin agents, I began to think suicide a preferable option, and, making an excuse, I made my way out to the street. Shortly after that, I was spectacularly sick down the carpeted stairs of the United Services Club, where Clark and I were staying. My credentials as an ambassador

24

from headquarters were from that moment almost certainly wrecked.

This experience augured badly for my future with the firm, as well as for any trip to the Middle East, which in any case was probably regarded as Clark's personal perk. Soon after the war ended, he had been on two overseas tours, looking around, setting up a network of agents in the Middle and Far East, assessing market opportunities and generally stimulating Menley & James's overseas trade. It had given him extra standing in the company, underlining the importance of his rôle in a period when overseas trade was becoming ever more necessary.

We were in The Age of Austerity – the phrase coined to characterise the era in which the priggish-looking Sir Stafford Cripps, the Chancellor of the Exchequer (Sir Stifford Craps – my father's standard joke), introduced harsh measures to restore the country's exhausted economy after more than five years of war. Foreign currency was what we needed: Export or Die, the motto we were urged to remember. Any firm that had something to sell abroad was being pushed, cajoled, exhorted and shamed into getting out there and selling it. The Duke of Edinburgh, famed for 'speaking out', and for what were then regarded as royal indiscretions, made a speech telling British businessmen to 'get their finger out', a remark that left us surprised, even shocked: out of what? could he mean . . . ? Members of the Royal Family weren't supposed to know, still less employ, such rude expressions. But then, he'd been in the navy, and was almost one of us.

Chiefly, the country needed 'hard' currency – i.e., US dollars. One problem for Menley & James was that although the firm earned a substantial commission from selling American drugs, the bulk of the profit went back to America again. In a modest sort of way, the firm was doing its bit, but we should have had greater prestige as exporters if the goods we were selling had actually been British. Still, we were at least in a steady trade, as my serious-minded older colleague Barnes would tell me: there would never be a fall in the demand for medicines, he would say sagely, especially now we had a National Health Service (which, as a staunch Conservative voter, he didn't really approve of: he'd joined one of the private schemes). On the other hand, the products we sold weren't particularly exciting or even very important: none of them really came into the life-saving category. They were for run-of-the-mill ailments, the small change of medical practice: medicines to treat blocked noses, infections of the bladder, menstrual irregularities, acne and athlete's foot; and by a mildly interesting irony there was one medicine supposed to create an appetite (the tonic Neuro-Phosphates), and another which was meant to dull appetite altogether and so help you lose weight.

As a matter of fact this last preparation was becoming quite famous. It was Dexedrine, then prescribed, in the form of pills, as an 'appetite-suppressant', and in addition as a drug to alter mood. In other words it was one of the first of the psychotropic or 'mind-bending' drugs, then being added to the doctors' arsenal and already beginning to provoke controversy. Two Dexedrine tablets, or even one if you were susceptible, would induce a bracing sensation of confidence and pep: the fear was that once you had tried them you wouldn't be able to stop.

The drug had arrived on the medical scene later than another, even better-known Smith Kline & French product, Benzedrine. This was the pharmacological cousin to Dexedrine and was SKF's first 'mood' pill; its effects were similar to those of Dexedrine but a little coarser, and it had made its first appearance during the war, when it had allegedly been available to American troops in a state of battle-fatigue. In post-war Britain, the pills weren't available without a prescription, though there were ways of getting round this regulation and there were alarming tales about the effects it could have on people who did. One story, probably apocryphal, told of an Oxford undergraduate who had taken Benzedrine before going into the Schools to sit an exam he was especially scared of. He emerged three hours later, convinced he had handed in a paper of daring originality and brilliance: it turned out there was nothing on it but his own name, written over and over and over again.

Benzedrine came not only in tablets: it was also the main ingredient in the Benzedrine Inhaler, a neat little torpedo-shaped object, coloured red, green and white, which you pushed up your nostrils and sniffed; whereupon it would shrink the nasal turbinates (a word I had learnt from our advertisements) and help you breathe more easily if you had a cold. You didn't need a prescription to buy an inhaler: it was what we called an 'over-the-counter line'.

Inside the inhaler were layers of white wadding impregnated with liquid Benzedrine, plus some kind of harmless aromatic that made it smell like a cold cure. I never found my Benzedrine Inhaler much help, because if you had a blocked nose you couldn't breathe in the vapour that was supposed to exert its decongestant effect. However, there were more sinister disadvantages to the product. It was discovered that if you removed the wadding and soaked it in liquid – gin was recommended, but methylated spirit would do – you could create a cocktail with an impact of seismic force. Prisoners in American 'correctional facilities' were credited with having worked this out.

On the whole, Benzedrine was being prescribed, at least in Britain, with more moderation than Dexedrine, which besides its (less potent) effect on mood was also recommended as a slimming aid: it not only diminished your craving for food, it simultaneously boosted your spirits, making it easier to forget the pork pies and pints your system craved. SKF chemists had also conjured forth variants of these two preparations: there was Edrisal, a combination of Benzedrine and salicylic acid (or aspirin), which was thought good for complaints like menstrual pain and severe toothache: 'Relieves pain, elevates mood', said Menley & James's advertising copy. Then there was Drinamyl – popularly known as 'purple hearts' because of their novel shape: they consisted of Dexedrine with amylobarbitone (another 'mood' drug), and supposed to induce a feeling of 'calm elation'.

All but two of the 'M&J lines' were 'ethicals': the two which weren't were Iodex and the Benzedrine Inhaler. However, all of them were advertised to doctors, either in the medical journals or through the efforts of a corps of so-called 'detailmen'. These were a species then new to the British pharmaceutical trade: of course, once again it was an American idea. Among the M&J detailmen there were a few pharmacists, and I believe one lapsed, or possibly failed, medical student, but most were professional salesmen. All of them had what I thought the worst job in the entire organisation: they had to travel round, calling on doctors, to try to persuade them of the virtues of Menley & James's products.

This was a demeaning task. The detailmen had to equip themselves with adequate information about what the product would do, how it worked (very difficult, that), what the side-effects might be, what research had been done to support the company's claims, what it would cost the National Health Service, and any one of a dozen other things a doctor might ask them. So equipped, they then had to hang around doctors' waiting rooms in the hope that the doctor would spare five minutes to listen to their 'detail'. Either out of sheer spite or to hasten their departure, some doctors took a cruel delight in deliberately flooring the detailmen with technical questions, the answers to which hadn't been in the script. A few were polite and friendly. Others were stand-offish, busy, bored, tired or extremely rude. However, it was up to the M&J reps to take it on the chin and make themselves agreeable to their clients. Free samples might help and were always to hand. Or sometimes they could produce some extra attraction, which might be anything from a ball-point pen stamped with the name of the product they were 'detailing', to a golfing weekend in Folkestone. In fact Menley & James didn't go in for lavish free gifts: free blotters were about the limit of the firm's generosity: we were not in competition with the more prodigal American or Swiss companies then coming into prominence in the British drug business.

From time to time, the reps would appear *en masse* at Coldharbour Lane to undergo a course in some new product or a refresher course in what was already available. The major part of the course consisted of lectures on the physiological processes concerned in the goods we were selling. Ronald Clark thought it a good idea for me to attend one of these courses, which were under the supervision of a certain Dr Bett, who acted for the firm in a consultative capacity. Bett was not a mesmerising speaker; but he prided himself on his command of English, particularly the written variety, and had published a paper somewhere with the po-faced title 'The Preparation and Writing of Medical Papers for Publication', a line that could have done with a bit of editing. What was also odd about this was that Bett was of foreign extraction: I am not sure where he had been born but he spoke with a noticeably foreign accent. His manner towards his class of reps and recruits like me was distant, verging on the brusque, and I learned very little from his lessons. I'm afraid my performance in the end-of-the-week examination made it clear that, as a detailman, I would have been a liability.

The junior executives of the Export Department get on well together. After lunch, that is, between 1.20 and 2.00 p.m, when Clark might come in, Barnes, Creightmore, Sommers and I play bridge or dumb crambo across one end of my desk. The gossip is about films we have seen, about people in the office, and about sex.

I pass on to them the view expressed to me by L/Cpl. McCann when I was in the army, four or five years ago: whenever a man or woman work together in an office, there is bound to be sexual electricity between them. New to office life, we try matching this with the state of affairs among the M&J types. It doesn't seem to apply very much to the Export Department. Sommers claims to have had a brief flirtation, no more, with Mrs Days, snatching a kiss on the platform at Loughborough Junction. I say I think Mrs Unt, as we call her, is sexier. 'I saw you regarding her bum with cool appraisal,' I remark to Sommers, who finds this killingly funny. He goes round saying, 'Mrs Unt, may I regard your bum with cool appraisal?'

That could have been the day when the same Mrs Hunt turns up to work with acute laryngitis. Her voice is husky and she purrs to us that her husband told her she sounds 'adorable'.

We all agree Mrs Harmer is not the stuff of which great courtesans are made. But I think Barnes's secretary Mrs Stevens is another matter. She has one artificial leg, the result of being run over by a tram in her childhood. Barnes calls her Dot-and-Carry-One, though not to her face. But she has a merry, beguiling smile and bright eyes behind her round, innocent-looking glasses. She and Barnes have a running joke. 'Mrs Stevens, will you come in and take down for me?' She replies, 'Oh, Mr Barnes!'

The daily round is exceedingly dull. A lot of it consists of writing letters, or rather dictating them to the coy, stiffly permed Mrs Harmer, about matters of shipping, delivery, insurance, stock returns, and so on. According to the custom of the day, these always have to be couched in the first person plural: We thank you for your letter of the 14th inst., and we remain, Yours faithfully, for Menley & James Ltd, Assistant Export Manager. Telephone conversations too are supposed to be conducted according to the same antique protocol: Good morning, We are Menley and James.

The grass looked greener on the other side of the old Fred Karno building. That was where you would find the advertising department, thinking up succinct, persuasive slogans. The department was fairly high-powered. The copywriters were graduates: one, a man called Woodcock, with startlingly white hair, had been conspicuous in the streets at Oxford. Another was a qualified doctor, and had the distinction of being brother-in-law to the Labour leader Hugh Gaitskell. I envied them. Their trade was in words rather than invoices and letters of credit and consignments of medicines bound for Africa or the Mediterranean. But they had a low opinion of Clark's young men: word leaked out that they called us 'the arty boys in the Export Department'. I thought this funny, especially the idea that our partner Barnes, ex-pilot and pillar of the Streatham Tennis Club, could be described as 'arty'. It became a point of honour to live up to this disparaging characterisation: we began to affect unusual items of clothing like velvet waistcoats and even bow-ties.

After years of dressing in any old thing except for special occasions, I was expected to appear at the office each morning in a suit of regulation grey or dark blue. I only had my demob suit, a chalk-stripe affair, complete with waistcoat, with trousers too large and jacket too small; and I had a two-piece herring-bone tweed I had scraped together £6. 0s. 0d for and bought from Walter's in the Turl, in Oxford. As a daring gesture I sometimes wore a green velvet waistcoat. Reflecting now on the conventional dress of the period, it occurs to me how badly, in those days, Britain must have smelled. These were the days before the laundrette came to this country and before dry-cleaners' shops assumed their present-day place in the scheme of things. Wash-day was Monday in a million households. Between times, to keep them looking neat and tidy, men would rely on a change of collar, rather than a change of shirt. I wonder how we should feel if we were transported back magically to an environment such as the evening train from Loughborough Junction, to experience the fug of stale clothes and BO, overlaid with exhaled tobacco smoke, that we then took for granted.

Whatever they may have thought of the frivolousness of the Export team, I think our advertising colleagues did once use a slogan of mine. It was for Benzedrine Inhalers: 'Quick relief for stuffy noses'. Not a prizewinner, I admit, but it had the virtue of plain speaking, like quite a few of the advertising department's own slogans, one of which, for Dexedrine, I thought commendably pithy: 'People are fat because they eat too much.'

A transfer to the Advertising Department? That would bring

me closer to what I hoped was my true *métier*. I didn't ask, confident something else was sure to turn up.

Nothing did. Obsessively, I pored over the Situations Vacant column in *The Times*. Many were the letters I sent off, referring with what I hoped was the right combination of nonchalance and pride to my small corpus of published work (mainly film reviews for *The Isis* at Oxford), and making the most of such other experience as I had had. None of them clicked.

In a mood of truculent despair, I wrote to the editor of the *News Chronicle*: no *curriculum vitae* this time, just a short letter telling him I was trapped in an office job and wanted to get out. Was there anything going? And this shaft did appear to strike home: I had a letter from the news editor inviting me to come and see him. I don't think I can have made much of an impression. He said he would think about bringing me in for a day here and there, perhaps once a fortnight, or once a week, to watch what happened in a newspaper office, and maybe send me out on a story – but he thought it mightn't be acceptable to the paper's NUJ chapel. He wrote a few days later to say he was sorry, it wasn't possible; and union rules, he hinted, were not the only stumbling-block.

I was demoralised, but a month or two later I followed this up with a letter to the features editor, enclosing an article which I should have realised hadn't the remotest chance of being published: it was about giving up smoking. It came back within a couple of days – but with it was a letter from the features editor, who was Tom Hopkinson. Encouragement at last: your article shows you can write, he told me, so try again some time with something really topical. But I could never think of anything. Another letter to the *Chronicle* editor might have worked; or maybe I could have tried any of the others. Or shouldn't I have just resigned from Menley & James, devoted all my time and energy to finding something else? Why didn't I? Lack of nerve.

I envied those men of my acquaintance who seemed to have

known from an early age they were going to be doctors, research chemists, schoolteachers, insurance brokers or solicitors. By this time, some of my contemporaries were well on the course they would stick to for the rest of their lives – journalism, the Civil Service, broadcasting. Derek Cooper was on the other side of the world, working for Radio Malaya with several other Oxford alumni. Amazingly, he had bought a car. Alan Brien was on the lower rungs of journalism but with a secure footing, his talent well recognised. Robert Robinson, another Raynes Parker, was working for Kemsley Newspapers in Liverpool, and another co-alumnus of both Raynes Park and Wadham was earning twice my salary working for Unilever. Apparently commerce did suit some arts graduates.

I should have been glad of some guidance from someone. But it was not available. The sad thing is, I hardly ever discussed my problems with my father, and he never raised the matter with me. Our relationship wasn't what it had been. He had now been 'in' linoleum for around twenty-five years (he was Secretary of the Linoleum Association), and although I was living in his house and seeing him every day, he never questioned me about the job I did.

I'm sure he thought being Assistant Export Manager of Menley & James was a perfectly acceptable way of earning a living, and possibly it didn't deserve comment; perhaps he thought I would be chairman of the board one day. But I think it likely he had more or less blocked off his family from any prolonged, serious thought, and he had no great interest or curiosity about the kind of life I was leaving.

Three

An M&J Type

IF I HAD to identify some hidden reason why my life in the grown-up world took the shape it did, I should probably point to the paternal model I half-wanted, half-hated to copy: a suburban ideal, the steady job from nine to five, suggested – and condemned – in some lines from Auden's and Isherwood's *The Ascent of F6*:

> The eight o'clock train, the customary place,
> Holding the paper in front of your face,
> The public stairs, the glass swing-door,
> The peg for your hat, the linoleum floor . . .
> Nothing interesting to do,
> Nothing interesting to say,
> Nothing remarkable in any way;
> Then the journey home again
> In the hot suburban train
> To the tawdry new estate . . .

'Why is my work so dull?' groans Mr A., that play's crestfallen Mr Average. 'Why have I so little money?'

It is a Saturday afternoon a few weeks after the end of the war. I have been given a weekend pass and I am taking some 'snaps', in the small garden of the three-bedroom suburban chalet on the Kingston Bypass in which my brother and I had grown up. They call them snaps. I call them photographs. In my pictures people have to adopt unusual poses or be taken from strange angles. The idea is to send some to my brother, now 6107870 Staff Sergeant Vaughan D., Royal Army Service Corps, a clerk at Mountbatten's headquarters in Singapore. He is also a member of the unconventional group of conscripts that includes Stanley Baxter and John Schlesinger, and Peter Nichols, who will make out of the experience the play *Privates on Parade*.

It's a sunny day, with blue skies, and billowing white clouds. My mother is wearing a pretty blue dress with big white polka dots. My father is in a white shirt with no tie, white flannels.

When the photographs came out I stuck them in my photograph album and, as was my adolescent habit, gave them whimsical titles. One of them showed my parents sitting side by side on our small lawn. All unknowing – though flaunting my Latin to anyone who happened to have a look – I wrote underneath: *Felix domus*.

If I look carefully at this picture fifty years later I can see several things I did not think important or significant at the time. My mother is smiling at the camera. She looks good, already in her mid-forties but pretty enough to pass for someone ten years younger. My father may be dressed not for cricket, as he would have been ten years earlier, but for golf, which by now had taken the place of cricket in his life. He is forty-six, but his hair has not yet turned grey. He looks at the camera with a wintry, guarded smile that doesn't get as far as his eyes.

Then there is another picture, this time of the three of us, looking away to the left of the frame. I forget which of my friends was holding the camera: probably Derek Cooper, on leave from the navy. I am adopting, a touch self-consciously, my 'visionary' look. Searching the horizon, with a faint smile on my face. This one I captioned *Cercle de famille*. Probably I chose to label it in this way in half-awareness of some lines by Victor Hugo that I could remember from school.

> *Lorsque l'enfant paraît, le cercle de famille*
> *Applaudit à grands cris. Son doux regard qui brille*
> *Fait briller tous les yeux,*
> *Et les plus tristes fronts, les plus souillés peut-être,*
> *Se dérident soudain à voir l'enfant paraître,*
> *Innocent et joyeux.*

I am very much afraid I may have unconsciously seen myself as the child who'd appeared, amid general applause, to effect a brightening of the eyes on the most careworn features. Innocent I was not, after a year in the army, and certainly not joyful, with the prospect of a return to the REME lines in Bicester a few hours later, and the nagging possibility of a posting to the Far East, and the Burma campaign.

Felix domus indeed! How little I understood what was really happening in that small, neat house with the pebble-dash walls and terracotta-tiled roof. The war had shaken and rattled the structure of our family life just as violently as the German bombers and rockets had unsettled ours and our neighbours' trim little houses. It is what war does, and our story was like many another: an inherently rocky marriage undermined, tossed about and raked over by the world-convulsing events of 1939 to 1945.

Suburban life wasn't what it had been. The raw newness of the great, sprawling estates had been tempered after a decade or so and the Luftwaffe had arbitrarily obliterated some of the houses: there were competitors for the title, but New Malden was said to have been London's most-bombed suburb. There would have been precious little justification for maintaining the optimism of 1934, when we had moved from Brixton to the new Wates estate on the edge of London's vaunted Green Belt. No. 248 Malden Way, purchased by my father for £1,000, was beginning to look shabby and neglected: the cream and green paint was peeling, the pebble-dash rendering stained by the effluent from the traffic on the Kingston Bypass.

Perhaps their marriage would have come to pieces anyway, war or no war. My surmise is that my father's inner restlessness was made worse by the realisation that, by now, his job was not going to change: he would only ever be Secretary to the Linoleum Association, unless by some chance one of the big lino firms offered him a seat on the board ... but it didn't seem to be happening. I like to think it was because he was good at his job – good at being the discreet, impartial official who knew things about the Association's member-companies that were unknown to their rivals but which he would not, in honour, divulge. So he had made himself irreplaceable.

Moreover, it would have been unforgivable for him to have been promoted to such a position in the absence of many of the trade's leading people, away serving in the Forces. As Secretary to a trade association, George Vaughan was in what was categorised as a Reserved Occupation. Had it not been so, he could have been called up: he was still not quite forty when the war began. Did it worry him that he hadn't volunteered – hadn't tried to take up again from 1919 his commission in the Middlesex Regiment? I shall never know.

Every morning and most weekends during the war's last stages, with whatever thoughts of escape he might have had in his head, my father did march away to do his bit – in navy-blue battledress, with gas mask, whistle and tin helmet. He was off to the ARP post that had been set up in the New Malden Tennis Club. The air raids of 1941 were over but you never knew what might happen, and now there were the V1s and V2s. We were lucky enough to escape the V2s, but the V1s, the 'buzz-bombs', were a recurrent nuisance, cruising overhead with a hoarse uneven drone, with flames issuing from their rear ends. My father said they were made of a new synthetic substance like bakelite, called arse-alight. His joke was typical of an attitude towards them shared, I believe, by many

Londoners: John Terraine, an Oxford friend who had got a job at the BBC, had said to me that as far as he could tell people tended to dismiss the V1 as a rather feeble and typically foreign joke.

In a perverse sort of way my father, like a lot of others, quite enjoyed dodging those missiles. Perhaps he was now 'seeing action' at last. One day I was with him on the steps of Waterloo station when a V1 appeared overhead. Its engine stopped. We retreated to the station wall. He gripped my wrist and we waited. Somewhere north of the river there was a bang. My father looked at me with a bemused expression and shook his head, as though we had witnessed a careless piece of driving. We descended the station steps and crossed the road to wait for a bus.

Another time, on the way home, there was a repeat performance. The Chessington train stopped outside Wimbledon and again we heard the sirens wailing. It was rush hour, and the carriage was full of men on their way home, nearly all of them reading their evening newspapers. There was complete silence. A cough or two, the rustle of a newspaper as someone turned a page. In the distance we heard again the noisy rumble of another V1 rocket, trundling towards the city. It came nearer. The engine cut out.

As one, the men in the railway carriage, in their suits and hats, leaned forward, still (as in Auden's verse) holding their newspapers in front of their faces. *Bang!* Everyone slowly sat back. And no one said a word: one or two men grimaced briefly at each other. The All Clear sounded, and the train moved off. I could only marvel at the utter Englishness of it, and at the fact that not even German high explosive could break suburban man's insistence on privacy in a public place. Perhaps when they arrived home they let it all come out ('Nasty business on the 5.15 this evening, dear . . .').

Soon afterwards the war was over, but it was too late to restore my parents' feelings for each other. The atmosphere at 248 Malden Way was ominously quiet: murmured conversations between my mother and her friends would cease swiftly when I passed near by. Worn out by the drabness and danger of it all, my mother could not offer any diversions to compete with what was available at my father's local pub, the Malden Manor. The ARP post being no longer in existence, it was there he would escape every evening – sometimes proffering some more or less plausible reason ('I promised to drop in and see old man Saunders about the darts tournament'). My mother was left alone with the BBC Home Service for company. Eventually the gossip reached her: he was spending as much time as he could with a woman who lived not far away on the same estate, who was another Malden Manor regular, known for always occupying the same place at the end of the bar with a large gin and It. She was the wife of a war correspondent-photographer who was somewhere in Europe.

One day, the marriage died. I had come home on leave again, to find the atmosphere even more frigid than usual. They didn't seem to be talking to each other. There were angry voices: well, that wasn't new. A door slammed. More shouting. Another slammed door: footsteps going away down the front path. A few days later when I was talking with Derek Cooper in my room upstairs, the doorbell rang. I went down to answer it. 'Who was it?' asked Derek, rising to the strained atmosphere of the household. I remember answering, outwardly *insouciant*, 'It was my father's mistress's husband.'

I can't remember which one of them came and explained things to me: my mother, I think. I had no words to talk about it with her, nor with my father; and as he moved out, my uncles rallied round. My mother's brother Bill Stocks said he was going to 'horse-whip' my father: it was the language of cheap melodrama. I thought it absurd. I didn't believe he owned a horsewhip, certainly not a horse. Perhaps there would be a pitched battle: my mother's three short and slightly-built brothers versus my father and my two paternal uncles, one of whom was a former army boxer, all punching and feinting and boxing each other in the back garden while my brother and I looked on from my bedroom window

39

upstairs. I had written to David: he seemed to have taken the news coolly. In his letter back, he said, 'We are too old to play the wounded children of divorce.'

Divorce was, of course, the outcome – even then, on the suburban estates, an uncommon event in the lives of middle-class people like my parents. It seemed to me I had lived for a long time under the shadow of this final solution: the word 'divorce' had been lying about in our household for years – perhaps as a threat uttered by one or other of them and, when I was a child, feared by me as the ultimate family catastrophe.

Did they really intend things to get to that point? I believe it was one of those occasions when marital brinkmanship went too far: neither of them backed down and both of them called the other's bluff. But this is only conjecture: they didn't seem to want to talk about it with me: I think the matter embarrassed them both, and their guilt and embarrassment infected me. I retreated into my own preoccupations: jazz, chiefly. The subject of their break-up became taboo, off limits, and remained so for years – until my mother was widowed by her second husband: then, at last, she seemed able to talk about her first marriage with greater freedom and candour. Each of them married again, my mother to a man who had served in both the Royal Marines and HM Submarines. He was a decent, simple man, and he thought the world of my mother, but from 1947 onwards she was never happy. The skittish, vivacious young woman of the 1930s belonged to the past. There had been a time in the family circle of aunts and uncles, when 'Rosie's turns' had been famous: anecdotes about people she had met, or seen in the street, or whom they all remembered from other days, these she would turn into great cadenzas of comic description and mimicry. 'Rosie's off!' Auntie Nell or Auntie Vi would say, as my mother's act gathered momentum. My brother and I hated these party turns, and thought she was 'showing off'; but the aunts and uncles responded with whoops of laughter.

That never happened now. The attractive, smartly dressed suburban *coquette* who had charmed the young masters at my school faded from memory: perhaps in an attempt to seal off her former life, my mother let her friends know she would prefer to be known by the romantic, Schubertian name of Rosamund. But it was not enough to soften or mellow the wan, worried-looking woman my mother became in her fifties, inwardly pining for the gawky, cocky young officer my father had been during their courtship.

As for my father himself, he married the woman who had consoled him in the saloon bar of the Malden Manor. She was an ex-nurse, which could have been part of her attraction: she was only a little younger than my mother, and my father had fallen romantically in love. He called her his Princess. They lived in a flat in Cadogan Square, a total change of environment that didn't suit either of them, for they both began to hanker after the tidy gardens, cosy lounges, golf clubs and pubs of the suburbs, and it was not long before they moved out again, to a more familiar district. The house they bought, three-storeys, five-bedrooms, built in the early 1920s, was in a sought-after road in Wimbledon – significantly, a house big enough to provide rooms for my brother and me, the sons of his first marriage. I doubt if this altogether pleased his new wife.

There he proceeded to create some kind of simulacrum of his pre-war life, taking the train to the same office every day, where he would spend the day dictating letters, filling in returns, attending meetings, helping to sew up the linoleum market. His office in Victoria, with its mahogany furniture, with leather armchairs in which he would take a nap every day after lunch in front of a coal fire – this represented for him a standard of achievement which never lost its allure and remained a cause for self-congratulation.

One difference in his routine was that his new wife would often go with him to the local pub or, his new-found alternative venue, the Raynes Park Conservative Club, where he rapidly became an elected officer and, soon, Chairman.

*

All these family changes were well established by the time I was going about my business in Coldharbour Lane. But they had warped relationships in the family, frozen off a lot of normal contact between the four of us. We were awkward with each other as if some big, unspeakable mess had appeared on the carpet before us, or as if someone had some fearful illness we had all agreed not to talk about.

My first marriage in 1951 marked the start of what may be termed my Welsh period. I came to regard myself as a member of the Welsh diaspora although I knew next to nothing about my own family's past, nor how we came to have a Welsh surname. My father, who was born in Birmingham, once described to me a frightening childhood experience of his, when he met a fearsome, unfamiliar grandfather with only one arm, and he also had a vague conviction that his own father, who had been a prison warder, had been born in Dublin.

However, my Welsh name stood me in good stead with the Prys-Jones family, who were patriotic for Wales and, most of them, Welsh-speaking. Chronically short of money, my new wife and I would spend our fortnight's holiday in towns where there were Welsh relatives who would put us up. Porthcawl was popular. My in-laws kept a small flat in that modest Glamorganshire resort, a place with slightly comical connotations, derived perhaps from the reminiscences of Dylan Thomas or a running joke in Timothy Shy's *News Chronicle* column about 'Gerald Barry, the Porthcawl flautist'. Its climate was unpredictable and it was a safe bet that a lot of your holiday would be spent sheltering from the rain on the Esplanade, or cringing before a fierce wind on the sea-shore with the fine sand stinging your face. But when the weather was fair you could enjoy the old-fashioned shops and local walks, the rickety funfair overlooking the sea, and the immense, empty beaches of firm sand pounded flat by huge Atlantic breakers.

Another place where there were obliging relatives was Rhyl: less popular – we only tried it once, for a wet fortnight relieved by outings to north Wales castles and to the pier concert party, named The Quaintesques. There was an amusement parlour on the Esplanade, which had an equally odd name, on the marquee outside – incomprehensible at first and, when comprehended, recognisable as false: UKANKUMINANAVSUMFUN.

I wondered if I could make some commercial use of such experience as I was getting. So I had the idea of creating a game, based on the daily round, called Export. With a few Oxford friends I would sometimes play board games, a little ashamed of such childish pastimes and guilty that this was all an expensive education had equipped us for. Alan Brien and I had whiled away the time between our job applications with Totopoly, Flotilla, and Buccaneer. In the last two games, players had to move tiny plastic ships around a map, and that may have given me the idea for Export, which I thought might make us some money if we could get someone interested. A board was made – a map of the world – and little boats, plus 'money' and cards of various kinds which awarded you certain penalties or advantages, or sometimes inflicted unlikely accidents on your vessel (*'Pirates board your boat and steal your cargo. Miss two turns then proceed to the nearest port'*). All that, plus a dice, and away we went.

But I had to admit that playing at exporting British-made goods was no more amusing and exciting than the real thing. Players sailed their tokens around the map amassing money and credit with nothing very much to stop them except the supply of fake money. A game of Export would last for three or four hours without even the arbitrary, cut-throat drama of Monopoly, with its unforgiving imperatives ('Collect £100', 'Advance to Mayfair', 'Go to jail').

Life seemed slow to get going, for I knew I was one of those young men who didn't have a very clear idea what they wanted to do with themselves. Probably we were, and maybe still are, in the majority. Something that involved writing, that was all I knew: I had started one novel, with a hero called Nick Jenkins, and then read the first of Anthony Powell's famous sequence with a hero of exactly that name. I abandoned my novel in a state of demoralisation. Then I began another, and it was about – but of course – a young intellectual working in a pharmaceutical company. He was turning out horribly priggish and I was dogged by the fear that I wasn't really a writer.

Hoping none of my successful friends would find out, I enrolled in a correspondence course for writers, the Anglo-American School of Writing Success. Their advertisement said NO SALES, NO FEES – what this ambiguous slogan actually meant was that if you hadn't earned the price of enrolment – twelve guineas – by the time you'd finished the twelve lessons, they would return your money. That seemed fair enough. I scraped the money together and off I went. Lesson One: an article on anything that interested you, bearing in mind certain rules, viz., no sentence of more than fifteen words, and no paragraph of more than three sentences. That seemed a bit restricting for my usual piece about the Victorian toy theatre, and I sent it in for their inspection, written according to what I considered more civilised stylistic criteria. Back it came. 'Try *The Lady*,' said the note from the man who ran the correspondence school, whose name was Henry Kowal.

My piece went off – and lo! it was accepted. Though I'd had many pieces in *The Isis*, and one or two other periodicals at Oxford, this was grown-up journalism. I received a cheque for two guineas.

Kowal's advice: when you've sold something to a magazine or paper, follow it up at once with an offer to write something else on the same subject. I asked *The Lady* if they'd like a second article on the toy theatre, but they declined the offer. Penalty point, Kowal.

Next, we had fiction: this was Lesson Two. You had to

nominate a magazine for which you would like to write a story: I chose *Good Housekeeping*, with an outline of a story about a marital tiff – a subject on which I had acquired a good deal of inside knowledge. Kowal didn't like it. Not only that, he informed me I would have to start again. I began to understand how his No Sales, No Fees system worked: you only got the money back if you completed the twelve lessons to his satisfaction, and they could go on indefinitely sending your stuff back until you got tired of the whole thing. Never all that strong, my initial enthusiasm was waning fast.

One day I was sent on some errand which took me into the middle of London. I have forgotten what it was, but it meant a couple of hours or so out of the office and the opportunity was too good to miss. I took a diversion on the way back to Coldharbour Lane and did something you were not supposed to do: I called in person at the offices of the Anglo-American School of Writing Success, Henry Kowal, Prop. The office was in Bond Street, on the top floor of a building with a shoe shop on the ground floor. You had to climb about eight flights of stairs to get there.

I expected something a lot more consistent with writing success than the dingy room I arrived at up in the eaves of the building, where I found Kowal seated at a desk on his own. His name, I learned, was pronounced to rhyme with towel. He was a thin, white-haired, stooping man in his early forties, evidently an American, which I suppose accounted for the get-up-and-go tone of his prospectus. He seemed surprised to see me and even a little embarrassed: well he might. It struck me forcibly, as it should have done already, that if he knew the secrets of writing success, he should have been keeping them to himself and writing prize-winning stories, newspaper features, and novels. I asked him for some advice on finding subjects to write about, and with a confidential air he let me in on his own method, dragging out the bottom drawer of his desk to reveal a shoe-box full of newspaper cuttings. Anything he saw in the daily papers that interested him

– a murder case, a comic accident, a story of personal heroism –
he would cut out and keep. Then, when ideas failed him, he told
me, he would riffle through the cuttings until he found one that
suggested a saleable piece.

There was something about his explanation that suggested this
was not the way to writing success either, and it was clear that
this sad, rumpled man in his shirt-sleeves was not the person to
help me find my way.

Life away from the office chugged along at about the same pitch
of excitement as that which marked the 8.32 to Loughborough
Junction. A keen amateur musician, I graduated from first clarinet in the Worcester Park Orchestra to second in the Wimbledon
Philharmonic. These advances are important to amateurs. It was
the difference between infrequent appearances in places like the
Shannon Corner Odeon (for a Coronation Concert) and a local
church fête, to ambitious concerts, three times a year, in Wimbledon Town Hall.

The Worcester Park Orchestra had been the first 'classical'
orchestra I played in, when on vacation from Oxford: with this
organisation I first experienced the fierce excitement that can
come from taking part in an orchestral performance. Somewhere
Mark Twain wrote about his envy of the musician who sits in the
midst of such a group of players with 'that great sound washing
over him' – and he was right. For anyone with any talent for
music it is an experience more satisfying than almost anything
else life has to offer. The first time I played with the Worcester
Park Orchestra, I could hardly wait for the week to pass so that I
could go again, and it was also an introduction to a phenomenon
I have come to know well: the immense, semi-submerged world
of amateur music-making in this country. I cannot believe that
whoever it was in the last century who dismissed Britain as a
'land without music' had dug below the surface. The taunt is
absurd today and it was certainly not deserved in the 1950s, when
there were many thousands of ordinary people whose unquench-

able aptitude for music-making was driving them to form chamber ensembles, bands, choirs, orchestras, musical societies and clubs, and to organise regular meetings and concerts at which to display their talents.

The Worcester Park Orchestra was typical of many such organisations in the London suburbs at that time. The conductor, a certain Alfred Swinscoe, had an office job somewhere. He also had a large library of orchestral parts which he would comb each week for likely pieces for rehearsal in a local church hall – once only, after which the music would be put away again, to be brought out a few months later. On the whole they were well-known classical works: *Koanga, Demande et Réponse*, Haydn's Farewell Symphony, Mozart's 39th. These were not so much rehearsed as hacked through, usually with an incomplete tally of players. But we did play in public now and then – Strauss waltzes at a church fête, or in a school. Once we were the pit orchestra for a home-grown suburban musical, written and composed by one of Swinscoe's friends, a fable about three lost children who encountered a succession of fairy-tale characters, each of whom had a song to sing. It played for three nights in Wimbledon Town Hall to surprisingly large audiences. Having a retentive memory for tunes I can still remember some of them, and their singers: a man rated star performer in the company who came on as a tree, dressed in brown tights and an army jumper decorated with oak branches: he sang 'I am the erk, the mighty erk, In the forest I am king.' When we appeared at the Shannon Corner Odeon at a concert for the wedding of Princess Elizabeth and the Duke of Edinburgh, the orchestra had the unexpected distinction of accompanying Anne Ziegler and Webster Booth, two popular duettists of the day. As a finale, the audience was invited to sing along with us in *Rule, Brittania*, but until we came to the last two lines hardly anyone knew the words.

The Wimbledon Philharmonic was several orders of competence higher than that. Its alumni included Colin Davis on first clarinet and several other well-known professionals. The conductor was a tall, stooping figure, a local bank manager named Kenneth Tucker who also moonlighted as director of a concert agency, calling himself Arthur Adams. I have played under worse conductors, but he was vain and short-tempered and, on the rostrum, rather more arrogant than was justified by the musical position he occupied. At our concerts we played big works: Brahms symphonies, the Enigma Variations, the Polovtsian Dances, Rhapsody in Blue, when the orchestra's ranks would be well stiffened by professionals, often from the Royal Philharmonic, with whom Tucker had some sort of understanding.

Of course, I lived for Wednesday nights and the orchestra rehearsals, the thought of them sustaining me through the monotonous journeys to Camberwell, the mundane letters and the piles of customs invoices. In 1953 my wife had our first baby, and parenthood was a huge burden on our cruelly stretched family budget. The landlord of our upstairs flat in Wimbledon was a man by the landlordish name of Pennycuick: he and his wife had decided to let the top two floors of their substantial house on the slopes of Wimbledon Hill. He was a crusty, rather irritable retired official of the London Passenger Transport Board and a former colleague of the famous Frank Pick, who devised large stretches of the London Underground system. Mr Pennycuick would now and then invite me to inspect his library, of which he was quite proud: 'Look at this,' he would say, handing me a copy of a Dickens novel. 'It's a second edition.' He also had a collection of old gramophone records – Galli-Curci, Paderewski, the classical hits of thirty years before.

One night as I came in quite late I heard him groaning in their front room downstairs. I tapped on the door and entered. He was sitting in his armchair clutching his chest: 'It's angina,' he croaked. 'I know it!' Unsure what to do, I thought brandy might be the answer, and ran upstairs to see what I could find in the reproduction mediaeval sideboard my mother-in-law had given us as a wedding present. But I had no brandy. Only rum.

I took the bottle down to the ailing man and offered him a tot, which he seized and gulped with suspicious zeal. At that point his wife rushed in wearing a dressing gown with her hair in curlers, and snatched the bottle from her husband's grasp. 'I'll deal with this,' she said grimly. I backed out.

Next morning I was led to understand that I should have recognised the signs of not angina but severe hangover complicated by alcoholic gastritis. However, the Pennycuicks quite liked us: we had got off to a good start when they saw their own double bed, which they had sold to a local second-hand furniture store, being carted back in again: we had bought it from the same shop. I learned afterwards from Alan Brien, who took over the flat when we moved out, that they always referred to me as 'the boy'. As for the flat itself, the rent, for four rooms plus kitchen and bathroom, swallowed two-thirds of my Menley & James salary and there wasn't much available for luxuries. In that category came annual holidays: two weeks was all we M&J types were allowed, though I was reminded I would get an extra day for every year I served after the first ten years. Ten years!

One luxury we indulged in freely when at home was the cinema. There were no fewer than five cinemas within walking or trolleybus-ride distance and television had not yet made its sweeping conquest of cinema audiences. Once or twice a week we would make our way to Regal, Ritz, Rialto or Odeon for whatever was going, sometimes no matter how boring and inane it might be. And 'Queueing all parts' was the cry frequently heard from the uniformed commissionaires, who have now virtually disappeared, along with the cinema organists with their bouncing golf balls, and other signs of the cinema's vanished supremacy.

We moved flats. My wife's parents bought a large Victorian house in Wimbledon which had once been the property of Gertie Morris, the music-hall star, and we divided the house into horizontal levels of influence. But the real loser in this transaction was my father-in-law. When I first met him he was a scholarly, pipe-smoking, sixty-five-year-old Welsh gentleman, who had published several volumes of poetry, and had a huge acquaintance in Wales, particularly its southern counties. On that first occasion, in Cardiff, I saw a carefully dressed, rather slightly built man in a grey suit and formal grey trilby, the kind of man it was hard to imagine as younger than fifty-five or so, still less as the nervous young schoolmaster he had been, during and immediately after the Great War, or the conscientious school inspector pottering around the valleys and villages of Glamorgan and Carmarthenshire. The son of a country schoolmaster, he had been at Jesus College, Oxford, during the reign of Edward VII, had played rugby football against the Prince of Wales and had been a friend of T. E. Lawrence, who was also at Jesus. He and T.E. had shared tutorials: both read History. Unlike Lawrence he had missed the Great War through ill health and had followed, first, his father's profession, and then become an Inspector of Schools. He ended his career as Deputy Chief Inspector for Wales and retired early to become Secretary of the Festival of Britain in Wales, a post doubtless requiring fine judgement as well as considerable powers of organisation and diplomacy. But when the Festival was over, his task was done. And at that point, his wife, my mother-in-law, talked him into moving to London to be near their daughter and the grandchildren.

What crushing blows husbands and wives can thoughtlessly inflict on each other! A. G. Prys-Jones, doyen of Anglo-Welsh poets, was removed from his large circle of friends, his connections with the Welsh Service of the BBC, for whom he used to read his own stories on the air, from the literary gossip of the Principality and its capital, and the leisurely proceedings of the Cardiff Literary Society ... all that, and with it the Glamorganshire landscape and the 'feel' of Wales which had animated his life and, for that matter, his poetry. A good deal of that had to do with stirring episodes in Welsh history, like the conquest of Wales by the Romans and the deeds of Llewellyn the Great, King Arthur and Owain Glendower. Now and again a poem would strike a genuinely lyrical note, but it was for the most part conventional stuff, of a pale, romantic, Tennysonian hue, and much dependent on terms like 'glory' and 'high heritage'. Still, his poems have appeared in Anglo-Welsh anthologies, and a good few of his light verses, often rather funny, have appeared in anthologies of comic verse. I doubt if he was ever truly reconciled to living in London, but he remained there, in the Wimbledon area, until his death at the age of ninety-nine – deaf, a widower, still immersed in his books and anecdotes of his life, his mind as sharp as ever.

One day in 1955 I got in touch again with the Oxford University Appointments Committee, in the hope that, having got me into this dead end in well-named Coldharbour Lane, they could now show me a way out of it. Once again I began to get their foolscap sheets of job descriptions: the Cocoa Marketing Board, Ingersoll Watches, Bowater Corporation, Office Magazine . . . and once, the British Medical Association.

The BMA were looking for someone to be appointed assistant to their Public Relations Officer. I applied, and was summoned to an interview, an unnerving experience because I had to appear before the organisation's entire Public Relations Committee – nearly twenty stern-looking, elderly doctors. The confrontation took place in the largest of the BMA's committee rooms in their headquarters in Tavistock Square. The committee sat around three sides of a square of tables: I had the remaining side to myself. Perhaps it was as well that I'd taken the precaution of swallowing a Drinamyl before I went in, so ensuring the right, subtle degree of artificial, euphoric confidence. Calm elation was exactly what I required.

However, it was even more daunting than most job interviews. They asked me why I wanted the job, what was I doing at the moment, and was I writing anything. I said, a novel. That was true, but it wasn't getting anywhere. One of them said he'd noticed on my application that three of my wife's relatives were doctors. Did that mean I had a closer acquaintance than usual with doctors' problems? Dangerous moment. I sensed a need to deflect any close, weakness-revealing interrogation on this level. I said I thought it meant I had a closer acquaintance than usual with my wife's relatives' problems. Loud and prolonged laughter. I realised this answer had a sort of unintentional, smart-alec wit. However, it wasn't enough. They didn't give me the job. It went to a man with what sounded like a far more suitable background – he was a journalist who was writing verses regularly for *Punch*.

Ruefully, I wrote it off as another failure. But a few months later, I was rung up with the information that the man who had beaten me to it had lost patience with the BMA. The committees and the endless discussions about money were driving him mad, and so he had resigned: to avoid having to go through the whole rigmarole again, they would like to appoint me, if I were still interested. It appeared I had amused the committee with my repartee, and had been the runner-up.

And so, not many weeks later, I tidied my desk and closed the door on my claustrophobic little office, and my humdrum office job, for the last time.

None of the Oxford graduates who were recruited to Menley & James in 1951 lasted long. Creightmore was the first to leave: he went off to study full-time for Bar examinations and eventually was called, and became a barrister. I was the next to go. Soon, Sommers left to work for another, far bigger pharmaceutical firm. Woodcock, the albino advertising copywriter, became an assistant secretary at the Association of the British Pharmaceutical Industry. I am not sure whether these defections indicated some deficiency in Menley & James's recruitment skills – in other words, they'd chosen the wrong people – or in the way they organised promotion for their junior executives. Probably both.

My career, if I may lay claim to so grandiose a concept, was tending inexorably in one direction, towards territory I was going to be in for the next twenty-odd years – to wit, medicine. Even at Menley & James. It's true, I might as well have been exporting currants, or toy soldiers, or lawn-mowers, as pharmaceuticals; but I was getting some sort of an oblique view of the country's doctors, their prescribing habits, some of the pressures they were under, and their social attitudes.

I was now about to move a great deal closer to that profession, to become familiar with its trials, torments, mistakes, splendours, miseries, and failures. Furthermore, it was at a time when doctors' rôle in society was changing, along with the techniques and medicaments at their disposal to help the sick. The pharmaceutical industry was changing with it.

For the last few months of my time at Menley & James, a representative of Smith Kline & French seemed to have taken up permanent residence at Coldharbour Lane. He was a man by the name of Richard Pfizenmaier. James Cagney could have played the part in the movie: Pfizenmaier was a short, self-confident American, with close-cropped gingery hair and a damaged right arm: he had been a fighter pilot in the US Air Force and took people aback when introduced by offering his left hand. He would wander around the building engaging us in conversation, asking innocent questions, sitting in at meetings and visible in the canteen at lunch-times. It was not made clear to us what his function was, but he was gradually recognised as a company spy.

His arrival presaged an upheaval in the fortunes of Menley & James Ltd. It happened a few months after I had left. Smith Kline & French bought the entire company and moved it to new premises in Welwyn.

My former colleagues were no longer M&J types. Suddenly they were SKF types. They now worked for a huge company they'd never seen, in Philadelphia, not Mr Menley and Mr James: those two had vanished in a puff of smoke, and all you could say was that, just like Mother Siegel, they had never really been there in the first place. The old 'family' firm was based on a myth but its title, Menley & James, was kept alive, to be dusted off and wheeled out later on when they were in need of a name to put on the label of a drug to treat symptoms of the common cold, called Coldrex. Some of the staff moved out to Welwyn, but only the ones deemed essential to a smooth takeover. My ex-colleague Barnes stayed on, though not in the Export Department. Clark, the Export Manager, became a director: not very long afterwards he was about to begin another tour abroad – but he didn't make it, for he collapsed and died in the departure lounge at Heathrow.

The Menley & James story at about this time was part of the accelerating Americanisation of the country; and also the process by which long-standing pharmaceutical firms of modest stature were being elbowed out of the way, and scooped up by larger competitors, usually American or Swiss, but occasionally British. Old-established firms were being swallowed whole: Barnes's former employers Allen & Hanbury's, for one, along with Duncan, Flockhart, and Evans Medical Supplies were devoured by the giant firm Glaxo.

It was also the end of the M&J connection with Coldharbour Lane and Camberwell, that Edwardian relic of an inner suburb with its moth-eaten theatre, the Camberwell Palace (sample attractions: *Why Cover Girls, Hell's Lagoon, Paris By Night, Nine O'Clock Nudes*), its rubber-goods stores, lavish funerals, army surplus shops, horse-drawn baker's vans and innocent *graffiti* ('Margaret has a horsey grin and is bats', I once saw chalked on our outside wall). It was also the end of an era in the pharmaceutical business. The Celery Tonics, Soothing Powders, Miracletts and Popular Pellets of yesteryear, the old survivors from the age of quackery like Fenning's Fever Cure (formula: powdered dragon's blood) were going the way of Mother Siegel's Syrup and Keene's One-Night Cold Cure. The drug industry was now controlled by huge corporations manufacturing antibiotics and anti-depressants and, gradually, all the armoury of scientific medicine. Ahead of them, too, were such disasters as the thalidomide and chloramphenicol affairs.

For me, it was farewell to the 8.32, the monthly Stock and Sales Returns, the customs invoices and the annual increments of £50. The BMA were offering the handsome salary of £1,000 a year, with increments of £100. Exciting times in the accounts department would never dawn for me now.

Four

The Appointed Day, and After

NO GREATER CONTRAST could have been imagined than
that between the drab, utilitarian offices of Menley & James Ltd,
Manufacturing Chemists, and the stately building which was the
seat of the British Medical Association.

BMA House, in Bloomsbury, was the headquarters of an
organisation to which more than ninety per cent of British
doctors belonged. In its layout, customs and activities, no less
than in the views on society and the world that emanated from
it, this building epitomised the whole spirit of this, in those days,
much-deferred-to profession.

It was and is a fine building. Through the archway that leads
off Tavistock Square there is a large quadrangle: the main wall
lining this space is punctuated by classical columns. Behind that is
the Great Hall, an impressive chamber with rows of fat lapis lazuli
pillars and banners hanging along the walls like battle colours:
they are the banners of BMA Divisions around the country. The
lapis lazuli is actually false, the mottled colours skilfully painted
on. Edwin Lutyens designed and built BMA House in 1913 for
the Theosophical Society – or rather, he started to build it. It was
unfinished when the Great War began and, though incomplete, it
was taken over by the army and considerably messed about by the
War Office Pay Department. Then in 1923 the BMA decided to
move their offices from Charles Holden's building in the Strand

(now Zimbabwe House) with the notorious Epstein statues. After a brief search they bought the Tavistock Square building. Someone must have had an eye for architecture – probably the Treasurer of the day, an eye surgeon and minor poet named N. Bishop Harman, who slightly spoiled things by proposing to have a tower placed on the roof of the new HQ. Lutyens ignored his suggestion.

The new BMA House was in a semi-derelict state, and the BMA commissioned Lutyens to finish it. He never did. N. Bishop Harman was alarmed at what it was costing to install the gold-painted coffered ceiling Lutyens had specified for the Great Hall. Pressed for a cheaper alternative, Lutyens procrastinated, then finally lost patience with the BMA and its Premises Committee, and snarled at Harman: 'Leave the bloody thing open.' They did, and the ceiling never was finished.

Outside, beyond the collegiate-style porter's lodge, was Tavistock Square, exhibiting few characteristics of the tranquil Regency square it must once have been: it was becoming what it is today, a large roundabout for traffic with green trees and an acre or two of grass in the middle. But this, too, made for me an exhilarating change from the streets of Camberwell: instead of Loughborough Junction, my destination was Waterloo and the bus across Waterloo Bridge, past the Shot Tower and the Lion Brewery and the site of the Festival of Britain only a few years before. Up Kingsway and Southampton Row to the affluent terraces of the other Bloomsbury squares, with their crop of blue plaques; nearby were the massive caryatids of St Pancras Church and, next to BMA House, the gentrified Dickensian ally of Woburn Walk. Part of BMA House had been built on the site of one of Dickens's London homes and another blue plaque commemorates the fact. Coldharbour Lane this was not.

Visible from the street when I approached BMA House that day in 1955 were large ornamental gates of wrought iron: these could be opened with a key of solid gold, or they would have been if royalty arrived, which they did from time to time. Within was a quadrangle, with a fountain in the middle and large stone figures in stiff, frozen attitudes around the water's edge – they represented Sacrifice, Aspiration, Prevention, and Cure. The main committee rooms and offices, and the Great Hall, formed the three sides of the hollow square around this area. Wings had been added to either side of the principal building, and across another courtyard on the southern side stood the Library Wing.

That was where the Public Relations Department was to be found. The room they'd given me was luxurious: you could have fitted my Menley & James office into it three or four times over, and it had the sharp, satisfying reek of new fitted carpets and wooden furniture, also brand-new. I could look out through my two large sash windows on to the courtyard, which was ornamented with another, smaller fountain and a tree which had been conveyed there from the Mediterranean island of Cos, where Hippocrates had lived: it was a stunted, unhealthy object, and it failed to 'take' in the fume-laden atmosphere of London. But under just such a tree, so they said, the Greek sage, father of medicine, had in days of yore framed the Hippocratic Oath, in the intervals of treating his patients.

This part of the premises was known as the Garden of Remembrance, a typical BMA trope: they liked ornate and important titles. They also had a Court of Honour and in the Members' Dining Room a Book of Valour, while the man who looked after the BMA's funds, who anywhere else would have been called the Chief Accountant, was called the Financial Comptroller.

The entire place served a number of different functions. Apart from being the administrative headquarters of the association and a meeting-place for doctors when they were arguing about doctors' pay (called 'remuneration') and kindred matters, it was also the editorial office of the *British Medical Journal*. It housed too the large and well-used BMA Library and it was a club for doctors, with a garage where they could have their cars serviced, plus a members' lounge and a dining room.

On the walls of the latter were hung the stuffed heads of

slain beasts – moose, wildcat, bison, caribou, etc., a sombre collection. They had been presented to the association by some loyal, long-dead member who presumably had shot the creatures in the first place.

When you studied these grim trophies, it was easy to believe they were telling you something about the state of the profession.

It took a while to get used to the modes and manners of organised medicine, especially after the smallness of life at Menley & James, and to understand fully the state of mind that prevailed there as doctors strove to come to terms with the conditions of practice in the 1950s. Eight years before I went to work at Tavistock Square, the BMA had gone through a period of prolonged convulsion, locked in combat with the post-war Labour Government over the introduction of the National Health Service.

At that time, medicine, in both outlook and habits, not to mention political allegiance, was an extremely conservative profession. Changes of any kind, let alone something as traumatising as the inauguration of the world's first comprehensive health service, were allowed to take place slowly, grudgingly and laboriously, if at all. In the 1950s, doctors even looked a little out-of-date. In the members' car park, Armstrong-Siddeley Sapphires and Rolls-Royces were far from rare, and certain doctors frequently turned up for meetings in the old-fashioned doctor's uniform of short black morning-coat and striped grey trousers. There were even one or two women doctors who thought it necessary to affect a female version of this dress – in black jacket and striped skirt.

For a long time the BMA had been pondering some ideas of its own for a post-war health scheme, and a Medical Planning Commission they had set up at the height of the blitz, with impressive sang-froid when you think about it, had produced a report outlining the kind of service they wanted: it was framed almost exclusively from the doctors' point of view, and was mainly about how they were to be paid. But they had been left standing by the speed with which the Labour Government sprinted ahead after the 1945 election. Also, they were haunted by the idea that they might find themselves conscripted into some kind of full-time health service, paid by salary and in the employment of local authorities, and liable to be 'posted' to whatever part of the country the Government decided was short of medical manpower.

Moreover, lodged somewhere in the association's group memory was the uncomfortably similar experience that had befallen them thirty-seven years earlier. Then, it had been the start of the National Health Insurance Service and the arrival of the 'panel' doctor. Their opponent through that campaign, during months of public wrangling, had been Lloyd George, who had pushed through his scheme for an assisted family doctor service in the teeth of the profession's objections.

History, as history tends to do, was repeating itself. This time, in 1947–8, they found themselves up against another mettlesome Welshman – Aneurin Bevan, Minister of Health in Clement Attlee's great post-war reforming administration and no less tough an adversary than Lloyd George had been. And as in 1911, so in 1948 the BMA's leaders had cast themselves as defenders of the tried-and-true usages of medicine against interfering, idealistic busybodies. Politicians, they would declare, knew too little about the diagnostic and moral dilemmas doctors had to face daily, and had no scruples about up-ending the tradition of centuries.

The National Health Service actually came into operation on 5 July 1948: strange to reflect now that only three months before that date, known at the time as 'The Appointed Day', sixty-four per cent of doctors had declared themselves opposed to the NHS Act and fifty-two per cent said they wouldn't co-operate with the scheme. Just under 5,000 were in favour of it.

Yet two weeks after the NHS had started, the Ministry of Health announced – I expect with some complacency – that about ninety per cent of family doctors had signed on and ninety-three per cent of the public had registered with a doctor.

Partly, it was a concession to the inevitable. But there were other factors as well. In spite of the gung-ho speeches of their leaders, the doctors, truth to tell, had lost their nerve. One of the BMA leaders of the time said colourfully, 'the troops are going home' – defeated warriors, weary veterans let down by their generals, anticipating the order to stand down. And the medical defences were well and truly turned when Aneurin Bevan 'bought' the support of the medical colleges with his scheme for Merit Awards – extra payments for consultants which would jack up their incomes to a gratifyingly high level. Bevan boasted privately that he had stuffed their mouths with gold.

The medical profession would never be the same again. Its oracular, God-like character was already compromised by the noisy public argument it had been involved in and the exposure of such matters as the purchase of 'goodwill' – that is, the custom by which a retiring practitioner could sell his practice to the doctor who was replacing him. Bevan hated it, and said it amounted to the sale and purchase of patients.

And when the new health scheme did start, there was a mad rush as the lame, the halt and the near-sighted queued up to have somebody do something at last about ailments they had been putting up with for years. Opticians had stocked up with three million pairs of glasses in readiness for the NHS's first year: two million had gone by the end of the first eight weeks. For the services of the country's dentists the demand was likewise prodigious: the Health Ministry forecast expenditure in this department during the first nine months of just over seven million pounds. In the event the amount was well over seventeen million. It was an ominous portent of what would happen consistently year by year, as the demand for medical services rose and rose and rose.

In the early fifties the BMA was still feeling bruised from its long slugging-match with Aneurin Bevan. At Tavistock Square, by the way, his name was usually pronounced Bev-Anne. Mostly it was Tory-minded people who did this: ostensibly the idea was to distinguish him from Ernest Bevin, the Labour Foreign Secretary, but round the tables in the BMA's Members' Dining Room, doctors usually managed to say the name with a sort of grimace. There were other names that, similarly, they tended to utter with a sneer. In the last, urgent, cliff-hanging, behind-the-scenes bargaining that had gone on before 8 July, a key figure had been Lord Moran, then President of the Royal College of Physicians, who had acted as a sort of broker between Whitehall and Tavistock Square. Moran had been Winston Churchill's personal physician during the war, but he had become thoroughly unpopular with the BMA in consequence of his rôle in 1948, and he was known at BMA House as Corkscrew Charlie, 'Corkscrew' for short. He did nothing to rectify his unpopularity when, a few years later, he published his memoirs, which included details of his most famous patients' medical history normally classifiable as confidential.

One individual who did not have quite the same bogeyman status, but by the mid-1950s had come to be regarded, strangely enough, with mistrust, was Dr Charles Hill. This was odd, because he had been Secretary of the BMA during the 'troubles': it was Hill who had managed the BMA's stop-the-NHS campaign but he was also that rare thing in those days, a doctor widely known to the people at large – usually referred to in condescending tones at Tavistock Square as 'the lay public'. Hill's celebrity had come about during the war as the Radio Doctor, giving regular five-minute talks in the early morning on the Home Service, just before the eight o'clock news, with advice to listeners about such everyday matters as travel sickness, sound sleep, the common cold, chilblains and stomach rumbles. Thanks to his ordinary-bloke manner and rueful, avuncular way of talking, many of Hill's bits of homely advice – in those days when radio was the supreme form of home entertainment – had entered the repertoire of the nation's amateur mimics, who would drone on about 'prunes, those little black-coated workers' and commercial laxatives that would 'stimulate the bowel into a chronic frenzy of irritable activity'.

That kind of personal publicity was itself suspect in the BMA, where, in those days, the Central Ethical Committee used to spend long hours over pedantic attempts to define how far doctors could go in, for example, writing articles for the popular press. Apart from that, there were those in the medical profession who believed Hill had 'sold the pass' to 'the Socialists' by not 'sticking to his guns', these being the kind of rousing Imperialist metaphor then in current use in Tavistock Square. However, the common touch Hill had demonstrated on the Home Service, and his political deportment during the 1946–8 campaign, had been watched with approval at Conservative Central Office: he had already stood for Parliament in 1945 as an Independent candidate for Cambridge University (and been defeated by a Conservative, Sir Kenneth Pickthorn). Now he was adopted as National Liberal and Conservative candidate for Luton; he resigned from the BMA and set sail on a Parliamentary career that took him ultimately to the House of Lords and Governorship of the BBC. Some of his ex-colleagues probably expected that once he was in Parliament he would be in a position to do the profession a bit of good. But as an MP he kept well clear of medical politics, and his failure to take up the rôle of Our Man at Westminster probably accounted for some of the animus felt towards him. As someone once said to me in the BMA, when I asked why he never visited it, 'He's soared far above this place' – and it was true, though he did once come down to earth sufficiently to appear, unannounced, in the Dining Room for lunch, causing a muffled stir of excitement, as though some famous film star had casually dropped in.

My own arrival at BMA House was a lot less worthy of note. The BMA Secretary at that time, Hill's successor, was a balding, white-moustached, self-effacing Scotsman called Angus Macrae. There were twenty or so other 'officials', paid employees of the association, who ran the place theoretically under the direction of elected 'officers' such as the Chairman of Council, the Treasurer, the Chairman of the Representative Body and the chairmen of the important committees. Most of the officials had medical qualifications: the others either had university degrees or some other professional qualification.

The rest of the people in the building were 'staff': the Nibelung horde of Tavistock Square, who were kept resolutely in their place, if not actually below ground. Some of them could remember a time, not long past, when 'lay staff' were forbidden to share a lift with a BMA member, or ring up medical officials on the office telephone lest they sully their ears with their tiresome questions and pleb accents: if they wanted to speak to one of the doctors they had first to get in touch with their secretaries, who would act as go-betweens.

Eight of the officials were on the editorial staff of the *British Medical Journal*, and they included the editor, Hugh Clegg, a prickly figure who now and again found himself in opposition to the views of the BMA as a whole, and didn't mind saying so. He had also kept Charles Hill supplied with material for his war-time broadcasts, but received no credit for it. Clegg was a man of formidable intelligence, but the omission rankled.

Of the remaining fourteen officials, who worked on the other side of the BMA's large Lutyens-designed building, nine were doctors. I was one of the laymen, along with the Librarian, the Financial Comptroller and his deputy, and my immediate superior, the Public Relations Officer. The PRO was John Pringle, another Scot. His job had been created by Charles Hill at the end of his time at the BMA: Hill considered too little had been done to 'present' the doctors' case to the public. Before that they had made do with a part-time press officer who also worked on *The Times*. Pringle's appointment was a sign they meant business.

The BMA mandarins considered they suffered from a poor public image. It might not have helped that they had employed some absurdly amateurish ways to plead their case *coram populo*. Pamphlets were handed out in waiting rooms: 'YOUR DOCTOR OR

THE STATE'S DOCTOR?' demanded one. 'Your Doctor should only owe one loyalty – TO YOU', said another. Yet another ran, 'Baby will HAVE to go to the Welfare . . . The Kids will HAVE to go to the School Clinic . . . Mother to the Ante-Natal Clinic . . . Father to the "Works" Doctor . . . And Granny – ?' The question hung in a pregnant silence. They also had a film produced which was intended to glorify the character of the old-fashioned family doctor – an admirable type, there is no doubt, but the creaking production and reverential tone of this film were enough to ensure it had no wide distribution.

Small wonder, all things considered, that after their struggle with Bevan the BMA was perceived by outsiders as an out-of-date, self-serving bunch of Tory stick-in-the-muds who had stood in the way of one of the most popular measures of post-war reform. Hill considered this could have been corrected by the right kind of 'public relations' and he had already done something to further this scheme by appointing, on a retainer, a certain Colin Hurry as the BMA's public relations adviser.

Hurry was a remarkable man. Tall, affable, courteous, dressed always in formal city wear but with a black stock tie and wing-collar, he was the last survivor of a group of wits who used to frequent the Savage Club and had included Sir John Squire, Hilaire Belloc, J. B. Morton and Hesketh Pearson. It was well known that one of the characters in A. G. MacDonnell's novel *England, Their England* was really Colin Hurry. He had published one or two volumes of light verse under a pseudonym, and he was a witty, well-read man of pronounced Tory views. He had spent most of his working life in advertising, but he viewed that profession too with the same cynical amusement with which he did the newer and more sinister one of public relations. His definition of public relations was 'the art of explaining away'. Nor was he much impressed by doctors *en masse*. 'Just because they can tell anybody, Duke or dustman, to take his trousers down and cough,' Hurry remarked to me when I first arrived, 'they think they're God Almighty.'

To a lot of the doctors involved in BMA affairs Hurry was a rather puzzling figure, in his old-fashioned get-up, courtly manners, and quietly devastating opinions. He had first been retained by the BMA as adviser on public relations in 1943. Quite soon afterwards he took them aback with a memorandum asserting that the appointment of PROs by government departments, business firms and other institutions was a symptom of a diseased social and economic system, and the thought that the medical profession should now require one of its own, he told them, was a very bad sign indeed. He also had a profound dislike of the idea of a state medical service, which he persistently referred to as 'collectivisation', a word with overtones of Bolshevik menace. Other Hurryisms included the statement that there was no such thing as 'Public Opinion' – the term was meaningless and obfuscatory and only used by people who knew it was so. He had a low opinion of the BMA as a political force: yet, paradoxically, Hurry was one of the men who helped gradually to convince them that if they were to have any hope of fighting the government they would have to get the public on their side.

I was very much indebted to Hurry: he had been responsible for my being at the BMA at all, since he was the one who had persuaded the Secretary to appoint me, the runner-up, rather than have a repeat performance of the laborious selection process of six months before. In many respects, his way of handling this and other BMA problems was different from that of the Public Relations Officer John Pringle. Pringle, a Cambridge man, had begun his career as a journalist on the *Manchester Guardian*, where he had become a leader writer. After that he had moved to the BBC in its Reithian heyday, and had had the distinction of producing the first current affairs radio programme, entitled *The World Goes By*. From there, after a spell in the Portland Place news room during the war, he had moved to *The Listener* as deputy editor. After that, it was the BMA.

Pringle was in his fifties, a nervous and almost unbearably twitchy individual, seldom if ever in a state of repose, who smoked heavily and seemed permanently exasperated by the people who employed him and paid his not ungenerous salary. His chronic irritation with the place had evidently shown itself quite early. More than once he told me the story of his first interview with the Public Relations Committee, when, after ten minutes of cross-examination on a level he had thought rather puerile, someone had asked him to say why he wanted the job. Pringle lost patience and answered, 'For the money.' This was seen as refreshing candour and he got the job. He was also fond of telling how, after being appointed, he eventually had to appear before the entire BMA Council – sixty-odd influential doctors, in the Council Chamber – to answer yet more questions, at the conclusion of which he was treated to a round of applause. As he led him outside, Charles Hill whispered in his ear, 'Make the most of it, cock; it's the last you'll get.'

At the age of thirty, I was by far the youngest official and was keenly aware of the fact. Colin Hurry said to me: 'Always remember you've got something all these types here envy from the bottom of their hearts. Youth.' The true weight of this wise remark didn't come home to me for a few more decades. Yet I wasn't hugely encouraged by it then, and continued to blush when spoken to, feeling nervous and out of my depth. When I had been at the BMA no more than a week or two, I over-heard one of my companions at the luncheon table asking his neighbour if he had been following a recent correspondence on the use of masks in the theatre. I thought this might be, at last, a conversation I could take part in – I could have thrown in a few remarks about, say, the earliest performances of Sophoclean tragedy. Then I realised it was surgical masks they had in mind.

There was a grown-up atmosphere about the place which took some getting used to. With public school formality, Pringle addressed me as 'Vaughan'. So did the others. After the genteel *politesse* of Menley & James I found this disconcerting and hard

67

to copy: it seemed rather rude to address by their surnames men old enough to be my father.

Once again, you were expected to be formally dressed: suits at all times. I compromised this unwritten rule by appearing now and then in an outfit of Irish tweed – but only on Fridays. The first time I appeared in it I was challenged by another non-medical officer, a rather haughty woman who helped to edit one of the specialist journals published by the BMA. I explained that I was going away to the country for the weekend (naturally this was a complete lie), and I was interested to note that other officials began to do the same thing. Tweed suits on Friday began to be tolerated without much more than a lifted eyebrow, and so I had been responsible for a small innovation in the conduct of BMA affairs.

Some of the conventions at the BMA struck me as more than a little laughable. I was also amused, once again, by some of the names at the BMA. There was a Dr Catto, never known to contribute anything to the committees on which he now and then appeared, provoking the comment a friend made to me once, 'Catto, as usual, lay doggo.' A Dr Leak was Chairman of a committee on accidental death through coal-gas poisoning. Another odd phenomenon was that the more important doctors about the place had done tricky things with their initials, contriving for themselves more important-sounding names than they had been given by their mothers and fathers: H. Guy Dain, T. Rowland Hill, R. Prosper Liston, T. Holmes Sellors, L. Dougal Callander, etc. I assumed the initials concealed something they were ashamed of, like Trevor, or Leslie. I think Liston's 'R' may have stood for Reginald. Dain's 'H' stood for Harry. He had been a powerful figure in his day, though well into his eighties by this time – Chairman of Council during the run-up to 1948, a pugnacious little GP from Birmingham. Nobody would have dared call him anything but Guy, and few were on those terms with him. Pringle called him Sir. At the end of his career, and a little late in the day, he was awarded a knighthood: Sir Guy Dain. Wonderful.

Meanwhile, by contrast, it so happened that the names of members of the clerical staff underlined their lowly status. There was a Mr Hacker, a Mr Towner, a Mr Currer, a Mr Prosser and a Mr Scrivener – oddly enough he was the Chief Clerk. There seemed a suspiciously large number of these 'tradesman' names ending in -er. I cannot think why, unless some inner compulsion had led the doctors to employ people who sounded like mere artisans, as if their proper place were a few rungs down the ladder. And some of the other members of the staff had names that exhibited a sort of Dickensian eccentricity: we had a Mr Makepeace, there was a Miss Marriage, a Miss Angel and the essentially palindromic Miss Middlemiss; also there was a sprinkling of names that sounded like anagrams of something else. There was a Mr Tarbox, and a Mr Srobat.

These employees had few illusions left about doctors; and viewed from close quarters, the medical profession did seem to have more warts than most others. Pringle must have become aware of this quite soon after he was taken on as the man who was going to win friends and influence people on their behalf. Moreover, I think he was consumed with private anger at the thought that his job at the BMA was a step down from the *Guardian* and the BBC. A well-meaning colleague once told him he would soon deserve to be recognised as an honorary doctor: it was intended as praise. Pringle, with icy hauteur, replied: 'I am a journalist.'

Well, he wasn't, not any more. He had forfeited his independence and, what was more, he had turned his back on the heady rewards of journalism: the company of other journalists, the excitement, the champagne exhilaration when a big story is breaking, the adrenalin rush of an 'exclusive' and the satisfaction of knowing, when the morning's edition has been put away – or the evening's programme has gone out – that you have contributed something to the ferment of discussion that will follow. In place of that, Pringle had opted for a life dominated by a top-heavy organisation of political innocents operating largely through committees. And his privately expressed hostility to 'this place' was one of the ways his inner rage came out. When the association acquired for themselves a coat of arms there was some discussion over the design of a suitable crest. Pringle suggested a boa constrictor. He would stand at the window of his handsome bow-windowed office overlooking the Garden Court, arms folded, balefully regarding the eminent members passing to and fro. One day, the Treasurer, L. Dougal Callander, made his corpulent, stiff-jointed progress past the Tree of Cos and the fountain. 'Waddling ass!' hissed Pringle.

The BMA constitution, as I was instructed to tell anyone who asked, was democratic. There was an annual 'Parliament', namely the summer meeting of the Representative Body, with members drawn from all over the country: they elected the Council, whose function was to execute the policies they agreed upon in debate – policies towards everything from drunken driving to fees for giving dental anaesthetics. To this end the Council set up numerous committees, perhaps with some short-term task, like collecting the BMA's evidence for a government inquiry; or received reports from permanent committees dealing with, say, general practice affairs, hospital medicine or the public health service.

Every day, it seemed, somewhere in the building, there were committees in session, and Pringle instructed me to attend them. My heart sank at this. I developed a lasting dislike of committees: I tend to perform badly if called upon to speak at them, and at the time I felt guilty at finding them unbearably boring. The BMA's were conducted along formal lines, with points of order, points of information, motions moved and seconded and committee members speaking through the chairman, often at exhausting length. No wonder my predecessor had preferred writing for *Punch*.

At first I had no idea what these committees were on about. I would choose to attend the ones that sounded as if they might be interesting – not a very reliable criterion given my ignorance of medical affairs at the time. Having dabbled in the works of Freud, Stekel, Groddeck and others I made a point of attending the Psychological Medicine Group Committee, whose members included some of the most distinguished psychiatrists of the day. I was surprised to find nearly all of them exhibiting signs of psychological maladjustment – one a pronounced nervous tic, another a bad stammer, another was forever fiddling with his asthma ventilator and another moved about in a personal cloud of expensive perfume. And like almost every other committee, their agenda was largely taken up with matters of, as the doctors called it, remuneration.

Doctors' pay was *the* subject at BMA House. It was generally assumed it was what the BMA were there for – to argue the point with successive Ministers of Health, hanging on to, and occasionally brandishing, their ultimate weapon, mass resignation from the National Health Service. This was where the Public Relations Officer came in. Pringle believed it was part of his job to bring influence to bear on people who mattered – politicians, peers, senior civil servants. He was a member of the Reform Club, and most evenings he would repair there, with the object, I presumed, of listening to the gossip and passing on the thoughts of the people at Tavistock Square.

Colin Hurry and others would assure the committees at BMA House there was a fundamental store of good will towards them through the very nature of their work, and urge them to try to put this to use, although this good will was chipped away whenever a doctor was rude, off-hand, or brusque to a patient, or displayed his incompetence in any one of a hundred different ways. One of the functions of the Public Relations Department was to field telephone calls and letters from patients with a grievance against a doctor, the usual practice being to send them on to some other organisation, like the Local Medical Committee or even the General Medical Council. All through the years I worked at BMA House, doctors kept coming up with bright ideas for emphasising the 'right' side of medicine: how to bring to the notice of the patients in crowded waiting rooms images of caring family doctors, desperately overworked house officers and dedicated pioneers at the frontiers of science. Of course there were such people. But in those days they generally gave BMA House, with its politically tarnished reputation, a wide berth.

The Annual Meeting of the BMA showed the association at its most eccentric. Each year they arrived like a travelling funfair at some large town for their Annual Representative Meeting, and the Representative Body would cobble together an official BMA view on a long list of professional and public issues: whether charges should be made for prescriptions (medicines were dispensed free of charge in the Health Service's early days); on drunken driving, and of course the fees to be charged for examining a driver suspected of being drunk; on contraceptive advice by general practitioners and whether that ought to 'attract' a fee; and so on and so on. The agenda for the ARM was immense, and the debates seemed to get longer every year as the BMA managers struggled to find ways of controlling those representatives, far from small in number, who were prolix, obtuse, naive or ill informed. The stars of the Representative Body could be worth listening to, but they were well outnumbered by the wild men, the bores, and the eccentrics. One RB regular, a Home Counties public-health doctor who for no clear reason would usually affect a kilt for the meeting, was well known for his furious onslaughts against people who wasted doctors' time with unnecessary complaints: such people deserved to be put in prison, he cried, face mottled with rage. Next day, a newspaper headline, 'JAIL FOR PATIENTS – DOCTOR'S CALL', left him thunderstruck, and even angrier.

The Annual Meeting also included two throwbacks to meetings of Victorian times. One was a church service, featuring a procession, in full regalia, from the main conference hotel to the local cathedral. The other was one it shared with Menley

& James, namely an annual outing – a steamer along the South Coast when the meeting was held in Torquay, or a fleet of coaches to the Giant's Causeway when it was in Belfast. There were social occasions of varying degrees of grandeur: wine-and-cheese parties, an annual dinner, a reception by the Mayor of the city in which the meeting was being held, and an Address by the President of the BMA – a new one was elected every year, usually a medical *éminence* from the location of the meeting. Both the latter events ended in a dance. Everyone, officials included, was supposed to turn up for the reception in full fig. In the BMA, this meant full evening dress with white tie and tails, plus medals and decorations, and on top of all that, your academic gown, hood, and square, hired for the occasion from Ede and Ravenscroft. The sight of a crowd of middle-aged and elderly doctors waltzing, foxtrotting or tangoing round the dance floor in this cumbersome rig in the heat of a July evening wasn't one you'd easily forget.

Five

The Art of Explaining Away

IT WAS TAKEN for granted that the BMA's annual grumbling session would be reported in the newspapers. Forward, the Public Relations Department: Pringle and a small squad of secretaries, with me bringing up the rear.

We were there to smooth the way for twenty or thirty journalists despatched by their editors to cover this event: not an assignment to be sniffed at since the meeting more or less guaranteed a few page-leads and prominent bylines, if not a front-page spread. The representatives of the Fourth Estate sat in front of and below the platform of the Representative Meeting, waiting for a story. On dull afternoons when there hadn't been a story all day, it was sometimes possible to manufacture one, by having a word with one of the more worldly doctors present and stimulating him to say something dramatic.

The press 'corps' at BMA meetings included a group of veteran reporters – specialists who, when I started out, all knew far more about what was happening than I did. They were mostly correspondents from the national newspapers, but there were also reporters from leading provincials, broadcasting organisations and the agencies. (I can recall from my first ARM Alan Whicker as reporter for the Exchange Telegraph news agency and Lynne Reid-Banks for Independent Television News.) Then there would be representatives from the local papers and, as time went

74

on, from the 'paramedical' press – those periodicals, including even newspapers, which are circulated to doctors usually free of charge, and financed by the advertising they carried – predominantly, advertising by drug companies.

The veterans were a hard-bitten bunch who on the whole treated me with tolerance and friendliness. The doyen of the press corps was the *Daily Mirror* Science Correspondent, Ronald Bedford. Many of the doctors assumed a patronising, contemptuous attitude towards him, partly because he suffered from a speech defect caused by a cleft palate, but mainly because of their lofty assumption that his newspaper, being a popular one, was incapable of reporting serious issues. How wrong they were. Bedford's daily task was far from simple – to report often complex arguments or scientific observations, accurately but concisely, and in a way that brought before readers more or less uninformed about medicine the main point of the day's story. It was a skill born of his many years of experience as a reporter and of his sharp intelligence.

On the whole, doctors didn't read the *Mirror*. They read *The Times*, or more usually the *Telegraph*. But here again many of them were uncomfortable with what was printed in the latter newspaper about BMA affairs. The *Telegraph*'s Health Services Correspondent was John Prince, a pensive, nervous man with an uncanny knack of picking out the most embarrassing aspects of a story. His work reminded me of the definition, 'News is what someone doesn't want published.' From many years' experience of BMA meetings, Prince had an instinct for asking awkward questions, and they were coloured by a populist enthusiasm for the National Health Service. So good was he at getting under the skin of the BMA leaders, so good at piecing together the scraps of information available to him, that on more than one occasion his reports prompted a kind of witch-hunt within BMA House, the object of which was to unmask the mole assumed to have been feeding him with his material. There wasn't one.

I mention these two journalists and the suspicion with which they were regarded in BMA House because they belong to a period in which doctors as a whole had failed so far to come to terms with the risk of exposure to popular scrutiny and criticism through the public prints. Medicine was now expected to serve society in a way few doctors twenty years earlier would have recognised, let alone approve of: many of them went down protesting heatedly. There was an organisation called the Fellowship for Freedom in Medicine, a kind of Ku Klux Klan of medical politics, though very much less sinister and shorter lived, dedicated to the impossible task of blocking further inroads into the profession's independence – which amounted, broadly, to making a fuss from time to time in the correspondence columns of *The Times* or the *British Medical Journal*. The FFM's 'muscle' was provided by a number of senior consultants, in mainly private practice, but the membership included, too, some resolutely conservative general practitioners who had managed to stay out of the Health Service. They were a dwindling band. At the opposite end of the political spectrum was the left-wing Medical Practitioners' Union, also now a vanished organisation, who had more influence than their small numbers would have led you to expect.

Tacked on to the end of the five-day Representative Meeting was a Scientific Meeting, when papers would be read on matters of medical interest. By this time in the organisation's history it was seldom that any truly startling or original scientific research was unveiled on these occasions, but the fact that someone had stood up at the BMA and talked about it publicly would give potential news value to the subject of any paper delivered. In the BMA's very earliest days, when it was the Provincial Medical and Surgical Association (it had been founded in 1832), papers on public health, new surgical techniques or (rarely) new ideas in pharmacology, were delivered before audiences consisting only of doctors anxious to learn. Now, in effect, the audience was the world, represented by the journalists in attendance who had sat more or less patiently through hours of long-winded debate on medical politics and welcomed a change of gear.

Some doctors resented this, and saw no reason why 'the lay public' should be let in on the arcana of their profession. Of course, the Public Relations Department shared a good deal of the odium directed towards the press. We were expected to 'control' what they wrote. 'Why can't you control these chaps?' doctors would demand testily, as black headlines converted yet another innocent observation or surgery anecdote into a startling 'breakthrough'. I wonder if doctors still ask such questions. I suspect hardly ever.

Nowadays every large organisation has a public relations officer. Government departments have them, and so do universities, detergent firms, big charities and probably public relations organisations themselves.

Indeed, among the organisations that had appointed public relations advisers at this time was even the one of which my father was Secretary, the Linoleum and Floorcloth Manufacturers Association. The firm whose advice they sought at this time was run by no less distinguished a man than Robert Carrier – distinguished, that is, as a cook rather than a PRO. However, it was probably Carrier who persuaded the L&FCMA to re-christen themselves the Linoleum Association (shorter, less cumbersome) and then to run a series of advertisements featuring a friendly 'expert' called Thelma (i.e., *the LMA*) in the hope that this would help fix the idea of linoleum in the minds of newspaper readers in a period when the trade was getting anxious about competition from newer ways of covering your floor.

If this sounds a little silly, one can only reflect that the public relations profession was still new. And the title had about it a stronger whiff than now of transatlantic euphemism. It was true public relations officers had a useful function as persons whom members of the public could go to with questions about the body the PRO represented. But there was another function, usually considered more important, which the title glossed over in its bland, up-front, cheesy way; and that was to put as brave a face on things as possible when your organisation was doing

77

something stupid or unpopular or, as Colin Hurry had put it, to practise 'the art of explaining away'.

Pringle was not over-fond of the medical profession but he cared deeply about what he believed to be one of the most deplorable features of the 1950s, namely the decline of the middle classes – their relative impotence, as he saw it, against the growing power of the trade unions and the general flattening-out of British society which denied them the respect (and the domestic servants) they'd been brought up to believe was their due. He devoted much thought to this problem as well as to his own latter-day profession, but not all of his ideas were especially far-sighted. An annual event, staged by the Public Relations Department, was something called the Hastings Lecture, which was held at a different city each time. An eminent doctor would be persuaded to read a thirty- or forty-minute speech to a public audience, in somewhere like the local town hall. The local BMA Division would be enlisted to make sure all the right people had invitations – mayors, town clerks, leading figures from local Chambers of Commerce, etc. – and there was usually a goodly array of ermine and chains of office to be seen in the front row. Afterwards there would be a reception.

None of the Hastings Lectures was very memorable, and it was uphill work for local doctors to make sure the hall didn't look embarrassingly empty behind the ostentatious first few rows. Moreover, the essentially authoritarian, patronising nature of the event guaranteed its early extinction, and the Hastings Lecture was dropped in the 1960s.

Another of Pringle's ideas was rather more confidential: he initiated regular, informal lunches for the public relations officers (or their equivalents) of what he identified as the four oldest professions: the church, the army, the law – and, of course, medicine. Each in turn would be the host, leading discussions on – as I understood it – how to maintain the prestige of the bodies they represented. I am not aware of these lunches ever producing any concrete result.

Pringle himself once read a paper at a medical conference in which he argued that the PRO of a medical organisation was like the Best Friend in the advertisement, who was the only person who would tell you about your BO. Actually, the point of the advertisement was that not *even* your best friend would tell you about the unpleasant way you smelled, but I expect his point was clear; and now and again he would be invited to speak to the BMA Council or to one of the committees and explain to them what he thought the public would think when they read in next morning's newspaper what the BMA was proposing to do next. On these occasions he could be bravely outspoken, just as Colin Hurry could.

Pringle had also scored a notable *coup* following an uproar in the newspapers over the surgical separation of a pair of infant Siamese twins at the Hammersmith Hospital. The surgeon was Ian Aird, and the operation was so rare, and the 'human interest' deemed so intense, that the hospital was in a virtual state of siege, with reporters and photographers, having been barred from the wards, clinging to drainpipes outside the buildings in an effort to see what was going on.

The hospital had no idea how to cope with the press in full cry; and Pringle was responsible for setting up a committee of newspaper proprietors and editors, sitting with representatives from the BMA and the medical colleges, who devised a standard formula for what to do if anything like it happened again – in any hospital. The formula could have been summed up in three words: appoint a spokesman.

It was the first time there had been any such high-level co-operation between the two professions and Pringle's reputation for diplomatic treatment of either side was much enhanced. But he also saw another function for the PRO, and that was to mount 'campaigns'. Soon after I arrived I was required to help in staging one about crash helmets. At the time, motor-cyclists were not obliged by law to wear any kind of protective hat: if they did so, it was by their own choice. Consequently the number of head injuries among motor-bike riders – usually young men – was very much greater than it should have been. Pringle decided the BMA should 'take up the cudgels' (characteristic BMA term) with letters to the press (mainly *The Times*), inspired feature articles and debates at the Representative Body. My part in this was limited to providing ammunition for a speech by one of the RB's regular entertainers, a surgeon called A. Lawrence Abel (one of those names again), who incidentally was one of the last consultants actually to live in Harley Street, rather than merely rent consulting rooms there. A large, genial man, Lawrence Abel was said to be in the habit of appearing in the operating theatre wearing nothing under his gown but green silk shorts, embroidered with dragons. At BMA House he wore more conventional garb – black coat and striped trousers – and arrived in a huge, silent Armstrong-Siddeley. He also had a large and valuable collection of surgeons' bowls, dating from the days of barber-surgeons: porcelain vessels intended to catch the customer's blood, with slices cut out so that the bowl would fit under the chin.

His appearances on the rostrum at Representative Meetings were as a rule warmly greeted. 'Abel, Marly-bone,' he would growl, in his faintly gorblimey accent. 'Hear! hear!' the answering cry would come from all corners of the town hall we had taken over. His knockabout oratorical style, though not very subtle, was effusive and usually effective, affording a welcome change from the ruck of speakers. When he moved the Marylebone Division's motion on crash helmets he climaxed his appearance during the debate by donning a succession of comic hats, declaring that every kind of headgear afforded some protection, but only a well-designed crash helmet, with a kite-mark, would do the job properly. Of course, this was as much for the benefit of the press, seated below the platform, as for the 330-odd representatives in the 'Doctors' Parliament'. Soon afterwards it was made compulsory for riders to wear helmets, but I cannot pretend I played a significant part in bringing this about, and it is arguable whether Lawrence Abel did, either.

Pringle was responsible for a much more seriously waged campaign in the autumn of 1955, when the Conservative government tried to ban heroin. From the beginning of 1956, it was going to be made illegal to manufacture it in Britain. The government took this step to support the World Health Organisation's efforts to control international traffic in the drug. But Pringle, bristling with indignation, immediately interpreted the government's move as interference with clinical freedom. He set up press conferences at which eminent consultants thundered that it would be the first time in history a British government had prohibited the manufacture of a medicinal drug and that it would be recklessly inhumane to deprive doctors of such an effective means of relieving severe pain. And just because other countries, especially America, had addiction problems, it didn't mean the drug had to be prohibited in Britain, where the problem was virtually non-existent. In England and Wales that year, there were fifty-two known addicts. In Scotland, there were two. At this distance, one can only shake one's head in regret at how things have changed since 1955.

The BMA's opinions – the Voice of British Medicine – were all over the newspapers. It was the kind of issue that made good material for leading articles, features, and discussions on *Any Questions?* Pringle flung himself into it with huge seriousness and zeal – so much so that he developed acute urticaria, diagnosed over lunch in the Members' Dining Room as clearly psychogenic in origin. His evening visits to the Reform Club, the chats with members of the Establishment about questions of the day, seemed to have fresh point. He was forever on the telephone, pitching restlessly about in his chair as was his wont, talking confidentially to MPs and senior civil servants, bandying the names of other influential men and generally orchestrating the BMA's protests, which by then had begun to be a serious embarrassment to the Eden government and, especially, its Health Minister. In the end, it was a mole in the Home Office who settled the matter. Pringle learned from this anonymous official that there was some technical flaw in the legality of what the government was planning to do. He prompted Lord Jowitt, the former Labour Lord Chancellor, to challenge the government in the House of Lords, and the ban on heroin was dropped. Pringle was jubilant. His urticaria cleared up.

Watching all this from the wings (I was not allowed to be privy to the wire-pulling in high places), I had been given a lesson in the art of political persuasion.

A short time later, the public relations machinery was wheeled out again. It was June 1956. This time, doctors' pay was the issue. Five years had gone past since doctors had been given a hundred per cent increase, and when the BMA put in for another increase, this time of twenty-five per cent to match the increased cost of living, the answer they got from the Eden government was the predictable raspberry.

Pringle called a press conference, and addressed the assembled journalists from a table placed in front of more than a hundred doctors from the BMA Divisions who that day had been attending a conference on how to present the BMA case to the public. The event was intended to be, among other things, a demonstration of how it should be done. Perhaps spurred on by the medical presence behind him, Pringle made a bellicose speech, asserting loudly that the BMA had its sleeves rolled up, and could and would 'push the government about', at which the doctors behind him burst into frantic cheering and applause. The press observed all this with wry faces. I recall Ronald Bedford prefacing a question with the remark that not only had the doctors got their sleeves rolled up, they had steam coming out of their ears.

While the country was in torment over the Suez crisis and the Russian invasion of Hungary, the BMA was making faces at the Health Ministry, pushed on from behind by the rank-and-file membership, who in letters to the *British Medical Journal* were demanding mass resignation from the National Health Service, a kind of ultimate weapon which, like the hydrogen bomb, could only be used once. And like the H-bomb, in the event it never was used. The government's response to the dilemma was to set up a Royal Commission on doctors' pay, which had the useful effect of shelving the whole question. In the Public Relations Department, Pringle would once more lament the downfall of the professional middle classes, complaining of the disappearance of the servant class and seeing the doctors as front-line troops in a class struggle they couldn't win. In the Dining Room, the talk would be along similar lines, doctors mourning the way the profession was no longer regarded with the old respect: 'Do you know,' said a doctor to me with incredulity, 'the patients never stand up now when you come into the room?'

Another bright, PR-oriented idea came to Pringle, and that was for the BMA to set up a 'Royal Commission' of its own which, he explained enthusiastically, would make the Royal Commission look like 'a row of beans'. The BMA inquiry would investigate the entire National Health Service and tell the country what was wrong with it: the Chairman was to be a surgeon to the Queen, the popular, ex-Olympic champion, a New Zealander, Sir Harry Porritt.

Beyond the walls of BMA House, I had to remind myself, there were doctors who enthusiastically 'worked' the National Health Service, but not much was heard from them in Tavistock Square. Emigration was frequently talked of as the only way out of an unbearable system. A doctor who was on the point of leaving for Canada told a Representative Meeting, 'For the National Health Service I have nothing but hatred and contempt.'

Between them, Pringle and Colin Hurry had a plan that whoever was chosen for the job of Assistant PRO should prepare a pamphlet of some kind about the BMA. The idea was that when anyone asked, 'What *is* the BMA?', you could smile, nod, and hand him one of those Your-Questions-Answered booklets. It is possible that people only ask questions of that kind in the minds of professional PROs. However, I was instructed to get on with the job of writing something, after a necessary period of indoctrination during which I was supposed to identify all the things an outsider might want to know about the place. Was it the same as the GMC? Did the BMA strike doctors off? What for? Were doctors compelled to belong?

Along with the BMA Annual Handbook, a Committee Schedule, Diary, Calendar and so on that I was handed on arrival, there was also a copy of a *History of the British Medical Association* by a medical historian, one Ernest Muirhead Little, which the BMA had published in its centenary year, 1932. It was a solid and unexciting volume but the more I read it the more intrigued I was by the BMA's history – founded in 1832, year of reform, a radical ginger group impatient to allow the fresh breeze of social change into a chaotic, ill-organised profession . . . but then, over the decades, turning into something far more respectable and worthy, and much less sympathetic. The man who had founded it, Charles Hastings, was a Worcester practitioner who, like many of his friends, resented the assumption that London doctors were superior to everyone else. Until not long ago this had still been a cause of vexation in the profession and Bevan's scheme for Merit Awards for consultants was designed partly to put this right – by encouraging the spread of medical talent throughout the country. In the 1830s, however, Hastings and his circle had good reason for animosity at the stifling influence of the London medical cliques, especially the Royal Colleges, of Physicians and of Surgeons.

Hastings's portrait, or a copy of it, painted in 1839, hung in the BMA Members' Common Room: handsome, upright, curly-haired, a Byronic figure gazing at the artist with clear, open features, smiling confidently. It contrasted sadly with a photograph I found in the archives, of the same man in the 1850s, 'the able, laborious, never-wearying Dr Charles Hastings', as someone described him, with the face not of a romantic poet and idealist but a medical politician well versed in the art of compromise. And as the story continued, the Provincial Medical and Surgical Association became the BMA and hardened still more

84

into a pillar of the medical Establishment, the Tammany Hall of medicine.

This was roughly the position the BMA was still in by the mid-twentieth century. Even its internal politics reminded you of certain elements of the national political scene. In the Representative Body, I became aware of unsuspected cross-currents in what was supposedly the democratic focus of the profession's affairs: the 'Northern bloc', a confidential association of GPs from Birmingham and points north who could fix elections to Council and the General Medical Services Committee, loading the vote in favour of their candidate, communicating with each other across the crowded hall like tick-tack men at the racecourse – only less conspicuously (no white gloves) – and holding surreptitious meetings in hotel rooms to determine in advance their policy towards key issues.

However, my 'pamphlet', probably called *About the BMA*, or *What is the BMA?*, seemed to be inflating itself almost of its own accord, increasing in bulk like some barrage balloon. Little by little, it was becoming a history of the BMA. Pringle sportingly agreed that what he had thought of as a pamphlet should be allowed to continue its haphazard and involuntary expansion. Eventually it achieved book length, was finished, and accepted by a real publisher – Heinemann. I called it a Short History of the BMA, in case anyone thought I had pretensions to real scholarship, and gave it the title *Doctors' Commons*: this was intended as a polite reference to the 'Parliamentary' character of the BMA constitution, but unwittingly ignored the true meaning of the term as the ancient college in London for doctors of civil law. Hence, it was not a good title.

The book's tone of what I would now criticise as eager, callow respect, sharpened by mild sarcasm, made me dislike it more and more as the years passed, though at the time I was as proud of it as any man in his early thirties would be of his first book, and I was exultant when Heinemann's said they would take it on. Still, some of it I can read without a blush, and on the whole it was well received on the literary pages, with the exception of the *New Statesman*'s, where Barbara Wootton was so rude about it that I did what no writer should do to a hostile critic, and wrote her a pained, huffy letter. In reply she said her review could have been a lot worse: she had hated my book so much that had it not been for the duty laid upon her by the literary editor she would never have finished it. Served me right. But as a regular *Statesman* reader from schooldays, I took it hard.

Doctors' Commons was published in 1959; and by this time I had more or less dug myself in as assistant PRO, though there were aspects of the work I had begun to dislike very much indeed. The whole idea of 'PR' was one of them. The notion that I was there to make myself useful to this self-centred and self-important profession grated badly. Furthermore, I had the distinct impression I was there to take some of the odium felt for the press – to be a kind of decoy for the real journalists down in Fleet Street whose attentions were so unwelcome. Some BMA figures used to make ponderous jokes about the term 'PR', based on the fact that it was medical short-hand for 'per rectum'. I dare say it reflected their own secret annoyance at the intrusion of this new profession into the healing business.

It didn't do the BMA's prestige any harm – nor did it damage their claims for better pay and conditions – that the Public Relations Department was usually the place journalists got in touch with first when they wanted some elucidation of not only BMA policies but, far more often, of news stories which concerned medicine and which newspaper readers found much more interesting than 'remuneration'. This could be embarrassing. Now and then, for instance, the *Daily Graphic* news editor would ring up asking me to explain some peculiar or recondite item of news that had come his way, and with the help of someone in the building or some friendly nearby expert I would concoct a comment and read it out to someone on the *Graphic* news desk.

I was surprised to see these comments printed in the paper with the tag-line, 'The *Graphic* doctor writes . . . ' I thought I should point out to the news editor that although I was a BMA official, I had no medical qualifications whatever. Didn't matter, he said.

I had not been at the BMA very long when an annotation in *The Lancet* reported that certain small fish called guppies had been suspected of producing their young through the process of parthenogenesis – reproduction without the intervention of the male guppy, or in other words virgin birth. These creatures – rather quaintly named, by the way, after a Mr Guppy who first sent some to the British Museum – generally reproduced themselves through fertilisation of female by male. But some had been observed to produce young, even though they had been segregated from males since birth, and *The Lancet* said it meant we should think again before deciding parthenogenesis in human beings was out of the question. The report caused a small sensation: one newspaper translated *The Lancet*'s comment into the statement, 'Doctors now say: "It doesn't always need a man to make a baby." ' The *Daily Mirror* announced it had received a large number of letters from young women readers, 'All of whom say, "Parthenogenesis happened to me." ' Those whose claims could be authenticated, God knows how, were promised generous cash rewards. Unfortunately, in the event, none were confirmed. However, I was rung up by the editor of the weekly journal *Truth*, George Scott, who assumed I would know what the story was all about. He asked me to write a piece which would explain this odd story, and I duly sent over a thousand words which I hoped didn't reflect the struggle I'd had not only to write them but to understand what the virgin birth business was all about in the first place. This was my entrée to medical journalism, the first time I appeared in print writing about a technical scientific matter.

While I was learning, in my laborious way, the virtue of topicality, I still remained a little detached from BMA life. I was still by far the youngest official. I was surrounded by men – and one or two women – who at some time in their lives had spent years in the study of human anatomy and morbidity, who knew things about the human race I would never know. They seemed very superior to me. What's more they tended to set themselves on pedestals: 'We are the God-profession,' said one of the editorial staff of the *British Medical Journal*, 'with too much power for our own good.' All too often one could observe, going about association business, members who exhibited what this same doctor called the Jehovah Complex.

Of course, in the enclosed world of BMA House, within those Oxford-college style gates, titanic power struggles would take place. My *Journal* friend told me of a moment when he had stood in the office of the *Journal* editor, Dr Hugh Clegg, a brilliant and irascible man. There was a silence while Clegg, arms folded, grimly looked down from his third-floor window on the passing to and fro of Council members, Division officers and official staff. In the words Captain Scott had used in the diary of his last Polar expedition, Clegg had muttered, 'Great God! This is an awful place!' I thought of Pringle and his baleful contemplation of the Treasurer in the Garden Court.

I expect it was on the day of a Council meeting that Clegg had made his observation. These meetings were held on the first Wednesday of the month. Sixty or so doctors, elected by local Divisions or by the Representative Body, met in the Council Chamber, a lofty room in the basement in which each Council member had his or her own desk. The Council included some strange characters. There were some members who wouldn't keep quiet, others who never said a word. One, a Dr J. B. Wrathall Rowe (another trumped-up name), was never seen without a cigarette between his lips *which he never lit*. He didn't smoke and was often seen waving away helpful colleagues who advanced on him with lighters blazing. I presume he derived some oral comfort from this curious habit.

Not long ago, on a return visit to BMA House, I crept into the Council Chamber: a weird experience. I could almost hear the impassioned voices of long-gone medical politicians whose names were inscribed in letters of gilt on mahogany wall panels. From each desk now sprouts a microphone, and gone from behind the back row are the brown curtains that used to shield many a confidential aside. There came back to me with irresistible force a memory of many tense and dramatic debates, but, equally, the hours of grinding tedium I had spent in that Chamber. We officials had no recognised place to sit. We perched where we could, on single chairs or on benches, the discomfort of which was a necessary aid to staying awake as the committee reports dragged on and on. I usually made myself inconspicuous at the back, listening out as usual for the malapropisms and speech blunders. 'I think,' pronounced a Bristol doctor with slow, sagacious emphasis, 'Dr Macrae has hit the nail on his head,' and 'You know the saying, "I fear the Danes when they bring gifts" ' ('Hear! hear! from around the Chamber). Dr Derek Stevenson, Macrae's successor as Secretary, was an especially good source of such solecisms. 'It's good to have someone on Council,' he said of one straight-talking new member, 'who talks like a spade.' Down they went in the notebook my headmaster, John Garrett, had urged me to keep, and in which I was storing a rich harvest.

Then on the third Thursday of each month it was the General Medical Services Committee, the most powerful of all the BMA's committees, representing 20,000 family doctors. It was by far the most effective committee and some clever men chaired it while I was there, none more so than a Birmingham GP, Solomon Wand. Ruthless and able in debate, generous and kindly in private, Wand was a priceless asset to Tavistock Square. He was a broadly-built man, not very tall, and his square shape was accentuated by his habit of wearing double-breasted suits, which he would button up menacingly when rising to speak at meetings of the Representative Body, staring down the assembled members like a lion-tamer entering an unruly cageful. The coat-buttoning routine could imply outrage, weary resignation, stubborn opposition, comic despair, derision, or finality. He also had a trick of feigning a kind of innocent astonishment that his opinion could be doubted. In earlier times, as a young GP, Wand had been a thorn in the flesh of the Establishment, a rebel and a know-all who had probably made himself unpopular with the BMA brass of the day. Now he in his turn had become part of the Establishment, but I used to watch him from the press bench during Representative Meetings, or in Council when he was Chairman, wondering if he was the only medical-politician in sight who could be said to possess true greatness of character – a combination of courage, strong intellect and genuine magnanimity.

The Labour Health Minister Aneurin Bevan once said of him in the House of Commons, during the rows that preceded the 'Appointed Day', that he was aptly named, since he proposed to perform a miracle. He got a laugh from the House for that, but it should have frozen on their faces, because a miracle, in due course, is exactly what Wand did perform: he managed to get family doctors a sensational pay increase which worked out at no less than a hundred per cent. This triumph, famous in the annals of medical politics, was the Danckwerts Award, when the BMA had for the first time unveiled its H-bomb equivalent – the threat of mass resignation from the Health Service – and the dispute between them and the Health Ministry was submitted to the arbitration of a Mr Justice Danckwerts. Pringle used to maintain that Wand had carried the argument with the Health Minister of the day by simply saying No. No matter what the proposal, Wand's answer was always the same: No. True or false, and the story surely undervalues Wand's abilities, the BMA Council marked his victory with a resolution praising his 'stupendous exertions' and the General Medical Services Committee organised a kind of national whip-round, finally presenting Wand with a cheque for the tidy sum of £12,956, plus a gold cigarette case. He used the money to set up a Fund for helping needy GPs.

In the summer of 1959 the BMA's annual meeting was held

jointly with the Canadian Medical Association, a riotous trans-atlantic medical jamboree, which took on extra colour from the fact that Canada was the chosen destination of a growing number of British medical emigrants. The chosen host city was Edinburgh, and the President, no less a person than HRH the Duke himself, with whom I was, as it were, on waving terms.

All the BMA's 127 years' experience of organising big events of this kind was summoned to deal with the problems of looking after royalty, not to mention the many hundred Canadians who swelled the numbers of British members, thronging the meetings, relaxing the pompous tone of the social events and heading enthusiastically for the Scotch. The City of Edinburgh staged a special midnight Tattoo for the BMA's benefit on the approach to the Castle. I recall the lights suddenly going out – a single spotlight picking out the lone piper on the battlements, the unearthly, blood-curdling glissando as he began his Lament. It was almost too much for the Canadians: an equally blood-curdling yodel of primitive excitement cracked the darkness from the spectators' benches.

But off-stage, a drama just as electrifying, and much more relevant to my own career, was being played out. A kind of festering rivalry had developed between Pringle and Stevenson, the BMA Secretary. Pringle liked him well enough, but had little respect for his intellectual powers. He had more than once muttered to me that if there were ever a conflict between medical and non-medical officials, you couldn't win: the doctors would close ranks against you. His sour prediction turned out to be all too accurate. Stevenson, backed by Solomon Wand, who was now Chairman of Council, accused Pringle of trying to usurp his authority. None of this was done out in the open: only two or three officials were involved in the accusations that flew to and fro. These included vague charges concerning Pringle's expenses, which seemed to include too many taxis and unidentified acts of hospitality towards mystery contacts: the suspicion was that they came down to rounds of six o'clock drinks in the bar of the Reform Club, followed by assisted transport to Waterloo Station. Pringle was an able man, but his fidgety, abrasive personality did not suit Stevenson's diplomatic, watchful, slightly pedantic approach to medico-political matters. Stevenson had the well-groomed, good-looking, smooth appearance of a moderately successful actor. 'Who's the Gary Cooper type?' the TV newscaster Reginald Bosanquet asked me once, as Stevenson took his place at a press conference of the fifties, but it wasn't Cooper as Mr Deeds he resembled so much as some Shaftesbury Avenue professional – say, Nigel Patrick or Tony Britton – in an Anyone-for-Tennis domestic comedy. I once made a note of a description of a certain sea-captain in one of Jane Austen's novels, which I thought could have been applied to him: 'He did not want abilities, but he had no curiosity, and no information beyond his profession.'

So, while Canadian doctors and their wives toted their cameras around the Trossachs or caroused in the lounges of the North British and the Waverley, Pringle's career at the BMA slowed, then came to an abrupt and premature halt. He resigned.

The BMA now had to decide who was to take his place. I was thirty-four. Was I too young? Did I, in the phrase Stevenson would use of people angling for office, 'carry the guns'? He sent for me and told me of Pringle's departure, 'by mutual agreement'. I was to take his place as head of the Public Relations Department, but it was to be clearly understood that 'public relations' in Pringle's and Colin Hurry's understanding of the term were to be the responsibility of the BMA Secretary. The Public Relations Committee, the PRO's bulwark against interference from anyone else – with none other than H. Guy Dain in the chair – was to be wound up. In future Stevenson would do all the political work himself, if there were any, with the backing of the Council.

I told Stevenson I didn't want to be a PRO anyway. I mistrusted the idea of public relations and would rather take the title of Chief Press Officer. Nor was I very happy with another of Pringle's schemes – finding a back door into Parliament. For this purpose he had arranged to pay a retainer to a well-known lobby correspondent, who was supposed to give advance warning of whatever stirrings there might be in the Whitehall undergrowth which could presage any moves affecting doctors. He was also expected to sound out sympathetic MPs and suggest whom we might persuade to take up a cause on the BMA's behalf.

I believe it was comparatively rare in those days for organisations of any kind – political, professional, commercial – to use either House of Parliament in this way, and to me it had a slight whiff of – not dishonesty, perhaps, but interference with democratic process. Naive of me, I'm sure. But I didn't want anything to do with it, nor would my job include 'explaining away' – only furnishing the information needed urgently by the man at the typewriter in the news room when he was trying to get to the heart of a story, racking his brains for the right 'intro' and desperate for the clinching 'quote'.

When Pringle resigned he expected Colin Hurry to resign with him: he had always been Pringle's ally in the inner counsels of the BMA – another reasonable voice to warn of the consequences of a foolhardy decision, someone who was in touch with political realities and the ebb and flow of public opinion.

Hurry stayed put. I don't know what remorse it cost him, if any. He continued to turn up at meetings of Council and the GMS Committee, and at annual meetings. Now and then he would take me out to lunch; he would ask me what kind of relationship I had with the press, and we would compare experiences of the Jehovah complex; but we never discussed the kind of political manoeuvres I used to imagine him talking about with John Pringle, when they would be seen taking a confidential coffee in the BMA Dining Room. In any case, he was growing old: his former suavity and dated elegance were looking a little forced. Pringle was in a worse position: in his mid-fifties, he was out on the street – with no wish to return to journalism, even if any jobs had been going. It had to be Public Relations: he managed to get a job as PRO of the Bee

Research Association, an organisation with, it had to be said, a somewhat lower profile than the BMA's. I don't believe Pringle was able to raise it during his time there – but luckily that didn't last long, for shortly afterwards he was appointed PRO to the newly created National Economic Development Council, where he could once again indulge his liking for political intrigue, but in an organisation closer to the centre of affairs even than the BMA.

I admired and respected Pringle, although his attitude to life was different from mine. My inattentiveness during committee meetings exasperated him. So did the fact that I showed little interest in the principles of public relations which he tried to apply to BMA affairs, and often showed my amateurish ignorance of the way the grown-up world achieved its ends. I remember his consternation when he discovered, soon after my arrival, that I didn't read *The Times* but the *News Chronicle*. 'My dear fellow,' I can hear him saying now in his faintly Scottish accent, 'you must read *The Times*. It's the Establishment speaking.'

I fear I must have disappointed him greatly. But he was bored with the BMA and I imagine him dismissing his ten or so years there with a shrug, and one last, neurotic twitch.

Six

You and Your Ethics

MY VIEW OF the job was simpler than Pringle's. The BMA's dilemma could have been summed up roughly as follows. They wanted the media's support in their arguments with the government – whether over pay or anything else, but mainly over pay. (Enoch Powell once said pay was the only thing doctors and politicians ever talked about when they met.) But: medicine and publicity, they were always reminding me, didn't mix. They didn't want journalists poking their noses into medical affairs – giving away medical secrets, leaking information patients weren't meant to have, blunting the doctor's authority and generally spoiling things, like stage-hands eavesdropping on the conjuror's act from behind the wings.

There was something called *the doctor-patient relationship*: an ugly phrase – PR-speak for what used to be known as practising *the bedside manner*. But lurking behind this bit of modish word-spinning were such real and dramatic problems as how and when to tell a patient the truth about a terminal illness, and how a doctor could help effect a cure merely by being kind to a frightened and suffering person. On the other hand, times without number bombastic speeches would echo about the committee rooms in which 'the doctor-patient relationship' would be flourished like some potent talisman in the BMA's rows with the Ministry of Health, thrust out towards the dreaded bureaucrats like a garlic clove at a vampire.

In this there was a faint echo of Victorian romanticisation of medicine. BMA House wasn't well supplied with pictures (I once tried to get them to sponsor an art prize, which might have improved the position; but nothing doing. My colleagues thought it a frivolous and irrelevant idea: there were better things to spend doctors' money on). However, somewhere on the walls was a reproduction of a famous painting of 1891 by Sir Luke Fildes, *The Doctor*. It showed a solemn, frock-coated figure – one might cynically say stumped for a diagnosis, or for a remedy – sitting by the bedside of a pale and sleeping child, while her grief-stricken parents comforted one another in the shadows behind. Actually, the romanticisation wasn't in the work of the artist so much as the way it was interpreted, as an image of the wise, caring physician. In fact Fildes was keen to capture the reality of a medical dilemma and he went to extraordinary lengths to achieve the realism he was after, building in his studio a complete replica of the fisherman's cottage in which the 'story' of the painting was supposedly enacted. And incidentally, according to the art historian Christopher Wood, when rumours of what he was doing spread among the medical profession, he was deluged with requests from doctors wanting to pose for the principal figure.

Another attempt to convey pictorially the same kernel medical situation hung outside Committee Room A: it was a black and white print of another Royal Academy sensation of its day, *A Visit to Aesculapius*, painted in 1880 by the Academy's President, Sir Edward Poynter. It belongs in the Victorian-soft-porn category, a tasty subject artfully displaced to ancient times. It shows a group of maidens lining up to be seen in the garden of the Greek god of medicine. Their imploring looks argue their faith in Aesculapius' healing powers, but one might read a delicious fear of molestation in their shrinking postures. Rod and serpent to hand and thoughtfully fingering his beard, the old man is seated on a dais, staring at the ankle of one of the girls who, like the others in the queue, has been co-operative enough to shed all her clothes for consultation purposes. 'If only modern medicine were as simple as that,' I once heard a doctor say as he stood in front of this picture.

Neither Aesculapius nor Luke Fildes's harassed GP knew what it was to have the boat rocked by the media. Their successors in the new National Health Service were differently placed. A case in point happened during Pringle's time, in the spring of 1958, when the BBC launched a weekly television series of ten half-hour programmes called *Your Life in their Hands*. Their purpose was to show, each week, the work of a different provincial hospital, spotlighting each time a different disease. The BBC said they were putting on the programme to show off the quality of provincial medicine, and relieve people's fears about going into hospital. Also, they said they were out to satisfy 'the public's healthy interest in disease'. Each programme was presented by one Dr Charles Fletcher, a chest physician at the Hammersmith Hospital: very eminent, a Fellow of the Royal College of Physicians. He was also a TV natural. His calm, serious but friendly bearing made him just the man to 'front' investigations into orthopaedics, paediatrics, heart-lung machines, kidney dialysis and all the other wonders of post-war medical progress. Audiences were very large – larger, said the BBC, than for any programme since the Coronation of Elizabeth II.

However, at the BMA all this was watched through narrowed eyes. What was this 'healthy interest in disease', then? Annoyance simmered in the surgeries of the nation. Things came to a head when one week *Your Life in their Hands* featured open-heart surgery. I was present at a press showing of this programme, one of the crucial moments of which showed the surgeon making his first incision across a patient's chest: the lancet drawn swiftly, almost daintily, over the adipose flesh, leaving a thin line like a pencil stroke ... the line broadening as blood seeped, then flooded out, then the flesh and the rib-cage clamped back.

97

Now, in those days we were not at all used to this kind of thing. We didn't even see much property blood, let alone the real thing, and although the pictures were in black and white (colour television hadn't arrived) it was a sight to make you wince. I doubt if many of the television audience had ever seen anything like it, nor could many of them have seen what came next, a human heart not so much beating away as squirming about inside a patient's chest, looking a bit like a small hairless animal trying to escape.

There was a report that one viewer who was on the waiting list for this particular operation killed himself rather than undergo it. Two more viewers were also reported to have committed suicide after a programme on cancer: they became convinced they had it, though post-mortem examination showed it wasn't so.

Asked by Pringle to say what my reaction had been at the press screening, I admitted the open-heart surgery scene had startled me. I said I had been on the verge of syncope, which wasn't really true – it was just that I'd recently learned the word and how to pronounce it (sink-a-pee) . . . the vocabulary of medicine was soaking in, and one day this was going to prove extremely useful. Pringle wrote a memorandum on the matter and it was thereupon included in the next Council agenda, where my frivolously chosen term helped to inflame the Council's indignation. Another citadel had been invaded! The 'surgical insult', one member of Council thundered, was not for patients to see and fret over. I was amused that another member of Council mistakenly called the programme *Their Life in Your Hands*: I was working in one of the few places in Britain where this slip actually made sense.

The *British Medical Journal* accused the BBC of fostering hypochondria, pandering to sensationalism and invading the doctor-patient relationship. Angry letters came from doctors – and such was the prestige of the BMA that the BBC took the defensive, with an on-screen apology and, I suspect, many an internal memo, warning science producers to watch their step.

But *Your Life in their Hands* went on and, whatever the BMA thought about it, it went on drawing huge and generally riveted audiences. Before long the protests faded away.

What the BMA didn't mind, or not so much, was the craze for fictional programmes about medicine. These were the days of *Emergency Ward 10*, *Doctor Finlay's Casebook*, *Calling Doctor Kildare* and other series, milking for all they were worth the 'human' problems of medical practice and presenting doctors as, on the whole, upright, decent and well turned-out, if occasionally fallible, human beings. These series and others like them were regarded in Tavistock Square with a sort of condescending amusement. Those viewers – how little they knew! Anyway, these programmes weren't much different from the kind of stories you could read in magazines like *Girl's Crystal* or *Women's Weekly*, where doctors frequently appeared in the rôle of romantic hero: typically, craggy men with what were called then 'library frame' spectacles (signalling intellectual distinction), strong handshakes, and deep emotions concealed beneath a brusque exterior. Medicine had for long been the stuff of romance, and in a way that did no harm to the profession's public image. Now, through television, the audience was far, far wider. Throughout the media, as in popular fiction, a standard ingredient was the drama of medicine. Even *Mrs Dale's Diary*, the long-running radio serial, suddenly remembered Mrs Dale's husband was a doctor – and a London GP was recruited to give the series medical 'point'.

On a marquee outside the Granada, Clapham Junction (now a Bingo hall), I saw an advertisement for a new film: *Bound by Oath, Torn by Desire: These Are 'The Young Doctors'*. I would quote it now and then to my medical colleagues to illustrate the kind of limelight doctors were finding themselves in whether they liked it or not.

As I thought about it, that advertisement also prompted me to wonder how many doctors actually were, literally, 'bound by oath'.

There was a widespread belief that, at some time or other,

all doctors at the time of their qualification had stood before some authority or other and – perhaps with hand on heart, or raised in the air – sworn to uphold the principles enumerated by Hippocrates, the Father of Medicine, around 400 BC. Had this been so, they would have sworn 'by Apollo-Physician, by Asclepius and all-Heal' (whoever that was), 'by Panacea and by all the gods and goddesses' to preserve confidentiality between doctor and patient, to abstain from seducing slaves, to share their money with their teachers, not to 'use the knife' and not to impart medical instruction to any but their sons, their teachers' sons, and indentured pupils. The Oath also forbade doctors to help any woman procure an abortion – a hurdle that had to be negotiated in due course.

Mainly out of curiosity I decided to conduct a postal poll of the thirty-one medical schools in the British Isles, to find out if any of them did still require new graduates to take – i.e., recite in public – the Hippocratic Oath. The answer was: none of them. Nowhere was a newly qualified doctor to swear, upright or on his knees, the Hippocratic Oath itself, though there were places where special ceremonies were held and during which *an* oath was sworn – that is, usually, a copy of the text was handed around to each young graduate. I published the results of my inquiry in a press handout. I included the statement, 'It should not be necessary to add that the questions were asked in a spirit of inquiry, not of reproach.' Still, it was an act of questionable value to my employers, to say the least, and likely to prompt a lot of newspaper readers to decide medical ethics was an out-of-date notion. It was understandable that some of the BMA people were distressed – not by the fact that the Hippocratic Oath was evidently passing into myth, but because I had, so to speak, disturbed the soil beneath which it was buried, and by implication called into question the ethical standards of today's doctors. Also because I had made these inquiries without any authority from the Council or one of the major committees.

I used to wonder how I had got away with this subversive,

though not very carefully considered, piece of work. It was a good thing I hadn't asked the Central Ethical Committee, who would certainly not have given the idea their sanction. This was one of the most influential standing committees. Its chairman was a dry-as-dust, tight-lipped, silver-haired Scot named Robert Forbes, who was Secretary of the Medical Defence Union, one of the organisations which for annual premium payments will cover a doctor's expenses in the event of his becoming involved for whatever reason in a legal action. (The MDU's offices were in Tavistock House – the two wings of the building, north and south, fronting on to Tavistock Square.) Forbes had been a candidate for the job of BMA Secretary after Hill's departure, but the mild and diffident Angus Macrae had got the job instead – for the BMA, a lucky escape. I suppose the Chairmanship of the Central Ethical Committee might have been regarded as Forbes's consolation prize, for it was an important committee.

It had created for itself a dual function. Its original job had been to act as an arbitrary body when doctors disagreed not over clinical matters but over what came down in the end to matters of hard cash. A general practitioner might be suspected, say, of poaching another doctor's patients; or he might have stuck too prominent a brass plate outside the surgery door. Even the single word 'Surgery' in flamboyant capitals or, appallingly, in bright red paint on a corner site (I used to pass such a practice in the mornings if I drove through south London to Bloomsbury) was enough to cause head-shaking. The idea, of course, was that every doctor was equal – you'd get just as sound medical advice from Dr Lancet as you would from Dr Pillbox and Dr Liniment. In fact, as everyone was aware then, as now and throughout history, this was absurd. Some doctors were expert diagnosticians and kindly, understanding advisers, and some (rather too many for comfort) were incompetent bullies or idle bigots, and the only thing the National Health Service had done to change things was to make it easier for the latter types to earn a living. Often, members of the public would ring up BMA House to say they had just moved to a new address and needed to get on the list of a doctor: the calls were always put through to my department – could we recommend someone? I should say not! All the doctors in the district could have been members of the BMA and we weren't supposed to favour one above the others. So how was the caller supposed to find a doctor? Our official advice was that they could go to the local Post Office: there they would find a list of doctors in the area, and they could choose one of those. And how were they supposed to decide? These calls made me feel inadequate and unhelpful and I would sometimes recommend checking out the local doctors' qualifications: an MRCP, as opposed to LRCP, was probably worth taking seriously, and an MB suggested a university degree. If he only had an LMSSA (Licentiate in Medicine and Surgery of the Society of Apothecaries – a qualification now obsolete on its own), well, probably better make a few inquiries among the other patients, if you could find them.

Nowadays doctors advertise in the Yellow Pages and commonly have prominent notices on display outside their surgeries, while, inside, patients are invited to help themselves to nicely produced brochures about the services on offer. In the 1950s this would have been extremely bad form. Doctors weren't supposed to draw attention to themselves in any way, especially not in any way that might prove to be to their financial advantage. So if a general practitioner suspected another in the same town of 'unethical' behaviour, he could complain to the local division's ethical committee; if this didn't resolve matters, the affair could be placed before the Central Ethical Committee in Tavistock Square.

The Committee was the ultimate court of appeal. Like the General Medical Council it was emblematic of medicine's status as a self-regulating profession. And when cases of professional ethics came up before them, all non-medical staff were ordered out of the room. However, when abstract questions of medical ethics were on the agenda, we were allowed to stay, and we would do so, oft times to listen with growing incredulity.

For now in the 1950s, new and much more scandalous means of self-advertisement were to hand. The committee began to nourish the suspicion that a doctor whose name appeared frequently in the press, or, God help us, was seen on television with any regularity, would enjoy an unfair advantage. Would-be patients would see him, or read his words in the newspaper, and, next thing you knew, they would be in his waiting room raising his income.

Charles Fletcher, for instance, was vulnerable, appearing every week in *Your Life in their Hands*. But his name was never given and when challenged on the question he let it be known he did no private practice: he was a whole-time consultant in the Health Service and therefore wouldn't be available if any viewer should take it into his head to request a consultation. But, muttered the Central Ethical Committee, but what if he were tempted ... Well, he appeared anonymously, didn't he? No one knew who he was. Yes, but word gets round. But Charles Fletcher was a man of such manifest probity ... The Committee would nod its collective head, and try to arrive at a formula. This would be printed in the BMA Handbook – an annual publication for members only – and it would enable them to point the finger at obvious quacks, while they doffed their caps at senior men like Charles Fletcher and another TV 'face', a consultant from the Maudsley Hospital who had become known as the 'TV Psychiatrist': he too appeared anonymously but his identity as Dr David Stafford-Clark was rapidly becoming an open secret.

In a way you couldn't blame the BMA for getting themselves in this fix. The General Medical Council, the body set up under the original Medical Act of 1858, could strike a doctor off the Medical Register for 'infamous conduct in a professional respect'. Unfortunately, this phrase, for all its orotund resonance, had never been precisely defined, but it had been held to cover all manner of professional sins, from seducing a patient to indulging in flagrant self-advertisement. On the question of whether doctors should give their names when they appeared on radio and television, the GMC contented itself with the absurdly ambiguous pronouncement, 'It is advisable, in the public interest, that doctors should broadcast anonymously.'

Lacking any guidance from this quarter, doctors could only turn to the BMA for advice. And the Central Ethical Committee had terrible trouble with it, as they tried to define true charlatanry without actually using the word or indeed saying anything too precise: doctors, they recommended, should think very, very carefully about 'granting' (*sic*) interviews to 'the lay press', and even more carefully if they were asked to appear on radio or television. It wasn't the fact of appearing on either medium so much as 'the manner and frequency of their so doing'. But who was to define that? They decided to send a circular to every BMA member, 'drawing attention' to the increasing frequency with which doctors' names were 'receiving public mention through the several media now available'. The circular was like a sigh in a thunderstorm.

Both Stafford-Clark and Fletcher were distinguished and influential members of the profession, and this was generally true of the hospital specialists who figured in *Your Life in their Hands*. That a BMA committee, consisting largely of provincial GPs, should suspect them of touting for patients was ludicrous. Furthermore, the committee had no teeth and it could do nothing about its suspicions. The BMA *wasn't* the body that struck doctors' names off the Medical Register – that was the General Medical Council – and all the BMA could do was show disapproval, or, in the last resort, make a complaint to the GMC. That idea, too, was absurd. It was never done. But anyone who was aware of the BMA's past might have recognised in this story a faint echo of the Provincial Medical and Surgical Association's irritation and resentment at the prominence of the London consultants and the London Colleges.

Ah, those 'ethical rules'! Under Forbes's direction, the elderly medical boffins of the Central Ethical Committee wrestled long and arduously over the small print that under the heading

104

'Medical Ethics' was to go into the handbook, a publication I was warned never to hand to the press, though I generally ignored the instruction. As John Pringle once observed, the Ethical Committee resembled nothing so much as a conclave of mediaeval monks, arguing over how many angels could dance on the head of a pin. Their solemn deliberations became more and more separated from reality as the achievements of medicine were more and more the focus of interest in the media.

To make matters worse, the BMA itself was publishing a monthly magazine which was actually intended for that hydra-headed enemy 'the lay public': it was called *Family Doctor*, edited by a certain Dr Harvey Flack, a cheerful, clubbable man and a talented editor, with a mildly startling facial appearance. He wore spectacles with extremely thick lenses; but, also, he had been badly burned during the war, and as a result of some clumsy plastic surgery, in the early days of that medical specialty, he had been left with an oddly shaped, steeply upturned nose. After the war he had become an assistant editor of the *British Medical Journal*, and in 1951, with the support of Hugh Clegg, the *Journal*'s editor, he had started *Family Doctor*, price 1s 6d monthly. Very soon, Clegg started to hate Flack, and was widely believed to have placed him top of his far from short personal hit-list. The notion that there could be two editors at BMA House grated on Clegg, but worse was the fact that control of *Family Doctor* and its publication was removed from the hands of the *Journal* Committee.

Family Doctor called itself a 'popular health' magazine, with breezy articles about acne, heart disease, asthma, peptic ulcer, athlete's foot and anything else which could be deemed relevant to healthy living. They also published a series of *Family Doctor* booklets – *You and Your Ulcer*, *You and Your Asthma*, *You and Your* this, that and the other, and you could buy these publications for a shilling each in chemists' shops. Harvey Flack would commission recognised experts to write them and he would edit them into a form that would be readily understood by those likely to buy them. He was a writer with a sure, popular touch, and often the articles in his monthly magazine made headlines because, so newspaper readers were led to understand, it was the BMA speaking. For example, his impromptu, very much *ad hoc*, study of snoring, its effects and possible cure, made the sort of headlines that were dreaded in Tavistock Square, even though they made it seem, briefly, that the BMA was human after all. But how about the ethical rules? Wouldn't a doctor's appearance in *Family Doctor*'s pages tempt readers to write to him and ask for his help with whatever complaint he was writing about? There was no sensible answer. Once again, the Ethical Committee was left to drum its fingers balefully on the committee room table.

If medical ethics was a minefield through which the Chief Press Officer, among others, had to pick his way with care, so were the activities of some of the other committees at BMA House. Prominent among them were those appointed to give evidence to government bodies.

As the voice of medicine, the BMA was the organisation governments increasingly turned to when there were social problems under review with some kind of medical angle. Several of these were handed over to an assistant secretary of the BMA called Ernest Claxton. He was a supporter of Moral Rearmament: this always seemed to colour the reports his committees eventually rendered to whatever government body was taking evidence. The BMA report on Homosexuality and Prostitution (two 'vices', it was understood, deservedly linked together) was a case in point. It had been convened to give evidence to a Departmental Committee on the subject, and the BMA's Committee on Homosexuality and Prostitution was sometimes known in the building as The Committee with the 'Orrible Name, because this was how a Chairman of Council, an Ulsterman called E. A. Gregg, would refer to it when calling for its report at Council meetings.

Their report, published in 1955, is a quaint example of what were more or less orthodox medical views on this subject at the time, though flavoured with Claxton's rather dotty ideas about 'the control and cure' of the two entities they were 'investigating', with much talk of the 'moral dangers of illicit sexual activity' and the need for 'personal discipline and unselfishness'. The report regretted to say that the medical profession had 'no panacea to offer for the cure of homosexuality', the growth of which was attributed largely to moral laxity. Widespread irresponsibility and selfishness – the root causes of this double plague – could only demoralise and weaken the nation, the report intoned. 'What is needed is responsible citizenship where concern for the nation's welfare and the needs of others takes priority over selfish interests and self-indulgence.' Curiously, the BMA's report seemed less interested in prostitutes than homosexuals. The published report devoted sixty-five pages to the latter compared with six to the former.

Claxton also steered a committee on Venereal Disease and the Young, which he perceived to be an important issue. He managed to make sexual promiscuity, then a phrase much bandied about, the subject of investigation by the BMA. At the time, cases of infectious syphilis, having been on the decline in Britain, were again on the increase; while gonorrhoea was (as someone said) 'spiralling to epidemic levels', and rising sharply among teenage boys and girls.

Further evidence, in Claxton's view, of the collapse of moral standards – and he considered these infections to be a kind of divine punishment for sinful behaviour. He liked to question people about their sexual history. In collusion with Ronald Bedford, my *Daily Mirror* friend, I hatched a disingenuous plan for Adam Faith, then well known as a singer, to give evidence to this committee, making sure the press were informed of the day and time of the appointment. I was able to convince dubious colleagues this would do no harm to the BMA's popular standing, but some were alarmed at the possibility of screaming, sobbing teenagers milling about the front quad, and the uniformed gatekeeper in the front lodge was briefed on how to cope if trouble broke out. After his appearance before the Committee, Faith was in fact briefly mobbed by three or four girl secretaries at BMA House, one of whom stole a kiss for the benefit of photographers.

Adam Faith then agreed to answer questions at an impromptu press conference, when he kept referring to the subject under discussion as venneral disease. Perhaps awed by the dignity of his surroundings he was at pains to make it clear he had led a life unblemished by promiscuous sex. This was a tactical mistake. Later that afternoon his agent began to wonder if this might be taken by his client's fans to mean he had never had any sex at all. He and his staff had to put in time on the telephone to Fleet Street to correct this impression: on the contrary, Adam was as red-blooded as the next man.

Had the next man been Ernest Claxton, that would have required qualification. He nourished some odd beliefs: anyone who favoured the colour green, for example, he suspected of homosexual tendencies. The same was true of men who wore suede shoes. One of the senior members of the clerical staff used to make a point of wearing suedes and an evil-looking green pork-pie hat whenever he could in Claxton's presence: Claxton would regard him with consternation. Another of his exploits arose from a speech made by a senior BMA figure at an annual meeting, who spoke vehemently of 'the loss of moral discipline sweeping the country' and claimed that at one girls' school he knew pupils who had lost their virginity had started the custom of wearing in their lapels a yellow golliwog badge. The speech caused no small sensation at the time: so much so that a small production company swiftly put together a film called *The Yellow Golliwog*. At Claxton's invitation, some of this was filmed at BMA House, in a scene supposedly taking place at a university college, hence conveying the silent implication that the BMA was associated with the production. Claxton failed to realise that *The Yellow Golliwog*'s makers were more interested in fortifying the box-office returns than rearming the country's morals.

Another event engineered by Claxton, which also turned into

a fiasco, was a weekend meeting at BMA House to discuss adolescent promiscuity, under the title *Tomorrow's Parents*. At this, a general practitioner from the town of Musselburgh made a speech in which he claimed that, while waiting their turn to be seen, two total strangers had had sexual intercourse in the waiting room of a doctor he knew. They were last in the queue, all other patients having been dealt with. And by the way, as a result of this encounter, the woman became pregnant. Surrounded afterwards by journalists, the doctor withdrew his assertion: he hadn't actually any first-hand knowledge of the incident and thought it wise, on the whole, to withdraw his story. It seemed likely it hadn't actually happened. Probably he thought it had sounded right in the context of the meeting, which was further enlivened by the arrival of a group of leather-clad bikers and their girl-friends, who sat silently in the front row listening to a succession of teenage speakers giving accounts of their own sexual experience: only one, a boy who worked in an East End factory, said he had had sexual intercourse, but he was 'not proud of it'.

These were innocent times, and I doubt if many people at the BMA were aware we were witnessing the first throes of a revolution in sexual *mores*. At this distance the BMA's response to what was happening – horrified amazement modified by a fear of appearing hopelessly out of touch – now seems a little ludicrous, though it was not much different from that of the bulk of the population. Sex education, another hot coal, was described by one doctor as 'not altogether disadvantageous provided it were done by doctors and that all talk of reproduction and ethics were omitted'. It is difficult to see what the lessons might have consisted of.

You might have known Harvey Flack's *Family Doctor* would get involved in the sex sensations at BMA House. In the early sixties he published the first of what became a series of booklets called *Getting Married*. A good deal of the booklet was devoted to matters like wedding etiquette, choice of wedding dress, furniture and honeymoon destination. But sex could hardly have been left out of it, and Harvey willingly grasped the nettle, commissioning a piece by a psychiatrist, Dr Eustace Chesser, on premarital sex: should you wait until your wedding night? The article went in with the title *Is Chastity Outmoded? Outdated? Out?* His answer to these questions was equivocal: he merely concluded that in many courtships the bride and bridegroom-to-be had, as the saying went in those days, 'gone all the way', and – oh well, that was their decision. But once again, it was the BMA speaking and, said many association stalwarts, hinting their approval of sex before marriage.

The article was illustrated with a photograph of a young couple embracing in a field. This picture attracted particular attention in the BMA Council when *Getting Married* was the subject of a full-scale debate, with reporters lurking outside. The young couple were fully clothed, but a member of Council claimed to be able to detect that the girl was *not wearing a bra*. So the suggestion was that they were on the verge of *doing it*. Council condemned the publication and, at some loss to *Family Doctor* revenue, *Getting Married* was withdrawn, and all copies pulped.

Through these years, sightings occurred now and then of my former headmaster, John Garrett. I and fellow-alumni of Raynes Park County School, the school he created from scratch, came to observe with a wry smile the progress he made, back in his native West Country. A son of Trowbridge, Wiltshire, where his father had been a gents' hairdresser, he had now become Headmaster of Bristol Grammar School.

By this time this former fringe-member of the Auden circle (he had been Auden's collaborator on the anthology *The Poet's Tongue*) had become a somewhat different person from the innovative educationalist of the 1930s. As one of the country's youngest head teachers – he was thirty-two when Raynes Park County School opened its doors for the first time, in September

1935 – he had created within the space of only seven years what was acknowledged as one of the best schools in the country. He had resigned in 1942, and by the 1960s he had reached, at Bristol, the peak of his eminence.

He was also an Honorary D.Litt. of Bristol University (Dr Garrett from then on, thank you), a Governor of the Royal Shakespeare Theatre at Stratford-on-Avon and organiser of annual Shakespeare symposia there. The proceedings at these summer sessions were published every year under the title *Talking of Shakespeare*.

One year, he undertook to give a lecture himself. Rash decision: perhaps his pride pushed him into it. Too late he realised he was out of his depth. He had been accustomed to asking Shakespeare scholars and theatre people of considerable eminence to come and speak, but in terms of intellectual attainment, and in comparison with his speakers, Garrett was nowhere. His knowledge of the Shakespeare canon was superficial, limited to armchair enthusiasm, preferably before an audience of innocent, impressionable schoolboys. 'The glittering superficies of learning' he had accused me of pursuing at school when I wasn't working hard enough were of course, *par excellence*, his own preoccupation. The accusation used to rankle with me and I wish I had realised at the time that he was probably rebuking himself, through me. At any rate he was not up to so merciless an exposure as a public lecture on that platform. As the date came nearer and nearer, Garrett panicked.

One of the Raynes Park masters who had remained faithful to Garrett was a man named Frank Beecroft, one of those – fortunately not rare – schoolmasters who are an ornament to their profession in this country: clever, helpful, sympathetic, widely read, never troubled by the faintest disciplinary problem, the kind of man who inspires successive generations of pupils with his enthusiasm and wisdom. Beecroft was homosexual, as Garrett was, though this was only dimly perceived by the Raynes Park boys of the late thirties, when children were more innocent. French was the subject he taught, but he would have been equally at home teaching Mathematics or, for that matter, Spanish or Italian, and his gift for languages (he taught himself Chinese in retirement) was complemented, as it often is, by brilliant musical talent.

Beecroft was also the man who helped Garrett to put Raynes Park school on the map with school productions of Shakespeare which were reviewed in the *New Statesman*, the *Spectator* and the *Evening Standard* and *Telegraph*. One day years later, in conversation with me, Beecroft let drop his resentment that his name as producer of the play was *never* printed in the programmes. Why not? 'Garrett wanted all the credit, you see.'

Yet when Garrett left Raynes Park for Bristol Grammar School, Beecroft followed him there after a term or two. He was a friend Garrett could count on. And, desperate for a way out of his difficulty with the Stratford lecture, Garrett went to see Beecroft in his flat in Bristol and almost in tears, by Beecroft's account, implored him to write the lecture for him. Beecroft did it.

Perhaps there was more to the two men's relationship than friendship alone. (Their first meeting, in Neville Coghill's rooms at Exeter College, was said by the novelist Rex Warner, another Raynes Park master, to have been in compromising circumstances.) Many of the boys at Bristol Grammar School assumed it was so, and there was once a tense moment at a school concert when someone came to the platform and sang *Frankie and Johnny were lovers* ... Perhaps the Bristol boys were more knowing, not to say braver, than the lower-middle-class boys of suburban SW20, who were generally in awe of Garrett's posh voice and hectoring manner. Those attributes didn't go down so well at Bristol, and it may have been the reason why this – as it was thought – brilliantly innovative headmaster became more severe, more obdurate in character. His regime at Raynes Park had been progressive, enlightened and liberal, backed by a talented team of high-flying assistant masters. His headship at Bristol, on the other hand, has been characterised to me as

112

'essentially oppressive', particularly towards the staff. A history of the school describes him as 'authoritarian by instinct', adding: 'He made enemies, for he could on occasions be insensitive in manner and speech and ruthless in action.'

Not, in other words, a popular man.

Now and then, word would reach former Raynes Park pupils of his activities in the west of England: about, for instance, his visiting lectures. We would smile knowingly. At Raynes Park we had been treated to a continuous parade, term after term, of writers, actors, theatre directors, musicians and dons. Garrett's Visitors' Book had been one of the wonders of his headship. But talk about *déjà vu*! It looked as if every literary or theatre celebrity who had ever visited Raynes Park to lecture to the Sixth Form was doing the same at Bristol Grammar. Cecil Day Lewis, L. A. G. Strong, Neville Coghill, A. L. Rowse ... it was almost like a repertory company of obliging intellectuals ready to respond to Garrett's flattery. A few new names cropped up, politicians mostly: Tony Benn, Anthony Crosland, James Callaghan, who were local MPs – but also Lord Hailsham and Lord Monckton. Garrett's political views were turning round. Another newcomer to the Visitors' Book who would never have been seen anywhere near Raynes Park was Queen Mary, widow of George V. She lived not far away. Somehow or other Garrett had succeeded in striking up with her a courtier-like relationship. She would arrive at the school in an old-fashioned Daimler, with a high roof specially chosen to accommodate her Edwardian hat, the invariable silk toque for which she was famous. With Garrett, I can imagine, simpering obsequiously at her elbow and doubtless in full academic regalia, she inspected a Guard of Honour supplied by the school Cadet Force, and signed the Book. It was said Garrett had a special royal lavatory installed for these visits. One can only hope Garrett took the precaution of concealing any *objets d'art* he may have had in his study, the Queen being notorious for her acquisitive claims on such things: if she admired them, you were expected to hand them over.

113

This was the man whose portrait had been painted, after he had left Raynes Park, by Claude Rogers, a painter of repute: he was the school's first Art Master and had gone on to found the Euston Road School, with William Coldstream and Victor Pasmore. At Bristol, however, Garrett sat for a certain J. G. Codner, and the painting that resulted, from a viewpoint slightly below its subject, shows Garrett in his doctoral robes, with an expression of profound self-satisfaction. But there is a hint of accusation, as though upbraiding the Third Form for their dirty shoes, and slovenly grammar.

Seven

Changing Sides

ONE AFTERNOON AT the BMA I was hard at work preparing a monthly summary of press comment on doctors and their affairs, when a call came from a BMA member who had asked to speak to me. He didn't give his name, but told me he was telephoning to make sure I was doing my job and not sitting on my arse in some restaurant, boozing with bloody journalists (*sic*). He disconnected the call at that point.

In itself, this wasn't a terribly important event, nor was it especially rare. Until then, I couldn't remember receiving any calls of that sort, though the medical officials were used to them: there were even certain doctors who were regular callers when well oiled after lunch, or even after breakfast. But as it happened, I'd been spared so far.

I realised he was in all probability one particular caller – usually tight – who was notorious on the fourth floor, where the assistant medical secretaries had their offices. But on that particular day, for no special reason, it annoyed me that I was supposed to be polite to people like him and even make myself useful to him – and that, as a layman, I was probably regarded by him and a lot of others like him as a kind of footman or messenger boy. Another incident had stayed in my memory, and that was the doctor who had told the Annual Representative Meeting that for the National Health Service he had nothing but hatred and contempt. No one shouted 'Shame!' at this rhetorical flourish. No one rose to protest that the Health Service was the institution that had saved countless numbers of people from pain, anxiety and unhappiness. Hence you had to conclude that the speaker's opinion, in general terms, was the view of the 'Doctors' Parliament'.

Enough, already.

I had now been at the BMA for eight years. I was obviously one of those people who are slow to move on. On the other hand, I wasn't only working for the BMA. Those articles for George Scott's *Truth*, plus a few book reviews and other occasional pieces, were seeds that had fallen on fertile ground. Through a contact at the London office of *Time* magazine I'd been approached by a New York publication called *Scope Weekly*. It was a weekly newspaper for doctors (always known as physicians) throughout America: it had a 'controlled circulation' – in other words it was posted to doctors free of charge, and existed on the quite lucrative revenue earned from advertisers, who of course were almost entirely pharmaceutical companies. But the newspaper was written and edited by journalists.

Publications of this kind had yet to arrive in Britain. When they did, they were to make a notable impact on the medical scene. But when *Scope* first got in touch with me, in 1957, the idea of a 'free' medical newspaper was a novel one. The piece they wanted was an interview with Dr Ernest Jones, the friend, disciple and biographer of Sigmund Freud, whom they'd discovered to be an expert not only in the art of psychoanalysis and the interpretation of dreams, but also figure-skating. He had even written a reference book on the subject, entitled *The Elements of Figure Skating*. What's more, he had once partnered in a waltz the dimpled international skater turned film star Sonja Henie.

Jones was then seventy-eight. I plucked up my courage and telephoned him, and asked if I could talk to him. He was a little testy, and not too willing, but agreed to see me, on condition I sent him a copy of what I'd written before sending it off to New York.

116

The interview itself I found arduous, a journalistic skill in which I'd had no training whatever. It wasn't without its interesting moments. The best was Jones's story about his habit of taking a cab from Harley Street to the rink at lunch-times, where he would derive 'physical and mental refreshment' from half an hour on the ice. He wasn't the only distinguished person with this habit. Another was Viscount Templewood, better known as the Tory politician Sir Samuel Hoare, who remarked as he glided round, 'First-class exercise, don't you think?' Jones snapped back, 'First-class *moral* exercise.' When I sent the result off to the peppery Dr Jones, he sent it back with a snappish letter, complaining about inaccuracies in what I'd written – but it did eventually go off, and was published under the title *Dr Jones Makes Few Freudian Slips on Ice*.

He was the first celebrity I interviewed. The next was Nancy Mitford, and the interview came my way through my brother David, who was by this time living in New York. A new literary monthly wanted ten thousand words about Miss Mitford and her books. After hastily reading through the Mitford corpus, I flew to Paris – still something of an expedition in the late fifties – to talk to her. This assignment was not a success. Nancy Mitford received me cordially, and it was not difficult to be won over by her legendary charm. Accordingly, my contribution to the new magazine was rejected on the grounds that my 'stance' towards her, as they put it, was 'too sympathetic'. Evidently they had wanted a demolition job. The magazine folded soon afterwards.

With *Scope Weekly*, on the other hand, my connection began to prosper. The editor appeared to have a hearty appetite for news of medical matters in Britain, and of the National Health Service, which was regarded by the majority of American 'physicians' in the McCarthy era as dangerously subversive. And in 1958 I made my début before a microphone, recruited by a BBC World Service producer to take part in a discussion on the first ten years of the NHS – this was recorded, not 'live', and just as well, since I did what many a débutant broadcaster has done, and dried. In extenuation I can only offer the excuse that my knowledge of the Service was slight and superficial, and since the other two members of the panel were Members of Parliament I think the producer had made a poor choice by including me in the discussion.

I was luckier a few months later, when the BMA held its first Annual Clinical Meeting – a kind of junior version of the Scientific Meeting of each July. A headline in the *Sunday Times*, reporting the proceedings, ran 'New Ideas at BMA Meeting', and this attracted the attention of another World Service producer, who was in charge of a programme called, yes, *New Ideas*. She rang me up and asked me if I would write and read a two-minute report on what had happened.

I went to endless trouble with that two-minute piece. I honed and fine-tuned the prose until it shone with an unnatural glitter, timed it to the last second and rehearsed it over and over with a borrowed tape recorder – then a novel gadget.

That afternoon in October 1958 when I sat down in a Bush House studio and earned my five-guinea fee was, I suppose, the start of my career as a broadcaster.

Leaving the BMA was not as easy as I expected. Colin Hurry had said to me more than once, 'You know, you've got a job for life here.' The BMA was a benevolent employer: they seldom fired anyone. 'You'd have to be discovered rogering your secretary across the office desk,' Hurry had said, 'and even then they'd give you full pension rights.'

However, my feelings about doctors, I have to admit, were more than a little jaundiced by this time. The last annual meeting for which I had organised the press room had taken place in Manchester. Conspicuous on the Representative Body's agenda – conspicuous to me at any rate – was a series of motions criticising the work of the Chief Presss Officer and his department. BMA colleagues scoffed at them and told me not to take my critics seriously. It was a common experience that when things were

118

going badly medico-politically, the cry went up that the doctors' case was 'not getting across': what that meant was that the newspapers had the insufferable cheek to criticise BMA policy, and that was my fault. On the other hand, the reporters at the press table asked me if I would like them to stand up and walk ostentatiously out of the hall when the meeting reached this point in its five days' business. I said it wasn't necessary; but it was good to know I had some allies.

More important than any personal pique on my part was that, by a near-unanimous vote, the Representative Body carried a motion demanding that patients make some payment for their medical service at the time of treatment, in order to put a stop to what was described as 'widespread abuse' of the National Health Service – by, one presumed, sick members of the public. This resolution, which provoked a storm of criticism in Parliament and in the newspapers, was the reason for my only speech to the BMA Council in the eight years I worked for the association. The Council's first meeting of the new session takes place, by tradition, immediately after the Annual Representative Meeting has finished. Non-medical officials did not usually have a voice at the Council: for some reason the Chairman of Council, Dr James Cameron (perhaps in sympathy with my feelings), invited me to speak my mind. What came out was an angry, and I dare say not tremendously articulate, speech, but it expressed some of my disgust at their negative views on the NHS. It seemed the battles of 1948 would have to be fought all over again, but this time in the absence of Aneurin Bevan, let alone of a Labour government with a huge majority.

At any rate, my resignation had been handed in by this time, and the machinery for appointing someone else had begun laboriously to function. Partly out of loyalty to my own alma mater I strenuously backed the candidature of an Oxford graduate, R. A. F. Thistlethwaite, whose name, remarked the editor of *World Medicine*, Michael O'Donnell, sounded like some obscure Fighter Command station in the Midlands around 1942. Thistlethwaite had been PRO for the Egg Marketing Board, a chapter of his *curriculum vitae* he had to live down, for he was duly given the job, and remained in it for the next twenty-five years, an amiable, hospitable and endearingly insecure man whose *penchant* for writing poetry was, for me, a further reason for supporting him. We have become good friends.

Turning it all over to my successor, with mingled feelings of relief and regret, I felt like a child who had dared to escape from the sight of some watchful and well-meaning aunt. But at least I was now my own man. I had joined the ranks of – in the awful modern phrase – the self-employed.

Almost the first thing I did when I left the BMA was join the National Union of Journalists. Then I joined the Press Club – and considered my immediate ambitions duly realised.

I bought one of those hopeful-looking books with the black and yellow covers from the Home University Library: *Teach Yourself Shorthand*, and struggled with confusing mnemonics like *Pa May We All Go Too* which were supposed to help you choose the right squiggle for the vowel sound you wanted. I soon gave this up as too difficult and tried another volume in the HUL series, Dutton's Speedwords: ta v fr vi let b j p n fa z v di ... thank you for your letter but I cannot do as you say. At least, I think it was something like that. Once again, as with Henry Kowal's writing course, I never got to the end. In any case, this wasn't a lot of help when it came to writing 'the hypothalamus and the brain stem have been shown to contain norepinephrine' or 'each tablet contains 100 mg NNanhydrobis-hydroxyethyl biguanide'. With nothing but Dutton's Speedwords at my disposal, I found myself under-equipped.

Luckily, a good few publications seemed willing to take contributions from me about what was new in medicine and medical politics.

The Physicians News Service and I were now firing on all six cylinders. *Scope Weekly* was long gone but it had been replaced by a medical newspaper, published by the same organisation in New York three times a week, called *Medical Tribune*. Its liberal-minded management appeared to have an insatiable interest in British medicine, in the British Health Service and its social impact. I assume their readers shared this interest, or perhaps read about it for its gloat-potential when things were going wrong – or at other times with disbelief that anything so politically unacceptable could actually be made to work. I imagined them reading with grim nods of satisfaction the stories I would file about British doctors' restiveness – their chronic demands for more pay and the steady haemorrhage of numbers as British doctors emigrated. Their usual destination was the American continent, especially Canada, obeying mankind's deep instinct for westward travel but not exactly helping the cause of state medicine.

These were bad days for the Health Service, and for the BMA as well. Mass resignation by general practitioners was in the air again, with demands for a new contract of service and a rumble like thunder that was the sound of doctors voicing their dissatisfaction with the BMA's leadership. There is nothing like an angry doctor. The purple faces and apoplectic mixed metaphors, familiar from 1948, were once more on display in the correspondence columns of the *British Medical Journal*. 'Have we not learned from the past,' raged a correspondent, 'that we are dealing with a ruthless political machine, willing to pat us on the head as the backbone of the NHS, but quite content to run us into the ground before lifting a finger to help us?'

The cuttings book I kept at the time makes ironical reading now: all that hot air! The splinter groups, the threats, the late-night press conferences after twelve-hour meetings, the posters sent out for every doctor to display in his waiting room, calling for better equipped surgeries, more staff, more time to study, more time for each patient, more doctors and, last but not least, 'a new fairer system of payment for your doctor'. But the medical profession's agony was my bread and butter. Dolour for them,

121

you might say, meant dollars for me. 'British Society Urges GPs Quit Health Unit' ran a *Medical Tribune* headline over a story I sent over in March 1965, while in a Danish medical journal, *Läkartidningen*, then relying on me to fill them in on events in Britain, it was '*Varför Strider de Engelska Praktikerna?*' This I had stuck in the album alongside a contribution of mine to *The Listener* reporting an exhibition in London on medicine at the time of Waterloo: in this, first-aid measures for the apparently drowned included the instruction, 'Tobacco smoke is to be thrown gently into the fundament with a proper instrument – or with the bowl of a pipe.'

Something similar may have been secretly applied to British general practice, which, though apparently drowned in 1965, somehow survived. But not before the BMA had passed through a summer of sulphurous public argument and an annual meeting – at Swansea this time – when the Representative Body told the BMA's leaders to send 'ringing down the corridors of Whitehall' the message that, in future, doctors had to be allowed to charge their patients a fee: back to the good old days, as it were. Was this a resignation issue, Cameron unwisely asked the assembled representatives? There was an immediate, loud, angry chorus in the affirmative, after which the meeting swept on to discuss, of all things, how to improve its public image.

If that meeting proved anything at all, it was that the doctors' rank and file, as they were sometimes referred to in Tavistock Square, were not marching on quite the same parade ground as the doctors who were supposed to be leading them. But it was pretty clear the British medical profession had got the leaders it deserved.

I was probably biased against the BMA by this time but the spectacle of its Representative Body cheering madly as they demanded, in effect, the dissolution of the National Health Service, was not a pleasing one. From my own new and unfamiliar standpoint, outside the organisation, I was being reminded of saner and more responsible voices in the profession. In the very week the BMA meeting was yelling for mass resignation (*massuppsägning* was the rather interesting word in *Läkartidningen*), the College of General Practitioners (not then the *Royal* College, a subtle change some observers mistrusted: were they about to merge with the Establishment?) published a report on the state of general practice with a very different, non-BMA slant. This asserted that British doctors were not as overworked as they claimed, didn't see shortage of money as the chief worry and were not plagued by irresponsible and demanding patients. 'British GP Group Minimizes Plight of Family Doctor' (*Medical Tribune*).

As the year went on, there was even a detailed proposal for an 'alternative health service', masterminded by the Private Practice Committee of the BMA with touch-line support from the Fellowship for Freedom in Medicine. It was a project 'of a magnitude far greater than anything the BMA has ever previously sponsored', boomed the Committee's Chairman. He was a certain Dr Ivor Jones, a short, pugnacious Welsh GP, with a practice in Sunderland and an annoying laugh which used to precede him down the corridors of the Tavistock Square building. He reminded me of a character in Spenser's *Faerie Queene* called The Blatant Beast, 'who by his grinning laughter mote far off be rad'. And in the flushed and unreal climate of that year, it seemed not at all unlikely that Dr Jones, aided by a small committee of dissatisfied doctors, could invent, in the space of a few months, a practical scheme to replace the NHS, one that could look after the patients and pay the doctor what he wanted without intervention by the government.

Saner voices could be heard in the distance now and then. 'For many of us, to undermine the National Health Service,' said a doctor at an Edinburgh University 'teach-in' on the NHS and its problems, 'would be to return to the Dark Ages.' And the BMA's grandiose scheme to – in effect – take over some of the functions of the Ministry of Health was all shoved aside when the government announced its own 'new deal' for general practice, and so another BMA Big Event drifted into oblivion.

In that year, 1965, medico-political surprises seemed to keep on emerging, like the flags of all nations from a conjurer's hat. All these sorry events figured largely in my working life at the time. But one other phenomenon accompanied them, and it has to do with the way news of these great arguments was circulated around the profession. It was all linked with the rise of the controlled-circulation press. What the American medical profession was well used to was by now hitting the surgeries, common rooms and hospital canteens of Britain. A weekly called *Pulse* was first in the field, originally published by a drug company as a novel way of advertising its products. Not long after it was launched, *Pulse* was bought by an independent publisher who recognised the potential of this kind of periodical. The BMA didn't like it. Right at the outset *Pulse* adopted a critical, carping attitude towards the medical establishment. Feature articles brought up matters the General Medical Services Committee would rather they'd ignored, like deputising services and careless prescribing. There was an opinion column whose anonymous author (he signed himself 'Jotter') sniped sarcastically at Tavistock Square: to my surprise, 'Jotter' turned out to be none other than Hiram Creditor, the thin, angular, rather stand-offish doctor who had been in the Advertising Department at Menley & James, brother-in-law to Hugh Gaitskell.

Other periodicals followed: *Medical News*, and before long *Medical Tribune*, a British edition of the thrice-a-week newspaper which had kept me going for more than six years. Then came *World Medicine*, a glossy monthly. All of these, and others, arrived by post through the doctor's letter-box, free of charge, and paid for by the advertisers, predominantly pharmaceutical houses who were always on the look-out for acceptable ways of puffing their products.

You would have expected these magazines and medical newspapers to adopt a mealy-mouthed, respectful attitude towards doctors and their affairs – tradesmen to the posh profession.

On the contrary, what became known as the paramedical press, as opposed to the orthodox medical journals – *British Medical Journal, The Lancet, The Practitioner* – maintained an independent attitude towards the three major contenders in the National Health Service – the government, the pharmaceutical industry, and the medical Establishment. If they were on anyone's side, it was that of the patient and the average, non-belligerent doctor-in-the-street, who worked and lived his life far away from the uproar at Tavistock Square.

The main reason for this was that the paramedical press was, on the whole, staffed by professional journalists, who had been trained to ask awkward questions and publish information that showed up prejudice, incompetence and now and then villainy. The orthodox journals had long abandoned this rôle – although historically they had fulfilled it with conscientiousness and zeal. Under its first editor, Thomas Wakeley, *The Lancet* had been the scourge of the Royal Colleges and the medical politicians of the 1830s, just as, later in the century, the *British Medical Journal* had exposed all manner of social evils from baby-farming to quack medicines and even the regulation of the plumbing trade. Now this necessary task was being taken up by specialist medical journalists – questioning, treading on people's toes, flooding the surgeries with information on new discoveries, government reports, BMA activities, medical meetings and developments in Parliament.

It was the time, too, of the rise in patients' pressure groups. The Patients Association was formed, and got itself recognised as an articulate voice in medical affairs. Groups were formed for sufferers from specific illnesses, some with their own newsletters, with clunky titles like *Talk Back* for people with back pain, and *Beyond the Ointment* for those with eczema.

But the effect of all this was that gradually more light and air were being allowed into medicine.

Before I left the BMA I had managed to establish a foothold

in broadcasting, through the BBC World Service. There was a weekly programme called *Science and Industry*, which aimed to keep overseas listeners in touch with what Britain was doing in those two fields of human endeavour. The presenter of this programme was a veteran broadcaster by the name of Arthur Garratt, whose knowledge of the sciences appeared to me positively encyclopaedic. There was nothing Arthur didn't know. He seemed to have a working knowledge of every -ology in the scientific dictionary and he was a broadcasting professional whose bland self-assurance I longed to acquire. Arthur Garratt's advice to me when I left the BMA and hoped to get more work as a broadcaster was to buy my own portable, professional-standard tape recorder: in those days the German machine called the Uher was the recorder of choice. 'Get your own Oo-her,' Arthur said. He also, typically, knew where to go to get a professional discount. Even with one-third off the retail price, it seemed an absurdly extravagant piece of expenditure, but he was right: it paid off. Waiting to speak to someone in Radio-4's *Today* office a little later, I noticed a typewritten list of freelances on the office wall. My name was there, with the cryptic annotation, *Own Uher*. It meant they could ring me up and despatch me on a story without delay. Unlike other freelances, I wouldn't have to trek laboriously up to Portland Place to borrow a machine from what was then, oddly, known as the midget section of the BBC.

Most weeks I would contribute something to *Science and Industry*, usually something in the technological line – disposable equipment for hospitals, drugs that became absorbed in a novel way (new 'delivery systems' was the ugly phrase) – that kind of thing. I also took the chair – sweating with apprehension at first – at another weekly programme called *Asian Club*. This required a visiting celebrity – usually a doctor on my programmes – and a studio audience of Asians living in London who would fire off questions: my rôle was to act as moderator, host and presenter.

Asian Club was a bit of a tangent for me. Mostly I patrolled the medical and scientific beat. I had learned the freelance trick of getting maximum mileage from a story. Looking around a hospital to collect material for a *Family Doctor* article, say, I could at the same time file a thousand words for *Medical Tribune* and, if armed with the Uher, knock off an interview for *Science and Industry*. Better still, I just might be able to get an interview accepted by the radio freelance's most desirable target, *Today* on Radio-4.

Today in those days was not quite as it is now, in 1995. For one thing they used a corps of freelances. Also there was only one presenter, and he was Jack de Manio. De Manio was one of that vanishing species, a Radio Celebrity. He was famous for his cheery voice and his slightly thick-headed *bonhomie*. But listeners loved him. He was a broadcasting 'natural': relaxed and confident at the microphone even when, or perhaps especially when, he fluffed a few words of script or got the time wrong by an hour. (Then, as now, *Today* presenters had to act as speaking clocks as listeners bolted their breakfast and hurried for the train.) There were dozens of stories about de Manio and his mistakes – saying *nigger* when it should have been Niger (he had announced a feature programme that should have been called *The Land of the Niger*), or saying orgasm instead of organism. It was typical of de Manio that one day he inadvertently hit one of the row of studio lamps with his pen: he thereupon hit them all and picked out a tune. He had instinctive style as a presenter, but wasn't in his element as an interviewer, though he always wanted to do more. Once he persuaded a producer to let him go out and interview the wife of a famous golf professional on the eve of a great international tournament: *Today* was fond of finding 'the woman's angle'. 'Tell me,' de Manio asked effusively, 'I'm sure you must have some little sort of good-luck ritual you go through when you send him off in the morning on something really big and important like this?' The wife pondered the question briefly. 'Yes,' she said, 'yes, I do. I always kiss his balls.' Sensing ambiguity, de Manio helpfully prompted her: 'You mean his golf balls?' The oddest thing about this story was that the interview

127

was broadcast on a Saturday morning with this exchange left in, intact.

It was probably a great pity Jack de Manio wasn't allowed to go out more often with Uher over his shoulder and bring in more scoops like this. But still, there was no dearth of freelances like myself, pushing and shoving to get interview ideas accepted on such a high-profile programme. I think in those days *Today* may have seen itself as the *Daily Mirror* of radio journalism rather than, say, its *Guardian* or *Independent*. At any rate the programme's team of producers were always ready to consider gossipy, 'human interest' stories in addition to more serious fare, though my own contributions were generally in the former category, in the area of medicine and science. Thinking back, I can remember carting my Uher to a big computer company, to numerous Medical Research Council Open Days, hospital press briefings and medical conferences galore, including (of course) the BMA. But I also remember interviewing a man who was about to proceed down the Thames on a pair of ski-like rafts he called 'skinoos' ('Do you think this has a future as a means of transport?'), a Sotheby's porter who was retiring after twenty years holding up masterpieces at auctions for the audience to inspect ('Will you miss holding up these expensive pieces of merchandise?' 'Don't make me laugh.' 'Didn't you ever want to take any of them home?' 'No.') and an Aberdeen urchin who'd just been told the BMA had discussed banning the sale of sweets to under-tens (words failed him).

Then there were other programmes like the undemanding *Home This Afternoon*, a Radio-4 tea-time show produced with an eye to senior citizens just settling down to enjoy a nice pot of Ty-phoo and a chocolate Bourbon or two. There was *You and Yours*, a consumer-oriented programme, presented then by my former school chum Derek Cooper, who for some reason usually called it *You and Your Crutch*: it was the only occasion when we have coincided on a programme, with the single exception of the time when *Kaleidoscope* reviewed his book on Skye. There was

Woman's Hour, difficult for male freelances to crash, but for whom I managed to do one or two series along popular-health, *Family Doctor*ish lines. And there was a late-night discussion series, thoughtfully, perhaps a little arrogantly, called *What's* Really *Wrong with the National Health Service?*

The World Service continued to employ me. *Science and Industry* was renamed *Science in Action*, a title thought more in keeping with, in Harold Wilson's phrase, the white heat of the technological revolution Britain was supposed to be going through. Title changes were the thing: round about this time two other World Service programmes, *Farming World* and *Techniques for the Tropics*, were merged under the single title *Hallo, Tomorrow! Science in Action* also acquired a signature tune – one of those catchy, rhythmic, four-bar motifs suggesting a squad of mechanics double-marching into the future.

Over this, the programme title was announced. My voice, actually, speaking out in as resolute and confident a tone as I could manage.

My father's second marriage did not go so well. What had begun in the Saloon Bar of the Malden Manor had on it the taint of the gin bottle.

His drinking routine had altered: off the train at Raynes Park station at the end of the day's work and quick march to the Junction Tavern under the skewed railway arch. After a round or two, and it was whisky not beer, and then maybe a game of dominoes or shove-ha'penny, a ten-minute walk to his house up the road. Perhaps out again later for a quick one, taking the car this time.

But just across the road from the Tavern is the establishment that rivals and soon supplants the pub – the local Conservative Club: more rooms, including a billiard room, more liberal drinking hours ... and perhaps a slight social cachet. On the wall, large photographs of Winston, Anthony Eden, Macmillan. He takes to the cheery, comradely atmosphere and is soon an elected officer of the club. He is always pressing me to go there, to join him for a drink, bring my wife to one of the Club Dances, drop in at a bingo session.

But the romance has faded: she isn't his Princess any more, but a bored housewife once again, with nothing much to do. She has a son by her first marriage, and he hasn't taken the family upheaval well; nor does he get on with my father – one more reason for him to linger on the way home.

She's not a woman of strong resolution: he puts her in the shade, with his meetings, his business contacts, his trips abroad, his habit of speaking French or German at home or in the bar, impressing fellow-members but very soon boring them. Often, in the early evening, she joins him in the Club. But it isn't what she wants. What does she want? A cosier home life, probably – and she persuades him to move: the house in Coombe Lane is too big, and she has always had an itch to get out beyond the huge between-the-wars estates of suburban London. He isn't keen, but lets himself be persuaded.

He suggests a private arrangement – he'll sell me his house. It's the kind of deal he enjoys – all in the family, and cuts out agents' commission. So, there's a general post. We move out of the downstairs flat in my father-in-law's house – and take over my father's place. George and Lillian Vaughan go West, to Thames Ditton and, she hopes, beyond range of the Conservative Club. It's a doomed hope.

When we move in, the first thing we notice is a massive collection of empty bottles in the garden shed. Gin, mostly. Somehow, we hadn't realised what had been happening, but it explained a lot of things that had been family jokes – her way of repeating herself, her odd habit of disappearing upstairs during our visits and coming back with a contented smile, hair perhaps a little awry. It also throws light on a medical crisis she had had a few months before: she had been taken to the local hospital with a peptic ulcer. Lying in a hospital bed with a tube up her nose, pale and rueful, talking slowly but all of a sudden making more sense.

My father, in attendance at the bedside, sighing heavily, looking at his watch, grumbling that he is expected to turn up again for the next lot of visiting hours and stay until they're over.

Then, one night, in the small hours, the telephone rings. It is her son, now a young teenager, but his voice is small and scared. My father is away in Germany, but due back that morning. Lillian has fallen down the stairs leading up to their flat. She is dead. I drive over at once, and there is a young policeman there, asking questions: 'Was she in night attire, was she?' 'You say she had been under the doctor?' He isn't told this, but it sounds as if she were drunk, fell all the way down a fifteen-foot flight of concrete steps and perhaps brained herself. But later we are told she had another ulcer, and it had perforated.

My father was expected at Victoria, off the boat train, within a few hours, and a small group awaited him on the arrival platform: his stepson, his mother-in-law – a grim, resentful figure – and me. When he saw us waiting, he plainly knew something was wrong, and it fell to me to break the news to him. His face flickered in the sort of smile children give when they're told of a death: not amusement but an instant, instinctive fending-off of the truth, or perhaps a catching of the breath that, this time, the bell did not sound for him. He said, 'Oh, Lillian, I've told her so many times.'

No more business trips abroad. Now he retired: nothing to keep him in Thames Ditton, and it was back to Raynes Park, and a flat no more than five minutes' walk from 'my club', as he called it, as though it were White's or the Athenaeum. But he had precious little money saved, and his pension soon began to be whittled down by inflation. He earned a small stipend as club Treasurer, taking it all with great seriousness: meetings, memoranda, audited accounts – plus billiards and bingo. But the halcyon days had gone.

And the other father-figure in my life, John Garrett, came abruptly to the end of his career.

131

In 1960, in the phrase of F. Scott Fitzgerald, there was a flutter from the wings of God, and Garrett suffered a stroke. He resigned from the Headship of Bristol Grammar School and, probably obeying some inner compulsion, returned to the district where he had scored the first major success of his career. He set up house in Wimbledon, with a young clergyman and a mongrel dog. Facing death, Garrett had come out.

A few months afterwards he attended a dinner of Raynes Park Old Boys. It was a sad sight. The stroke had affected his powers of speech, and the booming voice, the italicised, C. M. Bowra-ish Oxford delivery, were now filtered through some poor-quality internal jamming device. The hooting vowels were more or less intact but the consonants were muffled and came out wrong: his mouth was all tongue. You could see him trying desperately to make sense, perhaps thinking that he was. It fell to me to propose the school's health at that dinner, and I spoke in eulogistic terms of Garrett's contribution to the school's brief history, aware of his rheumy eye watching me, his head trembling a little and his lips curved in a slightly daffy, Justice Shallow smile.

He invited me to his house for dinner a few weeks later. It was another painful experience, though his young companion acted as interpreter. The conversation was stilted and difficult.

I never saw him again. In 1966 the wings of God fluttered a second time: he had another stroke, and this carried him off. There was a memorial service at the local parish church, at which a small number of ex-pupils from Raynes Park turned up, one of them the man who as a boy had played Hamlet and Macbeth in the school's productions nearly thirty years before. There were, besides, perhaps a dozen other people none of us knew. A few weeks later it was reported in the *Daily Telegraph* under the nosy headline 'OTHER PEOPLE'S MONEY' that Garrett had left the sum of just over £32,000. He made one more news item: a four-paragraph story in the *Evening News* gave the information that all but £2,000 of the money had been left to his forty-one-year-old friend, who merited this mention because he had been adviser to the ITV series *Our Man at St Mark's*.

Eight

A View of Mount Ararat

WHEN I LOOK back at the bread-and-butter work I was doing in the 1960s, I marvel at my apparent ability to exhibit such sophisticated familiarity with subjects well beyond my professional competence. Of course, my knowledge was only skin-deep, but I had the advantage that I could ask the man who had done the work, written the paper or performed the operation to help me get it right. And as a general rule, the more eminent the doctor or scientist, the more prepared they were to help.

Even so, stimulation of central, alpha-type adrenergic receptors in the mouse brain, the experimental production of auto-immune nephritis in the frog, *in vitro* studies of agglutination in red blood cells when mixed with dimethyl sulfoxide . . . can it have been me who wrote about these matters with such apparent confidence? When I read these thirty-year-old cuttings now I seem to be stepping into someone else's biography, that of some younger, visionary brother, perhaps, who read biochemistry or molecular biology somewhere; a man with whom I must have quarrelled and who subsequently disappeared, emigrated or died. What a piece of work he was, who could write about medicine, science, and medical politics, with equal assurance. A pipe-smoker, too: drawing sagaciously on a long-stemmed briar. (The Royal College of Physicians' report on Smoking and Health had made me give up cigarettes. Instead I was now getting through six ounces of Player's Mild a week, and probably smelled terrible.) How I regret having lost touch with this versatile sibling, putting across his copy to the *Observer*, the *Sunday Times* and *The Times* (pre-Murdoch), and God knows how many editions of *Medical Tribune*.

Nowadays reporting scientific and medical matters in the daily press and the paramedical periodicals is the work of better-qualified writers: probably journalists who actually did read some scientific subject at university. When I began to write about these things, few of the science and medical correspondents on the national newspapers had any such qualification. Most were experienced general reporters who had somehow been given the job because they'd happened to be about in the news room when one of these technical stories came in, and there was no one else on hand to get on to it. The science correspondent of a respected broadsheet was by training an artist who had been painting a mural in the staff canteen: the news editor, stuck for a reporter, asked him if he'd like the job. He said yes. At least two of the press corps had been war correspondents in the African or European campaigns, or both; another had a degree in History and also wrote thrillers; so did another, who also had a past as a conjuror's assistant – and thus was considered uniquely qualified to make sense of the stories we were required to cover.

The approach we generally adopted was that if we could understand a story from the depths of our ignorance, then we could make our readers understand it. It was a reasonable enough starting-point, and it was equally valid when you were writing for a medical audience, most of whom at any one time would have been reading about something out of their own specialty. Slowly, though, journalists with the 'right' qualifications were replacing us self-taught individuals who had joined the Association of British Science Writers in an attempt to gain some extra purchase on the subjects that were our bread and butter. I was not a regular at ABSW meetings: it was on infrequent occasions that I would go to one of their lunches, at which some distinguished man or woman of science would speak, briefing us on their particular line of research and occasionally supplying us with a story we could follow up.

However, one benefit I did get from belonging to the ABSW was a visit to the USSR at a time when contacts between East and West were exceedingly rare. At the time – it was 1967 – the Iron Curtain seemed to be fixed immovably in place. But the horizon was lightening just a little. The great tyrant Stalin was dead. Khrushchev was Secretary of the Communist Party and the curtain had been raised a fraction of an inch, if only briefly, by such events as his state visit to Britain with President Bulganin ('Call them Khrushchers and Bulgy', the *Daily Express* had jocularly advised its readers). But contacts on what one could call a human scale were few. Famous artists, the likes of the Oistrakhs, Rostropovich, Richter and the Bolshoi Ballet – people of their celebrity were permitted to make their tours for the sake of the USSR's cultural prestige. We had even seen the Red Army Choir in the Royal Albert Hall. Otherwise, movement was at a glacial pace. Ordinary Russians could not get out. Ordinary tourists couldn't get in.

But the ABSW had the idea that a group of specialist journalists like us might be able to get visas, and had written to someone in Moscow to ask if an official party might pay their Russian opposite numbers a visit. Months went by with no response, then one day, out of the blue and to everyone's surprise, a letter arrived. It is possible it had something to do with the fact that 1967 marked the 50th anniversary of the October Revolution. Whatever the reason, the Union of Soviet Journalists was inviting ten ABSW members to come and see scientific institutions in Russia. There was a ballot of members: my name came out of the hat.

The ballot may have been ever so slightly rigged because it so happened that, besides the Chairman and Secretary of the ABSW, the other eight names included a quiet, well-mannered man by the name of John Moss, who was science correspondent of the *Morning Star*, the now defunct daily newspaper published

136

(with Soviet assistance) by the British Communist Party. No one felt disposed to complain about this: it seemed a diplomatic and possibly helpful move. However, not one of us, and that included John Moss, spoke a word of Russian, and it made the trip sound more than a little problematical. We all equipped ourselves with phrase-books, which, as usual, were largely valueless when it came to the point. Mine had in it the kind of slightly barmy anachronisms one is led to expect from such works, like 'I am in need of a chiropodist', 'Fetch a mirror straightaway to Room 101', and 'Has anyone been asking for me whilst I was strolling round the town?'

We also equipped ourselves, after mutual consultation in the *New Scientist* office before departure, with what we conceived to be appropriate presents for our hosts. I cannot now remember why we thought it advisable to take with us ball-point pens and Dinky car models of London red omnibuses, but that is what we did. I suppose the buses were meant to be slightly humorous, to hit an apt note of not-too-pushy national pride; the ball-points we perhaps saw as a useful Western novelty. At least they didn't take up much room in our luggage but they struck some of us afterwards as a little like taking beads to the natives. As we should have foreseen, they became a bit of an embarrassment. Every now and then we would remember we had brought them with us and look about for a 'hit', hoping to get in before some other member of the group. It was like some ludicrous game of forfeits: ten roubles for the first to get rid of all his buses and biros. It might have been easier if there had been something applicable in our phrase-books ('Pray accept this pen/model of a London bus') but in any case there were few suitable cues. One evening in a bar in Novosibirsk we did encounter a sitting duck in the shape of a young blonde prostitute called Nina, and though no one in our party did business with her as far as I know, I believe she finished the evening well equipped with ball-points. I think we drew the line at the buses.

Actually we were to meet very few ordinary citizens, though

in the matter of language we were naturally given some help. As we discovered on arrival at Moscow Airport, two interpreters had been assigned to us: their names were Karl and Mischa. Karl was the one we came to like the better. He was a young, nervous, Jewish man, a professional interpreter who had learned English in a state-run foreign-language school. He enjoyed his rôle as host, and had an eager, helpful, anxious manner as he marshalled us into our coaches or strove to have the waiters in our various hotels perform a miracle and bring us our breakfast (yoghourt and scrambled eggs, weak coffee) within sixty minutes of our placing the order.

His fellow-interpreter, Mischa, was an altogether different type – younger, sharply dressed, and speaking English with a faintly American accent. It seemed he had learnt the language while working in one of the Soviet Embassies in the USA. His English was better than Karl's, but there was something slippery and plausible about his manner that made you think he had other duties than acting as go-between for us and the people we were meeting.

Besides Karl and Mischa there were two other members of our entourage. One was a senior science reporter from *Iszvestia* who also seemed to represent the Union of Soviet Journalists. He spoke a little English. Not much, but it was possible to engage him in conversation – unless the talk turned to matters of censorship and editorial control, in which case he became vague and evasive and retreated behind the language barrier.

Then there was the fourth man. He was a lot older than the other three. He was called Kyril Gladkov – the sort of name you would give a typical Russian in a spy thriller. No one ever explained his precise function to us but he was generally, and I'm sure correctly, assumed to be the main KGB minder for the whole event. He certainly looked the part, being short, broad, and square, with a glowering, heavy look under bushy Oscar Homolka eyebrows. He also wore heavy boots and the kind of gangster suit worn by the men you'd see in the background whenever Khrushchev appeared on TV. He too spoke English, and he too said he had learned it in America.

He was more the grizzled NCO than Mischa, the dapper, ambitious subaltern. Now and then he would emerge from his habitual heavy taciturnity. In the course of one conversation Gladkov recounted to me his memories of St Petersburg in pre-Revolutionary Russia. He said he had seen, with other street urchins, the half-frozen corpse of Rasputin in the Neva: he remembered staring at the dead man's galoshes sticking out. Everyone had known, he said, about the plot hatched against Rasputin by a clique of disaffected courtiers, who this time made sure the mad monk would be finished off properly. 'Rasputin was *tripled*!' rasped Gladkov exultantly, in his inches-thick Russian accent. 'He was shot! Strangled! And drowned!' And as for the October Revolution, Gladkov insisted this was 'practically bloodless': few shots were fired, he maintained, and the violence had been exaggerated. And he himself had brushed elbows with history again, for he'd found employment at Lenin's headquarters as a messenger, for which he was rewarded with 'bowels of lovely kasha'. And did he once see Lenin plain? Yes, not once, but many times.

Out with the trusty Uher. I recorded a lengthy interview about all this for sale to some willing producer when we got back. Alas, I never found one. The Gladkov Tape is still collecting dust in a drawer somewhere.

These were the four men who greeted us when, a little nervously, we stepped off the BEA aeroplane at Moscow Airport, a place of which my chief memory is a strange smell of boiled sweets. It was the fuel they used, said my World Service colleague Arthur Garratt, whose name had also come out of the hat. From there we were taken into the city, past the huge stone memorial marking the limit of the German army's advance to Moscow in 1942, and so to the offices of the Union of Soviet Journalists for speeches of welcome. We were confidently expecting these to be lubricated by rousing sequences of toasts, but to our

139

disappointment this proved not to be the case. No alcohol was forthcoming. However, we eventually sat down to dine and were rejoined by one member of the party who had disappeared shortly after touch-down: Arthur Garratt. Somehow, word of his imminent arrival appeared to have preceded us, for he had been hustled away to be interviewed, live, on Moscow Radio on the subject of our visit. How had they known? Why him, and not the Chairman or Secretary of the Association of British Science Writers? Was it Arthur's fame as a World Service presenter? Surely not, when BBC transmissions were routinely jammed. No one could explain. Arthur himself professed ignorance. But I believe he dashed off a quick ad-libbed account of the experience for *Science in Action*.

Next, the hotel. An anonymous and rather boring building, and not, unfortunately, one of those immense Stalinist structures that dominated the city skyline and regularly amazed Western visitors – vast stone wedding-cakes standing about Moscow like super-extravagant, Gothic war memorials. The idiosyncrasies of their architecture – half-Gormenghast, half-Disney's *Snow White* – suggested there would be many impossible living spaces inside. You could only wonder who might be called upon to occupy the rooms created by those ridiculous and unnecessary turrets. I was hoping to find out, but no – our own hotel was the utilitarian Hotel Peking, which must have been due for a change of name, in view of the poisonous ill feeling at that time between Russia and China, with bellicose confrontations along their common border.

However, the Peking was comfortable enough. We were assigned rooms in pairs: I doubled up with Arthur in a spacious apartment with bathroom and sitting room. In this there were easy chairs, a huge, massive-legged dining table with six upright chairs around it as though the family were expected for Sunday dinner. There was also, incongruously, an upright piano. On the walls were ornately framed prints of woody Russian landscapes, leaning steeply outwards from the walls, in a style reminiscent of richly furnished Victorian interiors.

In the wide corridor outside, all was quiet: thick patterned carpets and, by every lift, a little, unsmiling old woman seated at a table, who kept possession of your room key but seemed to have nothing else on her mind. Some passed the time knitting.

We did not spend much time in our rooms. When we did, there were often mysterious telephone calls. When you picked up the instrument you heard a female voice at the other end, talking excitedly as though from a long way away, barely pausing for an answer. These calls seemed more numerous after we had exchanged travel cheques at the desk in the hotel lobby, so it seemed likely someone was touting for trade. Spies? Whores? Room service offering drinks? Black market operators? Someone calling for help? Who could say? Not Mischa and Karl, who shrugged off the whole thing. More important is our schedule: the Union of Soviet Journalists is leading from strength, whisking us each day to a string of scientific institutes – the Institute of Physics, the Institute of Geochemistry, the Institute of Genetics, and there is little time between these appointments. But the weather is fine as we file out of some official building into the traffic-free streets. Arthur also has his Oo-her and is constantly knocking off quick interviews: outside the Institute of Physics he can be seen, microphone in hand, interrogating a woman selling a type of root beer called *kvass* from the back of a lorry, with Mischa in attendance.

Off to another visit. This time, the Minister of Health. A very large office in the Kremlin. He is a Dr Petrovski, and the only Minister of Health in the world to have transplanted a human kidney: actually he has done eleven. He is also head of the Institute of Experimental Surgery, a title with a sinister sound, and he has just performed operations for a mediastinal tumour and a mitral stenosis. The USSR believes in having doctors at the head of its health service and Petrovski, a substantial-looking man in a smart, biscuit-coloured suit and maroon tie, holds the

141

Order of Lenin for his transplantation work. Someone asks him a question about the contraceptive pill – new in Britain and still a hottish science story. Will Russian women be taking it? The Minister says something Karl interprets as 'We do not want our children to be born without legs or hands.'

An aide appears and whispers in his ear. The Minister rises and spreads his hands: 'Goodbye, gentlemen. I wish you success in your work, and correct writing on medical problems.' That seems a broad enough hint.

One day, by special request, they lay on for me a lightning tour of the Russian Health Service – a polyclinic and the 2,400-bed Botkin hospital in mid-Moscow, undoubtedly a showpiece, where they exhibit little of the reticence customary in the British equivalent. 'We have a wide selection for you,' says an English-speaking doctor. 'Heart failure, acute respiratory failure, orthopaedic cases with shock, profuse haemorrhage . . .' He is like a salesman offering his wares. They show me a man who they claim died twenty-eight clinical deaths after a heart attack and is now waving cheerfully at me from his hospital bed. One of the Botkin's success stories? 'He's not home yet,' says the doctor, with a sideways look.

Then after dinner in the Peking, around the little Union Jack the management has thoughtfully placed on our table, it's the circus, an outing that has to be sharply curtailed because we have to leave at midnight for Armenia. Just outside Yerevan they have built a giant new telescope, and that's our destination. On the plane we pass through several time-zones, arriving at Yerevan around eight in the morning: a horrible journey during which sleep is hardly possible. They do serve us a meal, though. I can't tell whether it is supper, or breakfast: a plate with two slices of mutton, a small bunch of grapes, a plain bun, and a cup of tea. I drop off at one point, to be woken up almost at once by a female voice droning on in a bored monotone, like an alternative version of those frantic voices on the hotel telephone. What is it this time? Production statistics? Safety precautions? Hardly the latter, since

142

I had noticed some passengers standing in the aisle at take-off after a stopover at some obscure airport *en route*. One of them seemed to be trying to find room for a live chicken in the small space around him.

Three days in Armenia . . . a view of Mount Ararat in the distance . . . better, more exotic food in the hotel . . . a trip to an ancient monastery containing, they said, the oldest illuminated manuscripts in the world . . . and back to Moscow. More science. The predictable visit to the Bolshoi, in the days before anyone had defected: they perform in the theatre inside the Kremlin, and it's *Swan Lake*, with the up-beat ending – Odette lives, and gets the Prince after all.

Then, off to Siberia. Another long, long flight, but this time we touch down somewhere in the middle of the afternoon at a small airport, where John Moss takes out his camera and is immediately surrounded by armed security guards. Mischa intervenes to prevent confiscation of the camera – or maybe Moss's imprisonment. Had it been someone other than the man from the *Morning Star*, would it have been so easy?

Our destination is Novosibirsk, a name that means New Siberia, designated by the Russians 'Science City', created out of an obscure little hamlet where Lenin stopped off briefly, before the Revolution. It wouldn't have looked then the way it did in 1967 with rows of identical apartment blocks set out along the wide, empty boulevards: not a beer lorry in sight, let alone a car. But Novosibirsk has its attractions. On our first night Karl announces we are going to the opera. What's on? 'It's called *The Hairdresser of Seville*,' says Karl enthusiastically. My turn with the Uher. Somewhere, probably in the same drawer, is the live recording I pirated from the stalls of *Una voce poco fàr* and an interview I did afterwards in his dressing room with the international *basso* Nicolo Rossi-Lemeni, guesting as Don Bartolo and the only member of the cast to sing in Italian.

Sad to say, of the scientific achievements we had been invited to go and see, I can remember virtually nil. Extra-curricular events made a far stronger impression: a second visit to the Kremlin Theatre, to see *Rigoletto*, all in Russian this time; and in deep Siberia, a picnic on the shores of Lake Ob, when our minders surprised us with Bloody Marys of great strength which they mixed from two flasks they had carried surreptitiously to this lonely and picturesque spot. But as for nearly everything else – vanished from memory. If there is any excuse it is that there is something dreadfully colourless and bleak about information conveyed through an interpreter: details are smudged, overall intentions misunderstood as the listener's attention wanders between two people instead of focusing on one, while at the same time he is scribbling down a few Dutton's Speedwords. Jokes and analogies lose their sparkle.

For all of Karl's careful efforts and Mischa's sketchier, more improvisatory fluency, the barrier between us and the eminent members of the Academy of Soviet Sciences remained more or less insurmountable. The tour of the Moscow hospital aside, I have a clear memory of only one Soviet invention, and that was demonstrated to us in an open space at the rear of the Institute of Physics. It was the work of the Hydraulics Department, an immensely powerful gun which propelled a thick jet of water with murderous force and accuracy across a distance of nearly a hundred yards. Exactly what this was for we were not informed: open-cast mining would be a kind assumption, but I thought I detected a lazy smile on Mischa's features during the demonstration and a look of professional satisfaction on Gladkov's.

Part of the problem at these scientific institutes was knowing what to ask. This was where the wheat was recognisable from the chaff – I mean, where the correspondents who knew something about science, and had the appropriate degrees, came into their own, people like Tony Osman and Robin Clarke, Chairman and Secretary of the ABSW, and Colin Riach, then science correspondent of the BBC. And of course Arthur Garratt.

Arthur's performance during our question-and-answer sessions had earned him the nickname (at which he purred a little) Academician Garratt. Everyone felt he lent us all a bit of style with his questions and comments, which were bursting with information and experience. Good old Arthur! With his highly domed forehead, and his eyes half-closed as he smiled a cat-like smile at what sounded like a productive response. He was a good-natured man but I suspect he was the cause of one odd incident during the trip. At least, it was difficult not to connect it with Arthur's slightly mysterious way of life, and his association with an American company bearing the odd and slightly meaningless title Value Engineering. Whatever the nature of their work, it seemed to involve Arthur in a huge amount of travel and close inspection of industrial establishments all over the world, with the aim, I think, of helping them to become more efficient. Arthur liked to boast of his membership of something called the Hundred Thousand Mile Club, only open to those lordly individuals who had travelled at least that distance by aeroplane and evidently conferring on them certain special privileges, such as the use of the Hundred Thousand Mile Club lounges at international airports. I doubt if there was one at Moscow. Arthur was well informed about aeroplanes, as about everything else, and he would whip out a stop-watch to time our pilot's take-off, nodding with approval (or, in the case of Aeroflot, frowning with disappointment) when the manoeuvre had been completed and the rest of us relaxed our white-knuckled grip on the newspapers we had been 'reading'. Arthur's deportment throughout the flying experience – still new to the rest of us – was relaxed and super-confident. While my passport was pathetically blank, Arthur's was so crammed with visas and permits and other special endorsements he had had an extra volume tipped into it, and now that was nearly full as well. He also had a wallet of credit cards fully two feet long. At a time when hardly anyone had heard of such things, Arthur's were kept in a bulging pocket book that he would shake open with a flick of the wrist, as though performing a trick.

He was an entertaining companion, and one late afternoon

he and I left the hotel together, to buy presents to take home —
a complicated excursion to the foreign visitors' shop, involving,
audaciously, a ride in a taxi. Our hosts had taken us by surprise
by handing each of us an envelope containing one hundred
roubles (rubbles, Gladkov called them) for spending money.
Arthur also had some roubles from his broadcast, which they'd
paid for in cash up-front. In the Intourist store he bought one of
those astrakhan fur shakos which, when worn on the streets
of London, were a declaration that the owner had been to
Russia. My purchases included amber cuff-links, and various
papier-mâché trinkets — ashtrays, dishes, nests of dolls and the
like. (I had already bought a toy space rocket and from sheer
curiosity, for my wife, a maze-like dress pattern resembling a
Moscow underground map, baffling and incomprehensible.)

When we had returned to our rooms bearing our purchases,
Robin Clark came to see us. He had tried to find us in our
absence, but, when he had knocked, a stranger came to the door.
Assuming he had gone to the wrong floor or made a mistake with
the room number, he apologised in slight confusion and went back
to make sure. He had been right: it was our room. He went back
and tried again. This time, no answer. He tried several times. Still
no answer, and no sound.

We checked our belongings. Nothing seemed to be missing.
But . . . could those shirts have been left exactly like that? Hadn't
I put that book I'd been reading further from the edge of the
table? I couldn't be sure. When we reportd the incident to Karl
shortly afterwards, he seemed much concerned, marched out to
the *babushka* at the desk (Had anyone been asking for us whilst
we were strolling round the town?) and began to question her
severely. Angry shaking of the head, dismissive gestures. Nobody
had asked her for the key, she had seen nothing.

And so the matter was closed. Was Arthur the Gladkov
of our group? Perhaps. But, you had to admit, infinitely better
informed.

That evening, after the room-searching incident, if that was what it had been, was our last in Russia. We had invited Karl, Mischa and Co, and some officials of the Journalists' Union to come and drink with us in Clark's and Osman's set of rooms (no piano). We all contributed what was left of our duty-free Scotch, and the Russians, who had been able to drink unlimited quantities of vodka, which rendered us incapable, now proceeded to get maudlin-drunk on the small amount of whisky we were able to serve them. We for our part remained sober: a lesson in drinking lore – the less familiar the booze, the quicker the effects. We also had some Russian champagne, and Clark and Osman had managed to obtain from somewhere in the hotel some platefuls of dry biscuits and caviare. Presents appeared: small enamel badges commemorating fifty years of communism. Some of our group brought out copies of their books, and we were each given a small wooden inlaid plaque which showed two Soviet cosmonauts standing on the moon waving to the earth, or possibly giving a clenched-fist salute. Sadly, the prediction never came true, though it seemed safe enough at the time, since Yuri Gagarin had orbited the earth and been the first man in space. We were also given a mysterious small package which turned out to contain a quantity of Russian matchbox labels. None of our party collected such things, but it seemed a fitting retaliation for the biros and the buses.

I think the Russian trip finally convinced me I was a journalist. After we had returned, the Russians sent a message asking us to send copies of everything any of us had written as a result of the trip. When I assembled my collection of broadcast scripts and *Medical Tribune* and *Observer* cuttings, it looked quite impressive and I was pleased with myself. More so still when Osman told me that, in sheer number of words, I had outdone the entire party.

So, I no longer needed to apologise to myself for the way I earned my living. I could put my occupation in my passport without shame, and I was doing something closer to the grain of my character. About time.

Nine

Hats Off to Mr Vaughan

I HAD DONE some work for one of the first Sunday colour supplements, the one published by the *Observer*: the man who had commissioned it was an Oxford contemporary, Hilary Rubinstein. I had never met him there but I suppose this was a demonstration of John Garrett's principle that the main reason for going to Oxford was to make connections that would be useful to you in your life afterwards. I expect Garrett would have pursed his lips in approval (a habit he had) if he had been eavesdropping on a telephone conversation I had with Rubinstein a few months later.

Rubinstein had left the paper and joined the literary agency A. P. Watt. He asked me if I would be interested in writing a book about the contraceptive pill.

My education under Garrett had left me with the instinctive belief that writing a book was an achievement all educated men should aspire to. *Doctors' Commons*, with its clunky title, didn't really count – spoiled by traces of its origin as a public relations gesture: this new one would be something more serious. Hilary Rubinstein rightly described the subject as 'meaty', but it was dauntingly so, and I was not altogether confident about the complexity of the project – its obscure biochemistry and the tortuous commercial negotiations, to say nothing of the large question of the social impact of birth control by means of a daily tablet.

148

In my view there were few books on scientific subjects which could be read with much pleasure or comfort. But I had read two which I thought set an example of how 'science' should be written about for a general audience. Both of them still deserve to be regarded as classics of this limited literary form, presenting matters of medicine and biology in literate, precise and amusing terms, illuminated when need be by pertinent analogy. One was by yet another Oxford contemporary, Anthony Smith: *The Body*, a stimulating and gracefully written book, which treated the human body almost as an unknown continent, to be traversed and marvelled at, and on almost every page it offered new slants on extraordinary details of human physiology.

The other book was by a man I had known at the BMA, a witty and elegant assistant editor on the *British Medical Journal* who was also the author of several novels set against medical backgrounds. He was John Rowan Wilson, and the book was *Margin of Safety*, a brilliant account of the development of the polio vaccine – a medical advance of not much less significance than the pill. I admired Wilson's firm grip on the material and his pungent and entertaining descriptions of the personalities of those involved. If I were to write this book, I thought, I should strive to make it as good as Wilson's.

Anyway, without much hesitation I said I would do it. Hilary Rubinstein already had a publisher willing to take the book. And he thought he could more or less guarantee wide foreign sales and Sunday newspaper serialisation.

A Victorian physician, Samuel Gee, once said, 'Make haste to use your new remedies before they lose the power of working miracles.' The pill was still comparatively new to Britain in 1967 but it would prove to be one of those miracle-working medicaments to which Gee's remark was all too applicable.

Our attitude to contraception has changed mightily in the last few years, in the West at least. In the late 1950s, today's contraceptive arsenal was unknown. Condoms and Dutch caps were more or less all we had, apart from coitus interruptus. None of these was foolproof; and abortion was a very rare option. Things are different now. Contraception is wholly acceptable as a topic for dinner-table talk, as for the television screen, commercials included, though I imagine many thousands of people have been scared into practising it and do it for the 'wrong' reasons – not to prevent babies but to prevent disease, specifically AIDS, but before that it was genital herpes and gonorrhoea. And that means protectives, not contraceptives – not the pill but the condom, which in the late sixties was the poor relation of the contraceptive family, if the expression is permissible. The French letter, as my generation called it, was the cloth-cap contraceptive, the *All right for the weekend, sir?* precaution, handed over by the barber with a furtive but sympathetic grin. Of course, the barber's shop wasn't the only outlet – just the most painless. Slot-machines were coming in but they were slightly disreputable and attracted scandalised comment, and *graffiti* ('This chewing gum tastes awful', etc.). And from chemists, naturally: one of the rites of passage for men of my generation was the ordeal of entering a pharmacy and asking for a packet of Durex, hoping against hope the person serving you wouldn't be young, female and attractive.

Actually by the time the pill was taking hold, LR Industries, the organisation which evolved from the London Rubber Company, manufacturers of Durex (and surgical gloves and party balloons), were showing signs of uneasiness. In their worst nightmares they could foresee a time when 'mechanical' contraception (the peculiar term adopted by birth control specialists), or at least the rubber 'johnny', would be as dead as the vinegar-soaked sponge or the sheep's caecum. They even set up a public relations offensive against pill contraception using a front organisation called the Genetic Study Unit, which sent out cyclostyled bulletins and proclaimed a crusade dedicated to 'protecting the women of the world from mass conversion to faith in oral contraceptives'.

If only they had known, they needn't have bothered. For, as time went on, amid growing anxiety about the safety of the

150

pill and the threat of sexually transmitted diseases, we have all been witness to the triumphant return of the French letter – the latter word being used, incidentally, in the sense of 'hinder', as in Hamlet's cry, 'By Heaven, I'll make a ghost of him that lets me!' Now the colourless word condom (etymology obscure: was there really an eighteenth-century Colonel Condom, or – surely not – Conton, as some dictionaries tell us?) is in general, more or less unembarrassed, use and the articles are on ostentatious display in pharmacies and supermarkets.

What a change from the 1960s, when contraception was still a subject to raise blushes or sniggers. As a sort of spin-off to my book on the pill, Hilary Rubinstein negotiated for me a modest paperback for the Family Planning Association. It was supposed to break new ground by reviewing all the available methods of contraception in straightforward and easily understandable terms. There was to be no mincing words. At one point there was even a discussion on whether the four-letter words should be used: by then it would have been just about permissible to do so, the *Lady Chatterley* trial having cleared the way. But we decided not to, on the grounds that it would give the book a blunt, coarse, barrack-room air that would probably frighten off a lot of readers. Perhaps I missed my chance of notoriety by not campaigning for this in the Mortimer Street offices of the FPA.

Instead, we went for sobriety and restraint. There were two or three paragraphs: a dainty, well-manicured finger pointing to an intra-uterine device – that sort of thing. The anatomical illustrations were line drawings of an entirely unexceptionable, indeed almost po-faced, nature. Nowadays they would cause no offence at all, but my father was electrified by them. Perhaps most people over sixty-five at that time would have shared his feelings. He referred to *The FPA Guide to Birth Control* as 'your pornographic book', treating it, I am sorry to say, with a sly and irritating prurience. Once he brought it out in, of all places, the bar of the Raynes Park Conservative Club, and started flashing it about like something he had bought from a Books and Mags shop in Soho. The pages he found especially noteworthy were those describing sexual intercourse, illustrated by a drawing of an erect penis. It was helpfully labelled 'Penis'.

From the very beginning of my freelance career I had been an obsessive collector of cuttings. I labelled them as systematically as I could, part of a private reference system accommodated in a second-hand steel filing cabinet of the kind now more or less eclipsed by the floppy disk. So the exciting times at Menley & James were turning out not to have been entirely wasted. My envelopes labelled Contraceptive Pill were a beginning of sorts, and indicated the territory I was going to have to cover: how the pill was invented, how it was tested, did it work, what effect was it likely to have on people's behaviour and, the biggest question of all, was it safe?

There were no easy answers to any of these questions and the answer to the last was a matter of guesswork. No one knew if it was safe or not. Some workers in the field were able to convince themselves it was safe enough – no less so, anyway, than a lot of other drugs in daily use. Others reasoned that the risks, if any, were permissible in the light of the world population figures, on which subject alarm bells were then just beginning to sound. It was the time when demographers and ecologists (the latter a discipline few had heard of) were beginning to voice their anxieties about the polluted and overcrowded state of the planet.

But to the average pill-user all this was no doubt irrelevant, especially in the excitement of the moment. The important thing was that if you had taken your Enovid (Conovid in Britain) you could be as good as one hundred per cent certain you wouldn't get pregnant. Sexual intercourse was all of a sudden as available as water from the tap, and it could be as spontaneous as kissing – no fumbling around beforehand with caps or condoms (or calendars, in Roman Catholic households), and nothing to get in the way.

It was a singular stroke of irony, or possibly good luck, that the Pill Revolution occurred at just about the same time as the

Sexual Revolution that had caused so much panic and perplexity at, among other places, the BMA. The two developments couldn't have been better timed.

I doubt if the men who worked on the pill in the late 1950s could have foreseen what a Pandora's box they were opening. As I was at pains to point out in the book's opening pages, nobody called 'Eureka!' when the first contraceptive pill in the world was held aloft in a pair of laboratory tweezers. Nobody made a speech, and nobody opened the champagne. When you looked into it, the discovery or invention of the contraceptive pill – whichever it was – was the story of a succession of bright and not necessarily connected ideas, a thoroughly laborious crabwise process involving a number of different people, who were working to a great extent in the dark. The generally received view was that the inventor was a man by the name of Gregory Pincus, an American working in Massachusetts – ironically one of the most puritanical of American states. Some people even referred to it as 'the Pincus pill', a name faintly reminiscent, I always thought, of the 'pink pills' of yore, a popular and probably useless anaemia remedy, widely advertised during the 1920s as Pink Pills for Pale People.

Unfortunately Pincus had died in 1967, of an obscure disease of the white blood cells – come to think of it, the sort of condition for which, oddly enough, those Pink Pills might well have been recommended forty or fifty years earlier. But the three colleagues who had worked with him in the early stages were all active: they were Dr John Rock, Dr Min-Chueh Chang and Dr Celso Ramon-Garcia. They made up an interesting and polyglot group, and they had brought various skills to the creation of the contraceptive pill. Pincus's base of operations had been the resoundingly titled Worcester Foundation for Experimental Biology, in reality a quite modest building with a staff of fewer than twenty. He himself was an extremely able man: born in America of Russian-Jewish parents, a graduate of Cornell who had gone on to Harvard to take a

Master's degree and a Science doctorate and had also worked in Berlin and at Cambridge University. He was also, incidentally, one of those lucky individuals with a photographic memory, who could read a book three times as fast as an ordinary person. He liked crime novels, and read one a night.

His wife was still alive, and I went to see her in the sort of house everyone knows from the movies, typical of middle-class America, the property unfenced and surrounded by well-kept grass sloping down to the road: inside, a spacious living room on a lower level than the entrance hall. Porcelain and silver much in evidence, photographs of the two of them, tables crowded with mementoes of their journeys abroad. Mrs Pincus expensively coiffured and dressed.

She had been 'Lizuska' to her late husband: she was my first interviewee on that trip to America in the spring of 1959. What kind of man was he? I asked her, with the Uher spool revolving, the AKG microphone thrust forward and the cable wrapped around my fist. She swallowed, and said, all in one breath and her voice swooping low in a downward arpeggio, 'He was a romantic, the kind of lover a woman always dreams about but rarely finds, he was . . . ' And at that point, she broke down in tears.

After a short time, with me wondering what to do and Mrs Pincus stifling her sobs, she was able to resume, and afford me one or two more insights into her life with Pincus: 'Goody', everyone called him. It was hard not to sympathise with this outwardly hard-boiled woman even though the unworthy thought came to me that this little scene might have been one she'd staged a few times before and was doing it again for my benefit. But she was a good talker. Once, she told me, she had been feeling discouraged by their slow rate of advancement and had said to him: 'Oh God, it's all too much. Let's go out and let's get a cart and sell lemons.' Goody had answered, 'Stick with me, kid, and you'll be wearing diamonds.' All the misery of the ghetto, I thought, was in that anecdote. I could only hope she had been well provided for by Goody and the pharmaceutical house of G. D. Searle & Co, for whom he had worked as consultant.

Pincus had been one of the research scientists who had been busying himself for a long time with the idea of what was thought of then as chemical contraception, and had entertained the idea that manipulating the balance of hormones in the female body might be a fruitful line of inquiry. He had come to this from a general interest in the process of fertilisation of the ovum by the sperm: as a matter of fact he had caused a sensation in the 1930s when he had performed an experiment in which he managed to bring about fertilisation of a rabbit ovum in the test-tube and make the ovum start to divide. This was striking enough, but it became more so through the chance omission of the word 'not' in a newspaper report of his research, which said, 'Dr Pincus said emphatically that he is [not] planning to carry it on to find out whether human babies can be made by test-tube methods.'

During the war, his research was put aside (he spent the time working on the relation of hormones to mental and physical stress), but in 1951 he had an encounter with the sixty-four-year-old Mrs Margaret Sanger, founder of the International Planned Parenthood Federation – one of those doughty women, like Helena Wright or Marie Stopes in this country, who had taken up the cause of birth control and made it her life's work. Some of Mrs Sanger's ideas on the subject were decidedly odd and well over to the right: one radical method of birth control she favoured was sterilisation – not for everyone, that is, but for 'certain dysgenic types who are being encouraged to breed and would die out were the government not feeding them'. Among those who harboured similar views around that time were H. G. Wells and Winston Churchill.

All this was recent history. Mrs Sanger believed the time had come for a decisive step forward: was Pincus the man? At her disposal was some of the immense fortune belonging to Mrs Stanley McCormick, money which had been amassed by her late father-in-law from the manufacture of farm machinery. She was another of the same breed as Margaret Sanger, and not only rich but a forceful manipulator of other people. She was in her late seventies when Pincus and Mrs Sanger met: a woman who was used to getting her way ('A ramrod!' said Mrs Pincus. 'Little old woman she was *not*'), and so rich, according to Pincus's collaborator John Rock, 'she couldn't even spend the interest on her interest'. Mrs McCormick was taken to see Pincus, and out came the cheque-book: $40,000 down and another $85,000 to come. Pincus got down to his task, recruiting Min-Chueh Chang from Cambridge, in England.

Chang was the man who did the laboratory work that culminated eventually in the original pill, the compound first used in Puerto Rico in 1956, and obviously someone to be tracked down. I met him in circumstances vaguely suggestive of a Hitchcock movie and in a manner typical of Chang's curiously elusive personality.

I was told to take a bus from the centre of Boston – he would meet me at a certain bus-stop at a certain hour. The bus-driver put me down on a broad, empty highway on the edge of a forest, then vanished into the distance in a black cloud of exhaust fumes. Silence descended. There appeared to be no traffic. I waited for something like ten minutes. Every now and then a farm vehicle or a car would pass by – as a rule, very, very fast – and I would try to look innocent and inconspicuous. Then, rather suddenly, a fawn-coloured saloon nosed quietly out of a side turning I hadn't noticed, about fifty yards down the road, came softly towards me, and purred to a stop: Chang got out, a thin, polite man, tall for a Chinese person, wearing a beret and smoking a pipe. These, and the car, which was a Rover, somehow didn't quite match his appearance, and I supposed he had acquired a set of British accoutrements during his time at Cambridge. His command of English, however, wasn't brilliant and lent an air of cliché inscrutability to many of the things he said. You could never be sure you had read him aright, and whether there were depths of irony to his remarks not immediately apparent to a Westerner.

Chang placed it carefully on the record, for instance, that the first experiment he did on suppressing ovulation in laboratory animals was on the 25th April 1951, adding: 'Do not get upset when people do not recognise you.' He said it was a quotation from Confucius, but it sounded more like Emily Post. He appended a further comment, his own this time, and thoroughly mystifying: 'I hope Chairman Mao will say the same.'

Chang took me back to his office at the Worcester Foundation and conducted me laboriously through the stages of research that had preceded publication of a key paper on the effects of progesterone and oestrogen on the fertility of female rabbits. The paper itself, published in a learned journal, had Pincus's name on it (it was described as 'constructed' by him).

Then I went to call on Dr John Rock, in his office in a suburb of Boston. He told me about the clinical work he had been doing while Pincus and Chang were poring over Petri dishes: his line of business had been the treatment of infertile women, and it was about to connect significantly with Chang's. Rock, a gynaecologist, had been treating infertility by giving his patients doses of hormones in a way that mimicked the early months of pregnancy. When the dose was stopped, some of them became pregnant: not many – thirteen out of eighty women was the number – but enough to suggest he was working on the right lines. Then, Rock and Pincus happened to meet at a local scientific conference, exchanged explanations of what they were doing – and the first trials took place of a kind of primitive version of the contraceptive pill.

Rock was still doing research on contraception, he told me. One of his experiments sounded a little absurd. Acting on the well-recognised fact that human spermatazoa prefer a lower temperature than that of the body's internal organs, he was inducing some of his male patients to expose their scrotums to the heat of naked electric light bulbs, which they had to hold next to their testicles for varying periods before intercourse. He was trying to ascertain if this would tend to make them sterile.

He wasn't in possession of any results at the time of our interview.

The whole project of my book seemed to me to be gathering both interest and momentum: I hadn't remembered hearing about any of the details of how work on the pill came to be started and I felt a quickening of the pulse as I heard about the course of events that followed this Blind Man's Buff between scientists and well-meaning parenthood-planners.

So how had things proceeded from there? Pincus and Chang had gone off to Tokyo in the autumn of 1955, for the 5th Conference of the International Planned-Parenthood Federation. Neither of their contributions aroused any special interest: both papers were about trials with laboratory animals, and were regarded as old hat by the likes of Sir Solly Zuckerman, the distinguished British zoologist whom I went to see when I came back to England. His chief memory of the Conference, he told me, was of large crowds of earnest people enjoying themselves in buses: sight-seeing was an essential ingredient in such trips, evidently with jolly singing *en route*. This was not Sir Solly's idea of a good time. 'I'm not very good in buses,' he said, a little distastefully.

But when Pincus and Chang returned to the Worcester Foundation, they changed gear – and launched the first trial with human patients. They collected a group of sixty women: some of them were medical students, but the numbers were made up with seven psychotic women from a local mental institution who could hardly have been in the best position to make a choice in the matter. None of them were (as the mealy-mouthed saying went) 'exposed to pregnancy', but Pincus judged the effects of the pill by various means, measuring the length of their menstrual cycles and changes in temperature, taking biopsies of the linings of the uterus and analysing their urine.

For no very clear reason he also selected, from the same institution, sixteen men – also psychotic. The results with this meagre sample of the male population, the pill's first male 'guinea-pigs', were not very illuminating, although the trial lasted over five months. Pincus said he detected by the end of the trial a definite sterilising effect on eight of the men, a result which probably quickened Mrs Sanger's interest. One of the men was found to have smaller testicles than when he started: his scrotum had become 'soft and babyish' and his prostate gland had atrophied. These anonymous men must have been very unsatisfactory experimental subjects. And it wasn't clear how their infertility was measured, either, since it was said to be impossible to get specimens of their semen. Psychiatrists at the hospital tried to keep an eye on the luckless inmates, logging masturbation curves (no change), trying to assess whether their psychotic condition was in any way affected (it wasn't) and attempting to observe any changes in behaviour (none, except one man was reported to have behaved in a 'very feminine' manner – not described). I believe this trial led no one anywhere. But the incident suggests yet again the sketchy, extempore manner of the earliest pill trials.

As much of an eye-opener was the move to the first large field-trial. Pincus needed a more convincing group of guinea-pigs than his motley group of students, lab workers and lunatics, and he and Rock set about organising a really ambitious trial. The place they chose was Puerto Rico, an underdeveloped country on America's own doorstep, with huge problems of over-population and poverty, badly in need of some way of controlling its headlong growth in numbers. They chose a suburb of San Juan where there was a large slum-clearance programme in operation, selecting at first one hundred women to take part – but new volunteers kept coming forward as word of this new miracle pill spread through the district. The trial began in April 1956 and, as they say, the rest is history. But it was still far from clear whether the pill was safe or not; and it is hard to imagine the trial taking place in any town on the American mainland, least of all Boston, Massachusetts.

Equally revealing were the conversations I had at Syntex, the company in Palo Alto, California, who had been the first to make synthetic hormones that could be taken by mouth – a development essential for any large-scale production of contraceptive pills. Carl

Djerassi, then Vice-President of Syntex Research, had performed this remarkable conjuring trick on the basis of work done by a man called Russell Marker, an eccentric loner who had stomped through the mountainous country of Mexico with a team of mules searching for a vegetable that could be used as a basis for what he wanted. He had eventually found it in a species of wild yam.

But then when it came to exploitation of his discovery, and Djerassi's pharmacological *coup*, Syntex were outsmarted by the firm of G. D. Searle, who had Pincus on their payroll and were able to patent a process slightly different from Syntex's and get off the ground factory production of Enovid – the world's first contraceptive pill.

Altogether, the talks I had in America, with Chang, Rock, and others in Boston, then with Garcia in Philadelphia, had got things off to a promising start. The story of how the pill began was turning out to have an interesting cast; and it was also becoming clear that the earliest use of the pill in the field (or the bedroom for that matter) was partly a question of guesswork and intuition.

It is hard to imagine a drug so powerful, and destined for such wide use, being allowed so readily on to the market today. Launching any new drug is a procedure that takes many months, often years, of laboratory work and carefully controlled field trials which have to be scrutinised and approved by official bodies before there is any question of the product being released. (Nowadays it is a standard complaint of drug company executives that the present safety regulations are seriously impairing the rapid development and marketing of new preparations.) As time went on, and as information was collected about the unwanted effects of the synthetic hormones, new versions of the pill became available. But I felt it necessary to devote a lot of the book to discussing, or at any rate reporting, the more or less continuous mutter of critical comment in the medical journals, and the low-level argument about the fine detail of pill contraception and its physiological consequences, which now and then would explode into public view. When that happened, queues of women (so we were led to believe) would form at doctors' surgeries and family planning clinics, as the pill-users panicked. There was a distinct polarisation of opinion about the pill's safety. One of the most vehement advocates was a Dr Malcolm Potts, then Medical Secretary of the International Planned-Parenthood Federation. 'Once a woman has sexual intercourse she faces death whichever way she turns,' he pronounced, arguing that the risks from the pill should be weighed against those of abortion, complications of pregnancy and childbirth. His view was that it would be more justifiable to have oral contraceptives in slot-machines, and restrict the sale of cigarettes to a medical prescription. His wife's view – she was also a doctor, and ran family planning clinics in Cambridge – can be judged from the fact that she announced in April 1970 that for about a year she had been giving oral contraceptives to her two-year-old daughter. She had taken this bizarre step to prove to other women that the pills were harmless. The child had had ten or twelve without apparently suffering any ill consequences.

Lining up alongside the pill's critics in the medical profession – but occupying a somewhat extreme wing – was the writer and broadcaster Malcolm Muggeridge, given to dropping lugubrious remarks like 'What a dismal treadmill is love on the pill!' There were many doctors – biochemists, epidemiologists, oncologists, cardiologists – with more serious grounds for their misgivings. The liver, the kidneys, the circulation, the hair, the skin, the eyes, the breasts, the cervix, the connective tissue, the teeth and numerous other organs or systems of the body had all, at various times, been reported vulnerable to the pill's ingredients – not necessarily to any serious extent, and usually in only a small number of women. 'Fantastic, unbelievable,' a research worker at Harvard said to me, shaking his head in disbelief, 'we've got to the point where, if you can measure it, the pill can have an effect on it.' In reply to an eminent doctor who had written to the Drug Safety Committee, an official listed the reactions to oral contraceptives which had been reported to the committee from mid-1964 to 1968. It made disturbing reading: amenorrhoea, breast disorders, weight gain, oedema, depression, headache, migraine, unusual skin pigmentation, nausea, thyroid disorders, diabetes, porphyria, anaemia, thrombosis and haemorrhage of the blood vessels in the brain, high blood pressure, clotting of the veins, coronary thrombosis, inflammation of the arteries, jaundice, skin disorders, hair disorders, tumours, abnormality in a baby, abortion and, last but not least, pregnancy.

Nobody knew how seriously to take most of the entries in this extraordinary catalogue, and that is why I decided to call the book *The Pill on Trial*. Everyone's opinion seemed to have equal weight: what it came down to was that no one could say how safe the pill was until enough women had been taking it for, say, twenty years. All an honest person could do was reckon up as logically and accurately as possible the comparative arguments: the risks of pregnancy, the risk of illness to someone of your physiological make-up, and how important you thought the 'aesthetic' effects of using the pill (compared with other contraceptives) – and then make up your mind. And looming over all, the matter of over-population. I thought it a dilemma of some magnitude, and it also posed the problem of what weight to give to the arguments that buzzed like a swarm of wasps around anyone writing about the subject.

It was in the interests of maintaining a balance on the question of contraception in general that I paid a visit to the world headquarters of what had been called the London Rubber Company, renamed LR Industries, in a large building on the North Circular Road. They then controlled most of the world's supply of what they preferred to call protectives, and had also sprouted other interests, such as drinks (wine, spirits, beer and soft drinks), automatic machines and paper panties. Nine out of ten condoms donned by British men (about 700,000 gross a year) were made in that interesting factory, whose production line supplied its own wry comment on human sexuality: ranks of phalluses –

condom-moulds, like over-developed penises – rattled along the conveyor belt, quivering as though with expectation, then dipped themselves, in a gesture of salutation, into the liquid latex, before rising proud and erect with their brand-new overcoats of rubber. At the other end of the line, they went through an electronic apparatus which could detect the tiniest pinprick of a hole: anything suspicious, and that one was dumped at once. And every thirty-two seconds, a finished condom would drop through the ranks and disappear into a testing-room below, where a group of grey-haired, seen-it-all women in white lab coats would catch them, fill them with a measured quantity of water, and hang them up for three minutes to see if they burst.

No doubt since then the production process has been refined and made even more efficient to cope with massive rise in demand. But I hope chance onlookers, such as I was, can still experience the touching mixture of comedy and pathos that registered with me twenty-five years ago and that I noted down as I gazed in admiration and astonishment. They weren't so much obscene, those hurrying phalluses, as appealing. Whatever else they suggested as they queued up to be clothed in their rubber sheaths, they seemed to embody the world's impatient desire for a contraceptive free from all doubts about safety and reliability.

I came to the end of the book in the winter of 1969 and it was published a few months later, serialised for three successive weeks in the *Observer* and reviewed on the whole favourably, if patchily. Some medical journalist colleagues dug out stories which were used in the news columns: ' "BLOTTER" DOCTORS CHOOSE WRONG PILL' (*Daily Mail*), '20m WOMEN "RUN RISK WITH PILL" ' (*Daily Telegraph*) and 'IS THE PILL ON THE WAY OUT?' (*Sun*). Perhaps that helped to damp down literary editors' interest in it, for only a few reviews appeared on the book pages. Some medical publications noticed it, nearly all of whom had rather stuffy things to say about what they believed was the 'slick' or 'racy' style it was written in ('Deplorable lapses into *Time*-style'). I supposed that to be a symptom of doctors' mistrust for the requirements of popular writing. It was a matter of satisfaction to me that John Wilson, whose *Margin of Error* I had so much admired, said in *World Medicine* it was a pleasure to read, and was civilised, detached and wryly entertaining. Some of the pill's advocates complained that I had reported too many of the pill's alarming aspects. Malcolm Potts said I had failed at the last jump, for I hadn't come down on one side or the other in the controversy, only reviewed the evidence.

An American edition followed a few months later, which was reviewed far and wide: I was sent cuttings from all over, including the Orlando, Fla., *Sentinel* ('a lucid discussion of a subject close to every woman'), the Aubury, NY, *Citizen Advertiser* ('One must admire the courage of Mr Vaughn [*sic*] . . . in attempting to compress in one short book one of the most explosive, important and complicated issues of our century'), the *American Journal of Psychiatry* ('Highly recommended to all'), and it was the Jackson Hole, Wy., *Guide*'s Book of the Week ('Mr Vaughan must be credited with writing an exhausting [*sic*] study of both the development and evaluation of the pill . . . Hats off to Mr Vaughan'). In due course *The Pill on Trial* appeared in Brazil (*A Pilula em Julgamento*), Spain (*La Pildora a Juicio*), Italy (*Pro e Contra le Pillola*) and Holland (*Alles Over de Pil*). It then appeared in paperback in 1972 as a Pelican, price 45p. But – it has to be admitted – the book didn't set the world on fire. I think it had a certain *succès d'estime*. But sales remained disappointing.

Perhaps the trouble was, as a medical journalist colleague said: 'Women who aren't on the pill don't care. Women who are don't want to know.'

Ten

Voice Over All

THE LAST STAGES of writing *The Pill on Trial* would have been familiar to many a writer: a frantic attempt to make it by the deadline, while everything else had to be put aside in the scramble to finish on schedule. The flow of material to *Medical Tribune* and its three weekly editions was staunched and virtually the only words that flew from my Olivetti Lettera – apart from words about the contraceptive pill – were scripts for BBC radio.

There was now a weekly science programme on Radio-4 called *New Worlds*, started at the end of the sixties by the producer Mick Rhodes, who placed a heavy emphasis on what he called gee-whiz science. The series kicked off with some bright new ideas – the programme was to have immediacy and 'bite', everything was to be live, with on-the-spot reports telephoned in from radio cars, or over an ordinary GPO line. There would be no 'stand-by' interviews stockpiled in case of need, no cosmetically edited tapes, and therefore none of what is called in the BBC de-umming. Instead, the programme would sound real, fast, and urgent, accurately reflecting the forward rush of new science and technology in all its up-to-the-minute excitement.

It wasn't long before these razor-sharp ideas became blunted for the usual reasons: producers found it easier to get at least some of the programme material in the can before it was to be broadcast. Stockpiled tapes prevented panic, and the 'no de-umming' rule was soon dropped – valuable minutes were being squandered while a speaker made up his mind or found an acceptable circumlocution: if all the 'ums' in some speakers' contributions were removed (a favourite pastime of bored tape editors, by the way, was to splice them all together and play them – an absurd sequence of hesitations) it could add up to whole minutes of priceless air-time. Also the scientists whose research was being featured were either too busy or too bored, or sometimes too nervous, to come to the studio at 9.30 on a Friday evening, to be grilled, live, on the air.

Even so *New Worlds* kept a good bit of the flavour Rhodes had wanted. One evening it went out as the news was breaking of the first heart transplant to be performed in Britain. It happened at the National Heart Hospital, not far from Portland Place and Broadcasting House. I was sent to the hospital with a radio car and the usual Uher, to witness a scene of extraordinary medical flag-waving. Literally so. Before an excited crowd of reporters, the surgical team gave out the news seated at a table placed on which were I'M BACKING BRITAIN banners. I suppose there was some excuse for the tumult. The National Heart Hospital's success came when transplant operations – especially on the heart – were big news: Dr Christiaan Barnard's pioneering work in this branch of luxury medicine had prompted an unseemly rush to the scalpel, and someone must have complained Britain was lagging behind. Next morning the story was the 'splash', occupying the front page of the popular dailies. I achieved a vicarious, and entirely undeserved, celebrity next day when my photograph appeared on the front pages of the *Express* and the *Mail* standing on the hospital steps in the rain with microphone thrust forward. Neither newspaper had yet gone tabloid at that time. The *Mail* headline, 'THE 18 WHO DID IT', was so placed that it looked as if I were an extra, dishevelled member of the team of surgeons, nurses, anaesthetists, and others who had brought off what was hailed as a triumphant success for British medicine. Not long afterwards,

166

the patient died: but that's show business. Heart transplants were to become almost commonplace within the next year or two, but for the time being this first patient, a man of forty-five (given the heart of a twenty-six-year-old Irishman, we were told), enjoyed a brief, indeed tragically ephemeral, moment of fame.

Another *coup* for *New Worlds* – of less far-reaching significance – occurred by accident, when I visited the Science Museum to interview someone about his research on deep-sea diving, in the course of which there was some discussion of the use of helium. It is well known to marine explorers, though possibly not to the average listener, that because sound-waves travel more quickly through helium than through ordinary air, the human voice sounds somewhat different when you take in a lungful: it rises in pitch and makes you sound like Bugs Bunny. It so happened that I had some clarinets with me, and wondered how helium might alter the sound of one of those. I played a phrase of Mozart and it did indeed sound extremely silly. The sound was broadcast in our next edition: a *New Worlds* scoop, illustrating the old radio precept, Do anything for an original sound-effect.

After *New Worlds* had been going for a couple of years, I was asked to present it. It was the first time I had been in the chair of a radio programme on 'domestic' radio. For the World Service by this time, I had presented quite a few *Science in Action*s and, in addition, a more heavyweight programme called *Discovery*, which went in for longer, more cerebral items which I often had to struggle to understand. Fortunately my contribution was limited to recording in the studio a script that linked tapes already recorded by someone else, generally the producer. Once, while an interview on particle physics, or plate techtonics, or the rôle of messenger RNA in cell replication, was winding uneventfully through the machine in the control cubicle (audible on the studio loudspeakers), I went to sleep. The green light flickered in vain: I awoke to find the producer leaning anxiously over me. Luckily, *Discovery* was not live. Far from it, you might say: as I learned later, another of the regular presenters had also drifted off during a recording. One began to wonder what effect this programme was having on the listeners.

However, what I was doing for *New Worlds* and any other programmes that came along was not enough to keep the family fed or reduce a swelling overdraft. Bank managers may have been more indulgent then: mine actually took me out to lunch (a warning signal) in one of Wimbledon's most expensive restaurants. Soon afterwards he was rather abruptly retired: but it was a reminder I should have to take drastic action soon. But, disappointment was in store. When I finished the book, I informed my *Tribune* friends of the fact, hoping my career as a medical reporter would be resumed. But journalism doesn't work like that, and it was more or less the end of the *Medical Tribune* connection.

Luckily, another door opened as that one closed: the editor of *World Medicine*, a glossy monthly magazine, took me in out of the cold, and gave me a job as deputy editor.

It was a lucky break, though I wasn't keen on the idea of leaving the house each morning and heading for an office desk, keeping office hours again and having to take instructions from a superior figure in the office hierarchy. My situation would have been much less enjoyable had it not been for the benign character of my rescuer, Michael O'Donnell.

O'Donnell was a remarkable medical editor, a man who had ricocheted gaily between the professions of medicine and journalism, with an occasional lurch into the theatre. While reading medicine at Cambridge he had edited *Cambridge Writing*, and when he was doing his clinical training at St Thomas's he had written comedy sketches for BBC radio. He had also somehow found the time and the opportunity to be a member of the Abbey Theatre Company in Dublin before following his father into general practice. He had now contrived to bring all these talents together as editor of *World Medicine*, and in the four years in which he had been in charge of the magazine he had established it as a bright, entertaining and – in terms of medical politics – radical newcomer to the well-populated ranks of the paramedical press.

O'Donnell was only just into his forties at this time, a colourful figure who went in for rather loud corduroy jackets and bright shirts, with his tie tied in a Windsor knot. His appearance suggested a raffish, debonair, professional Irishman – perhaps one who had suddenly hit the jackpot by selling a hit comedy idea to an American TV network.

I am not sure the proprietors of *World Medicine* knew what to make of him, though most of the time they left us alone. The magazine was owned partly by the American magazine publishing company McGraw Hill, and partly by IPC: it was the only spot at which these two publishing giants touched hands. Now and again McGraw Hill would send someone in to take a look at what was happening in the office suite, on the top floor of a plain little office block between Leicester Square and the Haymarket. But we were just a face in the crowd of IPC publications, at whose apex flourished the *Daily Mirror* itself. I doubted if Robert Maxwell, the Chairman of IPC, even knew he owned it. It was like the *Tribune* in that it was a controlled-circulation periodical: doctors received it free of charge, but the messages we got from our public indicated it stood out among the heap of uninvited mail that landed on their doormats. *World Medicine*'s recipients actually opened it and looked at it. Many even read it. It was also unusual in being a glossy magazine, printed on art paper, usually with a rather striking cover design. It appeared every fortnight.

I was given a room in the magazine's suite of offices on the top floor of the building. My window overlooked a well in the structure, on the ground floor of which was a restaurant specialising in traditional English food: the waiters were dressed like Doolittle in Shaw's *Pygmalion*, with leather aprons and string tied round the knees of their heavy tweed trousers. Every day, at about mid-morning, a strong aroma of meat gravy rose from below, causing the *World Medicine* staff's digestive juices to flow freely: this may have been the reason why I put on an extra stone or two during my tenure of the deputy editorial chair.

The magazine was enjoying a healthy success: doctors liked the droll and mocking tone of much that was inside. They especially liked O'Donnell's own regular contribution to the magazine's pages, a back-of-the-book series on the life of a GP in a fictitious northern town called Slagthorpe. These pieces centred upon the adventures of an individual who represented a projection of O'Donnell himself, a talkative and unpredictable GP called Finbar Aloysius O'Flattery; and O'Donnell used the Slagthorpe Papers as a vehicle for satire at the expense of the sort of people who tended to make life hell for Dr Average: Health Service bureaucrats, incompetent colleagues, pompous consultants and bloody-nuisance patients. His mockery of such medical *bêtes noires* struck home like a shaft of sunlight to *World Medicine* readers, immersed in their practice problems.

Slagthorpe became part of the mythology of general practice in the NHS. Once, O'Donnell managed to doctor his entry in the semi-official *Medical Directory*, in which he represented himself as editor of the *Slagthorpe Medical Journal* and Fellow of the Slagthorpe Medical Society. When they found out, the publishers were not amused. Small wonder O'Donnell had become famous in the profession and was in great demand as an after-dinner speaker at medical meetings, a function he performed with great flair, sometimes with the artful use of visual aids. His speech on the perils of over-population included what he called Slagthorpe's contribution to the problem: a film of a Caesarian section run backwards, very fast, which appeared to show a new-born infant being tucked back into its mother's uterus, her abdomen zipped shut (the incision, in reverse) and the surgeons standing back, hands up, in their sterile surgical gloves. This was guaranteed to leave a slightly tipsy medical audience practically incapable with mirth.

O'Donnell's greatest asset as editor – and the main reason for

World Medicine's success — was his instinctive understanding of what went on in the ordinary doctor's head. Not only had he been brought up in a medical household in Doncaster, where his father had had his practice, he had also worked on his own account as a family doctor, at the coalface of medicine. In consequence, he had a nose for the sort of thing that enraged doctors: he had scored an early success in the *World Medicine* story by waking the profession up to the anomalous nature of the periodic elections to their ruling body, the General Medical Council. For years it had been left to the BMA to nominate the five members of the GMC who under the Medical Act were supposed to be elected, by ballot, from the profession as a whole. It had become the custom for the BMA Council to nominate five doctors to fill these places. Nobody else ever stood, except once in a blue moon, and if they did, they hadn't a hope. The 'outsider' was never anyone doctors out in the wild had heard of, nor did he ever have access to the space in the *British Medical Journal* which was automatically given to the 'official' candidates. In effect, therefore, the election was sewn up in advance. Though the procedure had been invented to give doctors a democratic voice on their own ruling body, it had become about as democratic as elections to the Supreme Soviet.

O'Donnell was genuinely affronted by this anachronistic arrangement, and conducted a campaign in the pages of *World Medicine* to get it changed. The simplest way in the end was for him to stand himself, and that is what he did. The magazine having made a lot of friends among the medical rank and file, he had little difficulty getting himself elected, and to the BMA's confusion he became a GMC member in 1971. (As I write this, twenty-three years later, he is still there.)

There were other independent minds on the staff of *World Medicine*, including a former *Sunday Times* medical correspondent, Dr Barbara Evans, and the ex-*BMJ* medical novelist John Rowan Wilson, who bore the title consulting editor. He would drop in a couple of times a week at the *World Medicine* offices near the Haymarket and pass the time of day with O'Donnell, occasionally letting drop a word of encouragement or perhaps languid criticism of the magazine's progress. Once, when I had been in my job for only a few weeks, I found a short story among the dozens of uninvited contributions sent in every week by hopeful doctors. 'Do we publish fiction?' I asked Wilson. 'Not knowingly,' he replied.

In fact the majority of the 'on-spec' articles arriving with the morning mail were the kind of facetious, inconsequential pieces doctors often seem to write: biblical parodies about golf tournaments or cricket matches, holiday adventures, general-practice anecdotes or experiences with awkward patients. Occasionally there would be heavyweight articles like a series on lead poisoning (the author, I recall, had helpfully suggested the galumphing title *Lead, Kindly Light*) or some new abdominal operation, and these were generally looked on more favourably.

The staff of the magazine weren't numerous. We had a science editor, a features editor, a news editor and an art editor: come to think of it, nearly everybody seemed to be an editor. Others on the staff – there were two reporters – gave the impression they weren't really journalists but might as well be working for *World Medicine* as anybody else. The news editor was a man named Peter Brock, who actually was a professional journalist. He was also an autodidact but beginning to develop a slight chip on the shoulder about his lack of an academic qualification. I remember him standing about in the office lavatory on the floor below, which we shared with a travel company, wearing a stethoscope round his neck and washing his hands vigorously, in the hope that one of the neighbours might take him for a doctor.

At least Brock's news pages were always ready on time and were the result of some diligent footwork or telephoning. On the whole, the pace of work in the office was on the slow side. I remember being surprised by the amount of time spent in the morning making and consuming coffee, chatting about nothing in particular, perhaps exchanging views about last night's TV programmes, before anyone got down to work. Once, the editor had one of those rare visits from an executive from McGraw Hill, a New Yorker who questioned him about his activities and asked if he could meet the staff. O'Donnell duly conducted him down the editorial corridor, where he found the art editor designing his family Christmas card, John Wilson correcting the galley proofs of his next novel, the science editor writing a piece for the *New Scientist*, and Peter Brock working on his Open University syllabus. The deputy editor was away from the office doing an interview for the BBC. Needless to say, O'Donnell didn't let on that no one was actually working on anything for *World Medicine*, and luckily it didn't matter. As our American visitor was shaking hands at the lift door, he said warmly, 'And thank you for introducing me to your staff – you've certainly got a great team.'

O'Donnell, a forgiving man, never made a fuss about the meagre output from the other staff writers, who always seemed to take weeks to come through with their finished pieces. To fill the pages we relied on regular features: these seemed to grow insidiously in number. One of the problems with the magazine was its sheer success: doctors' sense of humour was tickled by the Slagthorpe page at the back, and their sense of justice aroused by O'Donnell's leading articles or special features at the front. A popular back-of-the-book item was *The Other End of the Stethoscope*, a two-page spread, with photograph, in which a guest writer amusingly, as was the intention, had to describe his or her experiences at the hands of the medical profession. The guests were usually professional writers and journalists, but we also employed actors, a reflection of O'Donnell's varied acquaintance: the only people barred from this column were doctors, who were invited by means of this regular feature to see themselves as others saw them.

The consequence of producing the whole effervescent mixture was that advertisers queued to buy space, especially the pharmaceutical companies, whose executives also found *World Medicine* a better read than the *British Medical Journal* or *The Lancet*. But it meant fatter and fatter issues which had to be filled somehow, and often it was necessary to slip in by way of ballast some of the substandard material that arrived from readers – perhaps savagely edited for whimsy (and grammar) – and hope it wouldn't be too carefully read, if at all.

One of the regular features was a comic column entitled *Dr Jekyll.* I didn't find it particularly funny: medical humour generally inclined to the jocose, with plentiful use of exclamation marks, and this seemed to be given free rein in the Jekyll column. O'Donnell sportingly agreed to my writing an alternative column to go alongside the pseudonymous Dr Jekyll's, and this was called, naturally, *Mr Hyde.* The column was supposed to be not good-humoured, jolly and mirth-provoking, but spiteful, sarcastic, and snide. Part of Mr Hyde's role was to puncture the readers' professional pride a little, with stories of medical and bureaucratic folly: a regular feature, 'Hyde's History of Medicine', cited quotations from novels, memoirs and biographies to the detriment of doctors, and another, called *Penchewer's Corner,* quoted examples of flatulent medical writing, of which there was always a rich crop in the medical journals. The BMA, I fear, would frequently get it in the neck.

Hyde sprang balefully to life in January 1972, in the middle of the book, under a Victorian cartoon of a grimacing, Rumpelstiltskin figure. It took a few issues for the column to find its form, but it continued until March 1978, some time after I had left the magazine's staff. It was to be my last gasp as a medical journalist.

Meanwhile, what I was doing in *New Worlds* and other radio programmes had come to the ear of the editor of *Horizon.* BBC-2's flagship science programme had begun in 1964 shortly after the second BBC channel took to the air – at first as a magazine programme, introduced by Colin Riach, but then its format was altered, and it became the documentary film series it has been ever since.

The series had a regular narrator, Christopher Chataway,

174

athlete turned *Panorama* reporter turned Conservative MP. But in 1970 he was given junior office in the Tory administration of the day, and *Horizon* had to find someone else. Hence, I was summoned to an Oxford Street recording studio for an audition. When I saw the opposition, I felt like giving up straightaway: another candidate was just leaving as I arrived, and it was Geoffrey Johnson-Smith, a Tory MP, like Chataway, with quite a lot of television work behind him. Another person they had tried out was Tony Benn, who had worked for the BBC World Service before his career in politics got seriously started: he had actually done the commentary for a film called *The Insect War* and it had been broadcast – but the rumour was that it had taken two days to record.

Perhaps *Horizon*'s editor felt this prestige programme needed a prestige narrator, and maybe, moreover, he wanted one with a future in politics. Or perhaps the instruction had come from above. Either way I didn't think I could compete. However, one of the producers needed a 'voice' for a *Horizon* film due to go out within a few days, and he could wait no longer – accordingly, I was heard in the following week narrating the story of the million-ton oil tanker. Within the next week I recorded two more, whose producers had been waiting impatiently for the auditions to yield a result. And so, choose me they did, and I was the regular *Horizon* narrator for the next twenty years.

This development had an almost immediate effect on my way of earning a living, for I became known more or less overnight as owner of a voice that sounded right for heavyweight programmes. I began to realise the vast size of the 'corporate presentation' industry: video had arrived, and scores of small companies had been formed to make films for businesses large and small – films for staff training, for attracting orders, for 'public relations', for showing to government agencies. Side by side with that were slide-shows, whose split-screen techniques and clever use of music could produce the illusion of movement: cheaper than film, but, as an information medium, now totally eclipsed by video. The 'video presentation' was supplanting the printed brochure as a means of advertising – at trade fairs, sales meetings, medical conferences and every other conceivable kind of demonstration. It was, and remains, a buoyant industry.

Slide-shows and movies of this kind had one thing in common: both, as a rule, required that indispensable feature, the voice-over – the invisible spokesman for the manufacturers of ball-bearings, farm tractors, bedroom furniture, traffic control systems, fighter aircraft, costume jewellery and, of course, pharmaceutical products – the drug companies must make more videos than any other branch of industry. Anyone whose voice is heard with any frequency on radio and television is likely to be recruited to the voice-over brigade, and find himself (less commonly, herself – men's voices are still generally preferred) tackling the problem of How to Speak a Commentary. It isn't quite as easy as it sounds, or ought to sound: the voice-over artist has to make a script seem convincing without being didactic, conversational without being chatty, sincere without being smarmy, and sometimes he must deliver blundering jokes with some kind of an imitation of quiet relish even though they have left him entirely cold.

I found I had, by huge luck, a knack for doing this kind of thing. Nature had given me a voice that worked with a microphone, and I began to collect flattering reviews. 'The first invisible star of television,' said someone. Another critic, a bit later, said, 'When God speaks, he uses Paul Vaughan's voice.' The work needed a kind of neutral authority: it was no good intruding your own views or personality – you were the oracle, but the words came from some mysterious, other source.

Oddly enough, not many actors can do documentary commentaries. Instead of speaking the words so that the information comes first, they sound as if they are intent on putting themselves first – actors before a curtain. Instead of reading the commentary, they tend to give a performance as someone reading a commentary. They often miss the point altogether: 'It's so boring, this script,' one well-known actor complained at a recording session. 'You can't do anything *with* it.' Of course, that is not what he was supposed to be doing.

Many scripts are lifelessly written. Some are frankly terrible, when the writers have no special skill with words and see no reason for paying someone else to do the job. What's more, there is a difference between words written to be read, and words written to be read aloud. (The best written prose *can* be read aloud, and it has something to do with the sound of the words in your head.) Not every video producer understands this distinction, but the voice-over artist discovers it rather quickly as he makes his way resolutely through long, clumsy sentences, so arranged that the emphasis falls with a thump on precisely the wrong – that is, the weakest or least important – word. Some video producers are grateful for suggestions about how to improve what they've written. Others have spent hours putting them laboriously together and they are prone to interpret as criticism any attempt at improvement. Others, again, have groaned inwardly to see the script pass through a dozen or more committee meetings and foresee, usually correctly, any tinkering with the client's prose will inevitably bring on three or four more.

Horizon scripts were always written by the producers. Before I became its narrator, I had in the past been employed by the programme to write scripts, and I had learned it takes a certain skill to do it properly, so that the words matched the pictures, complementing them but not upstaging them: it is no good telling the viewer what he is looking at, nor (in reverse) merely illustrating the words. The BBC being what it is, *Horizon* scripts were on the whole better written than those for commercial videos, but producers on that programme were also, I found, the ones who kept the closest guard on what they had given you to say: suggestions for alteration had to be tendered with the utmost tact. Often, after arguing over a hanging participle, a maladroit construction or gruesomely fractured infinitive, I would have to resort to the argument that doing it my way 'made it easier to say' – balderdash, but unchallengeable. Of course the voice-over man has to make it sound as if he understands what he is saying, and there were times in the *Horizon* booth when this presented a knottier problem than elsewhere. Partly this was because I seldom saw much of the film itself: head down over the script or watching the cue light, you hadn't always much chance of keeping an eye on what was happening on screen. Producers would ask hopefully what I thought of their film: I used to give vague replies, not really having seen it, and usually made sure my replies, if vague, were still encouraging.

The commercial voice-over is a slightly different matter. Here, actors score heavily, especially when the advertisers actually want them recognised as who they are. What is wanted is generally manly enthusiasm, unassailable conviction and twenty-four-carat sincerity, though occasionally there are finer shades required, like grimly serious ('Think of it as an army, an army of bacteria'), carefree and satisfied ('A brighter idea altogether'), or anxiously sympathetic ('Don't leave home without them'). For a long while I resisted invitations to perform in this area of the business, feeling it would dilute my value as the voice of *Horizon*. Eventually I yielded to the persuasion of commercial producers and have done a good few voice-overs for various products, from credit cards and building societies to toothpaste, disinfectant and mobile telephones. I dare say I am responsible for a few of those frustrating I-know-that-voice discussions that go on round the TV in British sitting rooms.

O'Donnell was an exceptionally tolerant editor, and raised no objection when his deputy editor disappeared to a voice-over studio, or to Broadcasting House to put *New Worlds* on the air. Small wonder I look back on *World Medicine* with a warm glow of affection. The only thing that spoiled it was the sneaking thought that the controlled-circulation periodical wasn't 'real' journalism but a sophisticated form of advertising: your work was being given away, and dumped on readers' doormats whether they liked it or not. All the more reason, you had to tell yourself, to earn

178

the readers' respect, though that was uphill work. Now and then I would hear doctors refer to the tied-circulation, paramedical press as 'the comics'.

The requirement of *New Worlds* and *World Medicine* sometimes coincided: one such occasion was when the BBC despatched me to Stockholm for the first United Nations Conference on the Environment, a three- or four-day trip which as far as I am aware achieved nothing whatever in the face of the threat to the future of the globe posed by the use of fossil fuels and the world increase in population. The conference was addressed by some heavyweight environmentalists but the net result was the production of numerous official reports, which is to say the use of still more paper, throwing a further strain on the earth's resources.

My most poignant experience was an interview with an American Congresswoman who was there to talk about whaling: her name was Shirley Temple Black, better known by the first of those two names, as the former child star who had had cinema audiences at her feet thirty years earlier. She came to the studio we had borrowed from Swedish Radio, where for some reason the lighting had partly failed, so that as we sat and talked we were lit only by a desk lamp from within the neighbouring production cubicle. As an American, she immediately placed us on first-name terms: we were instant old pals. But that and the crepuscular lighting conferred on the interview an atmosphere of conspiracy and seduction, as though we were alone in a private alcove in some discreet restaurant and I was about to take her hand. It was nearly impossible to direct my thoughts towards the whale as I looked at that winsome face, the dimples and the curly brown hair ... something about the voice, and the angle at which she held her head, reminding me of the Good Ship Lollipop, Brighteyes, the Littlest Rebel and Wee Willie Winkie ... of matinées at the Tolworth Odeon of long ago.

Would she, I wondered, accept an invitation to dinner? Nothing venture, nothing gain ... Should I try? Was she free this evening? I teetered on the edge of asking her, and, with a silvery laugh, she said, Goodbye.

World Medicine came to an unfortunate end. It happened several years after I had left the magazine.

One of the freelance contributors was a former BBC science producer, Karl Sabbagh, who was then working for a large pharmaceutical house, producing films for postgraduate medical 'refresher' courses. It happened that he wrote an opinion piece to the magazine, the starting-point of which was an international medical meeting soon to be held in Israel. He invited any *World Medicine* readers who might attend to bear in mind an incident that had occurred thirty-three years earlier in a small Arab village just outside Jerusalem called Deir Yassin. The village had been sacked by members of the Irgun and Stern gangs, and 254 people, some of them small children, had been killed. Women had been raped and other violent atrocities had been committed. Sabbagh wrote that his father's family were among the villagers who had fled.

The leader of the force that had been responsible was Menachim Begin, who at the time Sabbagh's article was written was Prime Minister of Israel.

A few days after the article was published, letters of protest began to arrive. The final crop of letters, mainly from angry Jewish doctors, reached many hundreds, and in many of them the writers employed strikingly similar phraseology. Then, Karl Sabbagh was mysteriously fired from his job. Next, word reached the editorial office that McGraw Hill had been approached by that particular drug company with a demand that something be done to punish *World Medicine* for its audacity.

When informed of these events I could not help remembering that, not long before, the same company had attempted to strong-arm the magazine in response to an article I had written. The piece had been a not entirely frivolous reflection on the growing use of the word 'fuck' in film scripts, books and indeed in general conversation. The word was printed a number of times in the article. Forthwith, the advertising manager was the recipient of an angry telephone call from some highly placed executive of the firm informing him he was withdrawing his advertising at once. The news was taken calmly in the office: soon afterwards, the firm resumed purchase of space in our pages.

Shortly afterwards McGraw Hill informed us they were getting rid of their holding in the magazine, and selling out to IPC. Then O'Donnell was told the editorial office behind the Haymarket would be closed down, and moved to Croydon. Croydon! O'Donnell regarded this as the severest blow of all, and wrote a leading article in which he made sarcastic reference to this summary decision. He was forthwith summoned to IPC's offices and told he had until four o'clock that afternoon to clear his desk. The entire staff, with one exception, resigned in sympathy.

World Medicine didn't perish immediately. A new editor was appointed, and a new staff – but the resulting publication lasted only a few months. It lacked the mercurial wit and verve that were O'Donnell's trademark.

Eleven

Leaping the Gap

THE LAST PRODUCER of *New Worlds* almost made broad-casting history when, late in the programme's career, he set up a seance in the studio. I was disappointed not to have been invited to take part, but those who did included, I believe, the monocled TV astronomer Patrick Moore, then somewhat thinner and an occasional *New Worlds* presenter. One winter evening, they gathered in a basement studio and sat round the table with an Ouija-board and some Lexicon letters, then waited with joined hands for the Broadcasting House ghost, if it existed, to make its presence known. Nothing happened, although the would-be communicants sat in hopeful expectation for something like four hours.

There was plenty of life left in *New Worlds*. However, one day they informed me the programme was going to be taken off.

But *New Worlds* wasn't exactly finished: it was about to be reborn in another form – merged into something new, along with two other existing weekly programmes. They were *Now Read On*, a books programme, and *Scan*, which covered the visual arts. These, plus my programme, were to be subsumed into a new magazine programme, to go out not once a week but every weekday evening. It would be about the arts and the sciences together. It was to be called *Kaleidoscope*.

The idea for this new programme had come from the then Controller of Radio-4, Tony Whitby. What he wanted was something that could engage the attention of the intelligent listener on a wide intellectual front, embracing the Two Cultures. The concept had been first advanced by the novelist and sometime Civil Service mandarin C. P. Snow, and at the time the two words had almost the status of a catch-phrase. It referred to the opposite polarities of Art and Science: Snow had expounded this idea in, among other places, a much discussed article in the *New Statesman*. Snow, a man with a scientific training, pointed to the gulf that divided arts and sciences and separated those whose intellectual leaning was predominantly towards one or the other. He deplored this. Snow maintained a person could not consider himself educated if he were not familiar with the first and second law of thermodynamics. You might have been able to list all the plays in the Shakespeare canon or recite the *Ode to a Nightingale*, but that was not enough: you should also have a grasp of the basic principles of science. Tony Whitby's belief was that *Kaleidoscope* could vault the gap, offering news and opinions on the arts and the sciences, side by side. To anyone who considered it an impossible mixture he would answer that it was analogous with the feature pages of a national newspaper, where you could juxtapose, say, an article on theatre design with one on genetics. In fact it is hard to imagine such pieces appearing side by side: however, Whitby's notion for a new evening magazine programme sounded both novel and intriguing.

Apparently there was a place for me on the team, and I was duly offered a job as one of the *Kaleidoscope* presenters. There were to be three of us: one was a World Service broadcaster called Peter France, and the other was the novelist and playwright Ronald Harwood. I was invited because it was assumed I 'knew' about science, even though I had an arts degree: perhaps I was thought already to have made the leap between Snow's opposing peaks, though had I been asked to recite, let alone define, the laws of thermodynamics my cover would have been instantly blown.

183

Nevertheless, off we went, and Tony Whitby was delighted with the result, though he rather spoiled things by asking privately, so I was told, 'Where has this man been all this time?' He meant me – so I presume he hadn't heard much of the Science Unit's output: not a Two Cultures man. At any rate, he decided the *Kaleidoscope* mixture was an exhilarating one: attention-getting and different from any other programme then in the schedules.

It was a shame Whitby didn't live to see how his brain-child developed, for he died, young and unfulfilled, only a few months after *Kaleidoscope* took the air. Nor did he live to see what happened to the – by intention – stimulating mix of arts and sciences.

Although it isn't much discussed these days, I believe Snow's idea is still accepted as more or less valid. But I suspect many people would sympathise with the view taken by Vladimir Nabokov, that one of those Two Cultures is merely utilitarian technology, while the other is 'B-grade novels, ideological fiction, popular art'. 'Who cares,' he asked, 'if there exists a gap between such "physics" and such "humanities"?'

One of the *New Worlds* producers had been recruited to the *Kaleidoscope* team but all the other producers on the new programme, and they were five in number – one man and four women – were on the arts side of Snow's great divide. The ex-*New Worlds* producer was also interested in pop music, so I think he was believed to possess at least one arts-relevant credential. The programme editor, David Holmes, was probably deemed to be neutral, neither science nor arts. He had been a member of the BBC's diplomatic staff: this was a useful background given the potential clash of temperaments within the production office.

For when it came to practicalities, the combination of talents and the broad spread of the programme's remit didn't work. The lone science producer wasn't always on hand to give advice, and hence the arts producers had to fend for themselves when a science item came up for consideration. They complained of the difficulty of finding science stories, and if they thought they had stumbled on something, perhaps by turning over the pages of the *New Scientist* or even *World Medicine*, they had no means of judging its value. Ringing up the person who had done the work and interrogating him on the telephone was a job they weren't used to and they would soon begin to flounder, if they hadn't funked it altogether. As for the presenters, they too had problems trying to get to grips with questions of physics, chemistry and biology: although we weren't expected to understand everything about the matter under discussion, it was better to have at least a general idea of the territory we were in. Total ignorance was embarrassingly obvious.

Sometimes the arts-and-science mixture did work to our advantage. A case in point was in the autumn of 1973, when the programme, unusually for that period, was all live. None of it was pre-recorded. One of the guests, I remember, was John Trevelyan, the last Secretary of the British Board of Film Censors, who had just brought out an autobiography, called *What the Censor Saw*, and another was Martin Bax, a man who usefully, for our purposes, combined the professions of poet, small-magazine editor and developmental paediatrician. He was in the unusual position of editing two totally different journals – *Ambit*, a poetry magazine, and another called *Developmental Medicine and Child Neurology*. There were other guests in the studio but I have forgotten who they were. More important was the fact that, in the late afternoon of the programme day, word came in that W. H. Auden had died.

As is usual in such situations, in newspaper offices and radio and television studios, there was a scramble to contact Stephen Spender. *Kaleidoscope* fared no better than anyone else: he was not available, and instead we invited Laurie Lee. As we say in broadcasting circles, he 'came in live', to join a full table of contributors at ten-thirty in the evening. I think he had been doing his best to numb his sorrow with alcohol: at any rate, when I started off by asking him how well he had known the great man, Laurie Lee uttered a little grief-stricken sob, and fell silent. But the hand of Providence had, of course, placed across the table from him an alternative spokesman for poetry in the shape of Martin Bax, and we were able to proceed with barely a pause.

But this was an unusual occasion in more ways than one. My two presenter-colleagues were having a harder time with 'science' than I was, and there were awkward joins between items on the programme menu. 'And now for our science item,' said one presenter on one occasion, sealing off the 'science' from the rest of the programme's contents, and at the same time sounding perfunctory and dismissive. More and more, the science was indeed drifting into the realms of gimmicky technology: where Whitby had wanted discussion of the new ideas that were moving forward the frontiers of scientific thought, we were reporting work on spider's webs or a new kind of collapsible umbrella.

The former *New Worlds* man, representing the lone voice of scientific rationalism, was having similar trouble from the opposite side of the arts-science chasm: while his colleagues listlessly turned the pages of *Nature* he felt ill at ease with new writing and minimalist art. It wasn't long before he went to work in the Natural History Unit at the BBC's Bristol studios, leaving the others still further disadvantaged. Then the editor David Holmes resigned. One of the producers, Rosemary Hart, was promoted to fill his place, and the programme's policy was re-examined. And *Kaleidoscope* took the plunge: science was out.

From all concerned, there was a sigh of relief. The last science story I can remember presenting on *Kaleidoscope* was an interview with one of my former BMA colleagues, on the subject of hangover – what it really was, medically (a kind of transient diabetic coma), and how to cure it (take a sugary drink, plus Vitamin C and some paracetamol). This invaluable advice was broadcast just before Christmas 1973, and I am sure it earned *Kaleidoscope* a few new friends.

It probably earned some for the BMA within the *Kaleidoscope* unit too, for one of the memorable features of the programme at that time, but long since abolished, was a hospitality trolley of striking generosity. At about six-thirty in the evening the studio door would open and the trolley would be wheeled in by a uniformed member of the BBC's domestic staff: this was the time when there was a person on the Corporation strength called the BBC butler. He, or his department, did *Kaleidoscope* – and other programmes as well, notably *Today* – very proud indeed: besides plates of sandwiches and fruit there were wines, spirits and beer of every kind. This prodigality was too much for some of the programme staff to resist, and it was not seldom that the evening's edition went out in a euphoric glow.

I doubt if drink problems were any more common at the BBC than elsewhere in the media: probably less, because the effects tended to be more public. There were certain news readers of the old school who were still at work at that time, one or two of whom could sound, now and then, suspiciously slipshod – a phrase, come to think of it, that would have caused them extreme difficulty. But to be drunk at the microphone was a misdemeanour that, if noticed by the Fourth Floor at Broadcasting House, would have meant a premature exit.

The sensible thing for the presenter was to leave the drinks trolley alone until after the programme had gone out. But contributors who arrived to take part in the live broadcast weren't always as aware of the dangers as we were. Once, when the programme had been going for more than two years a film critic arrived to review a biography of Fatty Arbuckle, called *The Day the Laughter Stopped*. He didn't seem quite his lively self, and when I asked him, if I remember rightly, if the book enhanced or diminished Arbuckle's reputation as a comedian, he was struck dumb: he stared down at the studio table, spread his hands with a shrug, and muttered, 'I'm sorry.' There was nothing for it but to answer the question myself – but the same applied to my next question as well. After that, he regained enough of his self-possession to say a few more sentences, but when the interview was over and while I was letting

187

listeners know the price of the book, my *vis-à-vis* was leaving the studio in shame. He vanished into the night, determined never to broadcast live in Britain again. Soon after that, he went home to Australia. The explanation, it seemed, was that he had sampled not only the hospitality trolley but at the same time some cold cure capsules, and the combination, pharmacologically, had been enough to render him speechless. The curious thing was, the pills were a brand manufactured by Menley & James, and so I knew my past had returned to haunt me.

Not many contributors have 'dried' on the air. The more usual problem is to staunch the flow of words. This is true on the whole of dons, though not usually with actors, who tend not to be at their best when interviewed, lacking, I suppose, the safety of a text learned in advance. One who certainly did not have that problem was James Mason, who came to the programme to be questioned about his autobiography, an interesting volume, and gave an equally interesting and un-vainglorious interview. When it was over, I walked with him to the lobby of Broadcasting House. As we moved along the basement corridor, we encountered, coming in the opposite direction, the politician Tony Benn. I stood politely aside as these two major celebrities approached each other like two great ships cruising on parallel but opposite courses. Mason looked steadfastly forward. But Benn's eyes slid sideways. And as he passed me, I heard him say to the air, 'Golly. It's James Mason.'

Another early *Kaleidoscope* guest whose visit lingered in the mind was Lillian Hellman, whom I saw at the Savoy, already well oiled by eleven o'clock in the morning. The occasion was publication of her book *Pentimento*. I questioned her about Sam Goldwyn, who figures in the book. Their relationship hadn't exactly been trouble-free, but once, she told me, she had decided during a visit to Hollywood it was time to try to let bygones be bygones, and telephoned him at his house. She spoke to Mrs Goldwyn, who spoke to her warmly and said she would fetch Sam to the telephone. Lillian Hellman heard the murmur of voices in the background, then Goldwyn's voice, enunciating clearly the instruction, 'Tell her to go fuck herself.'

Hollywood celebrities have on the whole been predictable. Liza Minelli was eager to please, effusively friendly, animated and overflowing with sincerity. Otto Preminger was bored, off-hand, unsmiling. Yet Fred Zinneman, to my great surprise, was nervous and tongue-tied: so was Eric Ambler. David Niven was also a trifle nervous, but modest and almost embarrassingly polite, though wearing suavity like a well-cut suit: I had kept him waiting for fifteen minutes in a shabby studio – instead of walking out in a huff he almost apologised for having put me to the inconvenience of getting there to meet him. In my copy of his book *Bring on the Empty Horses* he wrote, 'Put this in the "loo" and someone will read it! Yours aye, David.' I had never met him before. John Huston a few years later was taken aback when I put to him a somewhat clumsy question, asking if he would consider himself one of the species I'd seen described as *homo Hemingwayensis*. I realised as I saw his expression harden that he wasn't sure what I was talking about but suspected I was casting doubt on his masculinity. However, we had an interesting discussion on his experience in Africa when the cook to his unit, filming *The African Queen*, was suspected of serving what was known as 'long pig' – i.e., human flesh.

Presenting *Kaleidoscope*, doing commentaries for *Horizon* and voice-overs for dozens of different small film companies, and – at the beginning – being deputy editor of *World Medicine*, added up to an over-full timetable. Soon after *Kaleidoscope* started, I left *World Medicine*. Once again I had become a freelance.

Preparing for the programme had been a somewhat perfunctory business: a private view, an early evening film preview or a theatre press night – these were all very well. But if it came to reading a 500-page biography or an epic novel, I was sunk. The review would in most cases have to be done on the strength of the publisher's blurb and perhaps a quick read-through of the

189

first and last chapters. Of course, we weren't like newspaper crit-ics, we weren't actually reviewing these events: strictly speaking, we only needed to find out enough about them to be able to write an introduction to someone else's review. That someone else was the critic, who came to the studio and answered our questions. We weren't obliged to have read the book in order to think of what to ask – but if we had, the questions, and the resulting discussion, would undoubtedly be more confident. An exception should be made for those occasions – fortunately rare – when the critic hadn't read the book either, resulting in a discussion of perfect futility.

It has been asserted that, on the contrary, the questions would be better if you knew nothing about the book, play, film, or exhibition: the presenter, this argument runs, should be in the position of an intelligent listener who wants to find out from the reviewer what the product is like. After all, a person reading a review in the newspaper is in exactly that position. But the *Kaleidoscope* presenter has to introduce the work on the pro-gramme. And the introduction may include – most usually does – an interview with the person whose work is being discussed. There are few things more aggravating for a writer, for example, than to be told by his interviewer, usually with a grimace of apology, that he is sorry but he hasn't had time to read his book. At any rate, *Kaleidoscope* became known for not placing authors and others in this position. No presenter, so far as I know, has ever dared resort to quoting Wilde's witticism: 'I never read a book before reviewing it. It prejudices one so.'

The pace of the work was quick, with a 'strike' rate of three programmes in every fortnight and sometimes more. In consequence it was hard to retain any detailed memory of their ingredients. An obsessive notebook-keeper, list-maker and stationery addict, I had for years had the habit of writing down the title of each book I read: friends are mildly disgusted to discover I can name every book I read in, say, 1957. But as the list lengthened, under the influence of *Kaleidoscope*, the less it meant: looking over it now, many of the titles mean nothing to me. What was *Introduction to 5*, by Adrian Kenny et al.? Peter Prince's *Dog Catcher*? Why in 1974 did I read Ann Turnbull's *The Frightened Forest* and Richard Stern's *Other Men's Daughters* or Roger Dixon's *Christ on Trial*? Who were these writers, and what were their books about?

Samuel Butler wrote: 'One's thoughts fly so fast that one must catch them. It is no use trying to put salt on their tails.' The notebook habit persisted, with observations, for my own benefit, on books and authors, plays and actors and directors, films and exhibitions and other events which have been noticed by the programme. I recognise its deficiencies as a record of creative movements in this country: the annotated extracts that follow are like handfuls of water scooped up from the ever-rolling stream of artistic life or, to employ a less florid image from my career on the sidelines of medicine, biopsy samples from a body that despite everything remains in reasonably good health.

Twelve

A *Kaleidoscope* Diary – I

KALEIDOSCOPE HAD BEEN going for three years before I began a few systematic notes on the programme, with an encounter on 10 October 1976 with a Hollywood personality with unusual credentials: Sheila Graham, who had been the 'paramour' (his own word, in a black moment) of F. Scott Fitzgerald.

I sat across the studio table from her wondering about her intimate moments with one of the finest novelists of the century. From her book, which she had boldly called *The Real Scott Fitzgerald, 35 Years Later*, I had formed the opinion he had seen in her a certain vulnerability. When I said as much to our reviewer Clancy Sigal he said, vulnerable be damned, she was up there with Hedda Hopper, Louella Parsons and the others, trading in innuendo and hearsay: she was as vulnerable as a piranha fish.

Unfortunately, Sheila Graham was listening. When I returned home from the BBC around eleven-thirty at night, she telephoned. Why hadn't I told her there would be a reviewer? Who was this Clancy Sigal, and what had *he* written? During the *mauvais quart d'heure* that followed I came to the conclusion Clancy Sigal might have been right.

But I had to admire her: a roly-poly figure in a black velvet trouser suit, wearing a blonde wig with the stitching rather

192

visible and large sun-glasses. How could you hate a person like that, talking about her grandchildren, moving about fussily in a cloud of perfume and BO? The trouble was, she thought she was the sole repository of the truth about Fitzgerald and resented anyone else challenging her supposed monopoly. There is no way of knowing what he thought of her: the words *Portrait of a Prostitute* she found scribbled angrily at the back of one of her photographs may have been put there in one of his drunken rages. She thought she appeared in *The Last Tycoon*:

> The curtains blew suddenly into the room, the papers whispered on his desk, and his heart cringed faintly at the intense reality of the day outside his window . . . What would happen if he saw her again – the starry veiled expression, the mouth strongly formed for poor brave human laughter . . .

If that is really her she had something to be proud of: if it was not, who could blame her for pretending? Knowing Scott Fitzgerald was probably the most magnificent thing that ever happened to her. But wasn't she also a solitary fighter, with not many assets – a pretty face, the guts to succeed on her own, and probably a knack for conning editors, and victims of her gossip column? Without her, *The Last Tycoon* might never have been written. On that same programme we discussed, in addition to the year's productions at Bayreuth and a new release of performances by Benny Goodman, a book called *Some Time in the Sun* by Tom Dardis; it was an account of the careers in Hollywood (where writers, said studio boss Jack L. Warner, were just 'schmucks with Underwoods') of William Faulkner, Nathanael West and others. Fitzgerald was one of them, and the book made it clear his relationship with Sheila Graham was heaven-sent – restoring his confidence in himself and bringing him genuine happiness, however short-lived. They met in 1937; he died in 1940. She is dead now: she died in 1988, aged eighty-four.

*

A few days later the bill of fare was again pretty typical: a book about the painter Randolph Caldecott, a radio play and some short stories by David Pownall, a biography of Percy Grainger and the memoirs of Tatiana Metternich.

I had never before met a genuine Russian Princess. Tatiana Metternich was a very, very tall woman in twin-set and woollen skirt that to my eye looked coolly expensive, with 'unobtrusive' gold necklace and bracelet. Her book was mainly about her experiences as a White Russian refugee, and life in Germany during the war.

Aristocrats tend to survive hardships that cripple the community as a whole. She once saw Hitler, but never spoke to him: she considered him insignificant in appearance and could not understand his reputation for personal magnetism. Presumably this was one case where the despot's evil chemistry simply failed to work, but it could have had something to do with Princess Tatiana's instinctive indifference towards someone of such grubby lower-middle-class origins. It was a somewhat stodgy book, though with moments of poignancy, but it was not easy to read and radiated blue-blooded superiority. It was reviewed by another White Russian, Kyril Fitzlyon, who, rather puzzlingly, was born a Zinoviev: it was not clear what had happened to produce this anomaly, nor whether it had any connection with the famed Zinoviev Letter. Like Princess Tatiana, he had escaped from the Bolsheviks in 1917 with his parents. When a family reaches a certain level of distinction, he explained with a knowing smile, it is customary to dispense with the 'von', and the absence of this syllable before the Princess's surname should have caused my eyebrows to rise in puzzlement – though they didn't.

No one could deny that the name Metternich had acquired aristocratic distinction at a positively pan-European level; and that book demonstrated how certain top families could manage to stay on top through two appalling wars. But these great nineteenth-century names now belong in some remote, distant world, like, I am afraid, their bearers. The Princess was doing something with the International Red Cross, the sort of charitable good works titled ladies have traditionally involved themselves in. When I put this somewhat jaundiced view to Kyril Fitzlyon, he treated it with disdain, and I dare say he thought I was talking dangerous nonsense. I am obliged to admit that I lied when I told the Princess I had enjoyed her book very much, but by such little hypocrisies does life proceed.

I doubt if hypocrisy played a large part in the make-up of Percy Grainger, whatever else may be said of him: indeed he may have been rather more unhypocritical, more outspoken and up-front than was comfortable. It turns out that he harboured sado-masochistic tendencies and incestuous fantasies: however, *Molly on the Shore* and *Room Music Titbits* ought not to sound any different now we know about this and, for that matter, his fondness for constructing life-size wood and *papier-mâché* dummies of himself and his wife, which he clothed in 'the towelling suits they used when relaxing around the house', according to his biographer John Bird. I find it hard to imagine a towelling suit of the period. Perhaps it would look rather *chic* today. What do we deduce from the fact that, *per contra*, Wagner preferred to relax in silk? Bird's book was rather good, and was reviewed for us by a not very well-known conductor, whose outfit was on a radically different plane from that of Grainger or Tatiana Metternich: striped brownish-grey tweed jacket, hound's-tooth check trousers, mauve shirt with white floral pattern and a red check tie, an ensemble that must have taken courage.

It is an odd task to be a *Kaleidoscope* interviewer. In the lobby of Broadcasting House I met Clancy Sigal, the writer and critic – which, incidentally, is a typical *Kaleidoscope* term: contributors are generally ascribed on the air two, and occasionally three, distinct occupations, viz., poet and lecturer, aviator and broadcaster, musician and traveller, automobile collector and heraldry consultant, etc. Clancy Sigal had displayed on that occasion an air of Mephophelian glee thoroughly appropriate to the day's task, namely to be interviewed by Jacky Gillott about a film called *Werewolf of Washington*. Jacky Gillott was another writer-and-broadcaster – a *Kaleidoscope* presenter who had written several novels, and who, tragically, committed suicide not long after this time. According to Sigal she was 'one of those interviewers who became tense and jumpy when you express a point of view opposed to hers – unlike you,' he added politely. I had never noticed this about Jacky Gillott and don't believe his remark about me was accurate either. However, there have been such presenters, who seemed to regard disagreement as a personal affront.

But what were we doing? Were we supposed to be 'discussing' the book with the reviewer, or merely firing questions at him in order to elicit his opinion on the book, film, or whatever it was? Was it permissible for the questions to be loaded with the presenter's opinion – if he had one? And – the old question – was it better to have read the book yourself, or better to ask the questions from a position of ignorance? Surely the former: we were the representatives of the listener, and the listener had a right to one who is well informed.

THURSDAY 28 OCTOBER 1976 Spoke to the writer Reg Gadney about some thrillers, one by Alec Waugh, who's seventy-eight. I am intrigued by Waugh's treatment of sex in his book *Married to a Spy*: he has the English spy's wife dithering on the edge of a lesbian affair with a Spanish girl who is in turn rather keen to get her involved in a troilist mini-orgy. All written, naturally, with a degree of frankness unimaginable forty years ago. Things have certainly changed since *The Loom of Youth* and its 'scandalous' treatment of homosexuality. Scandalous! You have to read that book, published in 1917, very slowly and carefully to understand what all those public schoolboys are talking about. *Married to a Spy* is Waugh's fiftieth novel, and it reminds me of Ben Travers's approach to sex in *The Bed Before Yesterday* and Priestley's in *The Image-Makers*. These septuagenarian writers have discovered to their delighted surprise you can write openly about the ever-interesting topic and you can even call it fucking, though none of them have, so far. You can also have people practising adultery, lesbian love play and troilism without feeling you have to punish them for it.

After lunch in BBC canteen, went to read a commentary on Horse Nutrition: long sequences of grazing equines on the monitor while I intone virtues of protein, carbohydrate, fatty acids, the rôle of oats and hay in their diet, and even longer sequences of girls in hard hats with names like Emma, Sarah, Samantha and Cressida reeling off information about how and when to fix on the nosebag and so on. I liked best the moment when a rag-and-bone man's winded nag was shown, with a cheerful voice telling us how he'd eat pork pies, potato crisps or fish and chips. One was meant to frown in disapproval.

It seemed worthy of note at the time, the arrival of what was intended to be 'acceptable' pornography. However, the London Casino, probably the least comfortable cinema in the West End, wasn't the best choice for the press show of *Emmanuelle 2* ('MORE sensual, MORE sensational ... MORE beautifully erotic than ever'). Maybe had we all lain on silk couches sipping sherbet there might have been a chance of the film doing what it was supposed to have set out to do. *Emmanuelle 2* must be counted as some sort of a pathfinding work for the number of orgasms depicted or, rather, faked: I lost count, but they were all experienced by the heroine, played by Sylvia Kristel, who had opted for a life of sensations rather than of thoughts and lived for nothing but her labia minora. Several times she was discovered stroking them languidly, but when not doing that she was succumbing to someone else's desires, male or female, or working herself up by means of conversation to yet another sexual climax. Was she the first individual to experience orgasm through acupuncture? I felt the London Acupuncture Clinic had been missing out. The love scenes were only explicit up to a point – that is, no penises were visible – and if they had it would presumably have been pornographic not erotic. Male orgasm, depicted explicitly, will no doubt be a feature of commercial films before long, and will that be the final taboo?

It was necessary to make it clear that *Emmanuelle 2* really was boring, even though this was what people were always saying about pornography ('I was bored,' he insisted, his eyes blazing with sincerity). The film never got anywhere, there was no plot, the people were just silhouettes, nobody said anything funny or interesting: they were merely pictures in a girlie magazine come to life.

Margaret Walters reviewed this mistaken piece of work and argued that its racist overtones alone would have been enough to put it beyond serious study. Meanwhile we evidently had to accustom ourselves to the notion that this kind of pale blue movie could become a film genre like Westerns, horror movies or biographies of great composers: but when I asked Margaret Walters a question on those lines she waved it away and said, 'That's too *Time Out* for me.' Nevertheless, I should not be surprised if some time in the future the National Film Theatre puts on a season of films like *Clockwork Banana* and *Danish Dentist on the Job*, complete with pretentious programme notes ('Klingtwort's macabre vision, no less than his feeling for high camp, together testify to a talent undeservedly ignored', etc., etc.).

Previews of plays – as opposed to those of films – constitute a trap for the presenter. If a play opened on the night of the programme (at this period *Kaleidoscope* was broadcast at 10.30 p.m.), a critic would come straight to the studio from the theatre and deliver his judgement piping hot (and ill thought-out, some listeners might think). But if the presenter wanted to see the play, it would have to be before opening night, at a preview.

Managements were – and are – uneasy, and quite rightly, about plays being judged on the strength of a preview, before the performances have settled down and the production has acquired the final polish – and the excitement of an opening has had its claimed effect. It has been a common experience for the presenter to emerge from the theatre convinced he has just seen a second-rate production of a play that needed more work, only to find on the night that for the reviewer it was the theatrical experience of the season. A small case in point from this period of *Kaleidoscope*: a piece called *A Seventh Man*, A Play With Songs (*sic*), by Adrian Mitchell, based on the book by John Berger. Here and there traces of Berger's vigorous language showed through like sound pine under paint, but blunted by fumbling and amateurish production. The subject, migrant workers, ought to have caught our consciences on the raw. I recorded in my notebook the presence next to me of an unofficial claque, two girls who at the slightest sign of a joke (words like defecate, or innuendo about underdeveloped countries, would do) threw themselves about their seats guffawing loudly, thumping their knees and whooping. Such neighbours in the stalls are guaranteed to turn one's face to stone. But: it was only a rehearsal. Our reviewer saw it on press night, and thought it wonderful.

MONDAY 8 NOVEMBER   Interesting to meet actor-and-traveller Duncan Carse, who turned out to be a nautical-looking person with faraway blue eyes and neatly trimmed white beard: Captain Kettle to the life, with his clipped voice still reminiscent of his Dick Barton of long ago, the rôle he must long to forget. Sometimes he does *Horizon* commentaries. The play-acted cannibalism of the film *Survive!* left him unaffected, and no wonder. Carse: 'The trouble was, they got off on the wrong foot.' Undoubtedly correct. It left me cold too, though I would not care to have been the man with the fruit-knife who had to butcher the first corpse up there in the Andes in 1972. Carse thought the human flesh looked like veal scaloppine. I suppose if cooked in marsala it wouldn't be too bad. By the way, who sang that song of my youth, 'From the Indies to the Andes in his undies?'

WEDNESDAY 10 NOVEMBER   All day reading Frank Tuohy's book on Yeats . . . he is not very informative about what the man was writing when he was involved in all those barmy ideas. In mid-read, an Irish voice on the telephone: it's the Irish Embassy, asking if they could buy a copy of my film on government support for the IRA. It was a moment or two before I realised the bloody nuisance of my life had crossed my path again: the *other* Paul Vaughan. I kept getting his telephone calls and fielding accusations of missed appointments, etc. I explained all this to my caller: there is another man called Paul Vaughan and although he is in the same line of work – well, he's an agent, or something – he won't give himself a middle initial to show which of us is which. At this the Irish diplomat made the sort of gasping noise appropriate to the discovery of buried treasure. He's your doppelgänger, he said, in his soft Dublin tones. Incidentally I read in Tuohy's book that the Blueshirt contingent that left Ireland in the thirties to fight on Franco's side in Spain returned with more men than went out. Could this have happened with any other military formation?

THURSDAY 11 NOVEMBER   Armistice Day. Spoke down the line from Radio Oxford with the modest-voiced Prof Richard Ellmann, who was good on Yeats, yet spoke in a manner suggesting diffidence bordering on panic. He told a story about his meeting with Yeats's widow, who asked if he believed in ghosts. Said Ellmann, 'a trifle too glibly' according to him, 'Only those inside of me.' She said, 'That's the trouble with you.'

Composer Stephen Oliver was more vivacious, bursting into song, carolling '*Deh vieni, non tardar* . . . ' while being interviewed. I thought it rather a welcome change but he provokes a kind of rage in one or two people, e.g., Michael Oliver (who indignantly denies being related) said he thought it was 'time somebody taught the little bugger a lesson', while Julian Budden was sarcastic about how little he really knew. Of course, they probably said the same thing about Mozart and S.O. must be nearly as prolific, with all his operas, oratorios, chamber pieces etc., not to mention performing in his own operas and so on.

Met Ronald Gibson of BMA in Upper Regent Street, greeting

him with enthusiasm. I was genuinely glad to see him ... but taken aback that he seemed decidedly cool and not anxious to prolong the conversation. He would have passed on with a wave if I hadn't stopped to talk. We talked briefly, circling each other like prize-fighters, I asking after Betty, how he was doing, was he busy, etc., and he fending me off with monosyllables. He's Sir Ronald now. His eyes looked sad, disappointed, though he is now supposed to be enjoying the fruits of eminence. He once told me, long ago, he was at Cambridge with Peter Howard, before that deluded man was overwhelmed by Moral Rearmament, and remembered him confessing brokenly late one night how desperately worried he was that he was masturbating too much.

I interviewed the actor and TV comedian Ronnie Barker, in a secluded house in a secluded road in Pinner. The room he showed us into had a grand piano, a chapel organ, a phono-fiddle and shelf upon shelf of books, mostly Victorian boys' stories, bound Boys Own Papers, Henty and Westerman novels, improving tales and moral tracts with hand-blocked covers. A large scarlet, gold and ultramarine pre-Raphaelite painting hung over the fireplace, and on another shelf there was a row of his trophies: Golden Roses, Emmys, BAFTA masks and the like.

His *nom-de-plume* is Gerald Wylie, which led me to commit an absurd speech-blunder as we began to record: intending to suggest he might prefer one of his identities above another, I wanted to ask 'Are you Gerald Wylie or Ronnie Barker?' What came out was, 'Are you David Willey or Ronnie Corbett?' However, he didn't seem to mind too much and sympathised with my confusion, though I was not surprised to hear he dislikes being interviewed and isn't too keen to talk about himself. Useless to explain that I find it extremely difficult to remember names and that this springs from some neurological anomaly.

Perhaps it is linked with the migraines to which I remain prone. For a programme at that time (before which as it happened

I was indeed visited by a migraine attack), I read Francis Huxley's book, *The Raven and the Writing Desk*, on Lewis Carroll and his mathematical mania. This book tells us Carroll suffered from respiratory ailments, rheumatism, ague-like fevers, and migraines, the latter accompanied by the 'castellation' phenomena familiar to migraine victims, when battlement-like or herring-bone shapes flicker, and sometimes revolve, continuously just beyond one's immediate line of sight. If it is true that Carroll had migraine with fortification spectra, surely he would have put them into the Alice books. Could they be the Cheshire Cat's grin, fading?

When the programme went out, Marghanita Laski reviewed the book in what she intended to be the style of Lewis Carroll. I am afraid it didn't work, and must have puzzled the listeners as much as it did the other participants – James Galway, Huxley himself, and Mervyn Levy. Galway had forgotten my name – we had met two years before at a music summer school – but doubtless he had the same problem with names that I had. He entered the studio, I recall, complaining cheerily of the cold: said he was wearing three pairs of socks. The diary note reads: 'Life is a flute concerto for him . . . ' A man who would make a flute concerto out of Vivaldi's *Four Seasons* was not going to jib at doing the same thing with the Scherzo from *A Midsummer Night's Dream*, which is what he had done on a new record. He said it was no worse than Rachmaninov playing the flute solo from *Orpheus* as a piano piece. Diary: 'He got comeuppance of a kind when on transmission the cocky young tape SM brought in his recorded interview at double speed, presenting the man with the golden flute talking like a chipmunk. Agonising moment, resulting in at least ten seconds of that dreaded phenomenon in broadcasting – total silence.'

MONDAY 15 NOVEMBER   Stephen Pettitt's biography of Dennis Brain is really the story of how English orchestral playing managed to lift itself up from a condition of mediocrity to its present brilliance, with Brain as one of the meteor-like figures who lit up the early days of this renaissance. Pettitt is an uninspiring writer who just gets by on detailed knowledge of horn technique, who played what and for whom, and a few good anecdotes, dully told. I have two memories of seeing Brain: one was with his wind ensemble in Oxford somewhere, New College, I think, doing things like the Ibert *Cinq Pièces*, Gareth Morris playing *Syrinx* – this before the repertoire-explosion of nowadays, when libraries and museums and cellars are being ransacked for obscure pieces for wind in order to satisfy the huge demand from players, professional and amateur. The other time was a concert at the Orangery, Hampton Court, when he played Britten's Serenade with the New London Orchestra, Britten conducting and Pears warbling. John Terraine was with us, and said he'd disliked the bedroom atmosphere of the performance, with Britten and Pears ogling each other. Later tonight, having finished Pettitt's book, listened to that 1950s recording of Ljuba Wellitsch singing Tatiana's Letter Song with the Philharmonia. Brain's horn notes, so wistful, so poignant and true, reduced me to tears.

WEDNESDAY 17 NOVEMBER   Benjamin Britten dying, it seems. Unworthy thought for today: hope he doesn't die on a programme day, when I might have to do the obit.

THURSDAY 18 NOVEMBER   To Manchester for Royal Exchange Theatre production of Harold Brighouse play *Zack*. Gormless, scruffy, idle but benevolent younger son (kind of Cinderella figure) continuously squashed by monster of a mother and miserly brother, gets beef and backbone put into him by sturdy heroine. We're left with awful thought that he's now condemned to forty years' servitude to another equally domineering woman, his mother and the heroine having merely changed places. Good performance by Patricia Routledge as the gorgon widow Munning, and likewise Trevor Peacock as Zack. In the Midland Hotel, passed Laurence Olivier in the foyer. He gave me a searching look, like a cavalry colonel inspecting an orderly.

FRIDAY 19 NOVEMBER   Not much good turning to our reviewer, an academic, for a reasoned appraisal of that play. Is he mad, I wonder? Not only did he drive from Sheffield and back in order to appear live in tonight's programme, he sat in the cubicle on arrival mocking other speakers (recorded on tape) by pulling faces and miming their speech; then, later, pretending to conduct David Munrow's Early Music Consort with more mugging and what he thought appropriate parodic gestures. Nor do I trust those gleaming little darting eyes, nor the script from which he 'ad-libs' his answers. As for what he said – well, a lot of rubbish about people being tired of kitchen-sink drama and sex-comedies and now turning to the Theatre of Reassurance. Honestly, what an idle statement. And those terrible prepared jokes, uttered with a well-rehearsed 'stifled chortle'. I can't get it out of my head that I knew him at Oxford. And I can vividly imagine the sort of man he would have been there.

Kaleidoscope presenters have a recurrent dream, probably common among broadcasters in general: there is half an hour, or less, to go before transmission, and something has gone wrong. You are at Piccadilly Circus, struggling through a crowd of shoppers, and *you haven't written a word of script.* Cut to studio: you are in front of the microphone, ad-libbing crazily. Perhaps the guest hasn't arrived or, more frequently, the studio is too big – the cubicle window, through which you can just make out the producer, is yards and yards away and you have no idea whatever what you are supposed to say.

On the occasion of the programme noted immediately above, this dream was very nearly realised. Six p.m. came and I was still wrestling with phrases for first item, an obituary note on Basil Spence. Only by a steely exercise of will could I prevent sheer panic, and I found myself guiltily hoping Britten would pass away so that we could shove on his ready-made obit and go home.

WEDNESDAY 1 DECEMBER   The Personal Probate Application Office about Grandma's will. The performance you have to go through is not without its ironies. The idly waiting, elderly people respectable-looking citizens come to attend to the last secular rites (fee, £15, payable to Principal Registry, Family Division, and who are they when they're at home). Stolid men in brown overalls who sort the post and make the tea and smoke cigarettes as though that, too, were part of their official duties . . . the dandy-ish young clerk self-consciously calling out your name, the plain official leatherette-upholstered 'easy' chairs, cream and green paint everywhere, copies of *The Motor Car* to read, etc. Summoned to be 'interviewed' by prim-looking spinster from behind a utilitarian sort of desk, nothing much on it, blank walls on which a Sisley and a Canaletto reproduction hung, not much larger than postcard size, without frames. She read aloud to me what I'd put on the form, asking was it true, were there any mistakes, kept referring to Grandma's 'aliases', which meant the difference between Elizabeth Jane and Elizabeth Gwenny Jane and, I presume, Betty and Bessie, but sounded a peculiar note as though poor Grandma had a police record. Then I had to stand up, Bible in one hand and khaki-coloured official form in the other, and read out a sentence in my best *Horizon* voice affirming that it was indeed all true (but what is truth?). Outside to pay your money – and that, I reflected, is a human life wrapped up.

Kaleidoscope: far too much time went to the London Film Festival and the too-knowing exchanges between Derek Malcolm and Christopher Cook, and far too little to what we'd collected that morning at the new Museum of London, a noble pile. What with that and a live interview with Sheridan Morley on *In the Boom Boom Room*, which doesn't sound bad but is surely destined for early oblivion, it seemed a very strangely constructed programme, under the direction of a new producer: about him there is a funny little toy-like quality, like a Rupert character – he looks, for one thing, at least ten years younger than he is and gives the impression you could pick him up and put him on a shelf for a few moments while you answer the phone. But still he has this rather disarming manner. I wonder if it takes courage to go around like that, with one gold ear-ring, a nursery-style Fair Isle

205

pullover, gaudy braces and tight denims. Perhaps the continuous slight sensation his presence causes is what he prefers, in which case life must be one long adventure.

FRIDAY 3 DECEMBER   George Scott's party. Derek just back from Germany and a tour of some vineyard or other. I remarked to Jonathan Miller that a mutual acquaintance was a wine-fancier and claret-discriminator. Jonathan Miller: 'I've never gone in for that. It always seems to me like the gastronomic equivalent of *Playboy*.' Unfair, but it's true one has misgivings about professional eaters. Question: why isn't Derek obese? All that provender he wades through! And all the wine he sups, yet his stomach is surprisingly flat. Must ask him what his secret is.

In the afternoon, the Syberberg film, *Confessions of Winifred Wagner*. Can't share the general enthusiasm for this, it's more like a TV feature: camera planted before the old person with about three changes of angle throughout. But what she says makes one gasp: the 'dark side' of Hitler's life she knew nothing about, she said, therefore can offer no opinion on. He was a friend, that's all, and when he came to Wahnfried he was off duty, evidently, with all the cares of screwing up Europe and slaughtering the Jews presumably left behind in his In Tray. And she is Wagner's daughter-in-law, sometime child-bride of the buttoned-up-looking Siegfried then in his fifties but for whom Daddy wrote the Idyll!

THURSDAY 9 DECEMBER   Roy Strong tonight, talking eloquently about Victorian narrative painting in his Malcolm Muggeridge voice, huge brown zoological eyes behind those spaniel-like spectacles, mournful 1914 moustache. Today he was all in brown, a *symphonie en brun majeur*. Earlier, buying some reeds in Boosey & Hawkes, there was a tubby, elderly American beside me paying for a new 10-10 clarinet, the pride of the company's range, in £20 notes, and on his departure was affably saluted by the assistant, who called him Mr Goodman. I asked if it was Benny. No, said the assistant, it was his brother Harry, buying the clarinet for his nephew. I left, feeling I had brushed against real eminence.

TUESDAY 14 DECEMBER *King Kong*, the remake. The peculiar plot makes you wonder why not a single one of the characters, living in the present and being frightened by a giant ape, appears to have seen that famous old movie by James Whale, called *King Kong*: they must be the only contemporary Americans who haven't. Met Lindsay Anderson *en route* with Matthew. He urged Matthew, aged ten, to watch the 1932 version on TV this Friday, and says it is 'one of the best films ever made'.

A reflection on actors, after an ordeal by boredom listening to Roy Dotrice reading *Watership Down* on three LPs. It was an ambitious venture quite beyond his powers, for a good theatre actor does not necessarily make a good radio performer – which is what was required for this task. Slightly worse was Spike Milligan, reading *The Snow Goose* on another LP, this time with syrupy musical score in the background. Both projects were a grave error: one, about as intellectually satisfying as the verse on a Christmas card, the other, plain silly. Who could believe in a rabbit hero called Hazel? No amount of epic prose could obscure the fact that *these are bunnies*.

The work compared ill with an exhibition at the National Book League on Peter Rabbit, whose adventures were first published seventy-five years earlier. The eccentric Beatrix Potter's meticulous, elegant water-colours sprang also from an anthropomorphic view of the natural world but there was no question which was preferable. There to support his wife Nanette Newman, who was opening the show, was Bryan Forbes, erstwhile juvenile character actor: he was always the one who cracked up in the submarine. I interviewed him traipsing around the exhibition, about which he seemed only half-informed: Margaret Lane, alias Countess of Huntingdon, who was also on hand and wrote Potter's biography, was much better value.

When it came to programme day, Patrick Garland thought *Watership Down* and *The Snow Goose* 'spellbinding', to which the only reply was that that is literally half-true. I pointed out that

Dotrice said 'reckernise', and gabbled, and forgot to keep up that silly Loamshire accent, and Patrick Garland began to agree, yes, it really wasn't all that hot, yes, he was a boring narrator who kept getting his stresses wrong.

SATURDAY 18 DECEMBER   What to make of Isak Dinesen, whose *Last Tales* have been waiting on my shelves for some eighteen years and now, thanks to *Kaleidoscope*, have actually got themselves read? Their Gothic imagery and speech (nay, thee/thou, upon a time, etc.), no less than the density of the plots, made this one of the hardest reads for months. My brother David's story about her: seen hobbling out of Carnegie Hall on the arm of the Wadham poet William Jay Smith, where there's been a performance of Beethoven 9. She is heard to say: 'Beethoven, I distrust you, you lead to Wagner!' She is one of those authors one is expected to admire, but these tales open up an artificial world of familial guilt, vendetta, fatal curse, gypsy vengeance, etc. Got to the end with a vow not to read any other books by her, and turned to matters like decorating the Christmas tree, checking time of the Cagney movie. Took a look at televised Hoffnung concert, which was about as witty as a wet Monday morning: someone please think of a musical joke that's actually funny, and doesn't consist of fartish noises, comical accents or feeble parody, i.e., 'quoting' from some other composer.

WEDNESDAY 22 DECEMBER   Reduced to impotent rage by terrifying experience of sitting with audience of hyperactive children through *Emu in Pantoland*, a show that feeds sycophantically off the telly-culture, and whose cast included Barbara New, whom I last saw when she was slender little elf in Tom Quad, *c.* 1942, and now a plump comedienne. Rest of the performers lost no time whipping up audience to a pitch that became insupportable: having unlocked this Pandora's box they hadn't the knack of controlling it. Victor Spinetti the villain and he should have known better; Irene Handl, a subtle comic talent, wandered lost and inaudible through the fray, her style quite unsuited to this coarse theatrical form. And I expected to get mobbed by screeching infants. Invited from the stage to suggest some fitting fate for Spinetti, they knew what to do, howling KILL HIM KILL HIM KILL HIM. Merry Christmas!

Thirteen

A *Kaleidoscope* Diary – II

I MISSED THE opening of the National Theatre, but I did happen to present the programme marking the night when the Cottesloe Theatre, the National's studio space, was opened for the first time – on 4 March 1977. The first production was inauspicious: an adaptation of an extremely long work of science fiction called *Illuminatus*. The director-adapter was the inventive and funny Ken Campbell but something had obviously gone horribly wrong: it ran on for scene after scene in an ill-prepared and ill-organised procession of not well-related short 'acts' relying on monologue narratives of past events, and jokes about fellatio and masturbation, and, for some reason, journeys. There was an amateurishly manipulated puppet with a prominent penis who sodomised another puppet; and a black mass featuring a live goat, thankfully not required to play any part except that of onlooker, which it did with a look of dumb, goatish perplexity and, occasionally, alarm.

Illuminatus began at two in the afternoon and was expected to continue, with breaks for meals, until 10.30 p.m. Because the theatre was so new, refreshment facilities were on the rudimentary side: I dined off stale sandwiches, ice cream, and Toffo. I broke the rules for once by leaving before the play ended: but when I slipped away at 9.30 the performance was behind schedule by some two hours.

Kaleidoscope presenters often see what happens behind the scenes. I had often enjoyed the talented Ken Campbell's work and I was interested to interview him outside the theatre in the van which did duty as his headquarters for the week: the small space inside was occupied by an Irish wolfhound, two small rough-haired terriers, Ken Campbell himself, his leading actor, the producer with the Uher, and me. As a prelude to the interview Campbell, who met us outside, pissed copiously against the wall of the National Theatre: a trickle of foaming urine flowed across the pavement towards the legs of his terriers, who I was glad to see avoided paddling in it before jumping on to our laps in the van.

As to the interview itself . . . There is a standard *Kaleidoscope* opening question to author, director, composer, artist, and it is a question which fits absolutely any eventuality. It is 'What first attracted you to the project?' Later, the question itself is edited out, and the interviewee is then heard starting things going with something like, 'I wanted to embark on this because I was concerned by . . . etc., etc.' In Ken Campbell's case the answer was he wanted to direct *Illuminatus* 'because modern theatre in this country is *shitty*'.

Well, some artists give better interviews than others, and I was probably talking to a disillusioned man. Listeners knew nothing of all this: it was merely an interview with the director with the bad words cut out, juxtaposed with a review by the late Louis Allen. Radio being what it is, I doubt if anyone took a great deal of notice: more would have been taken of an interview with the harmonica wizard Tommy Reilly – because sounds are the life of radio and the sound of his playing was so seductive and pleasing.

Actually, I thought Tommy Reilly himself looked less like a musician than a successful farmer: tall, brawny, strong-jawed, with a sunny disposition, and carrying a neat little velvet-lined case in which nestled two silver harmonicas. I became aware of the keen rivalry that existed between him and Larry Adler, the only other known exponent of the instrument. I had met Larry Adler in similar circumstances, after the release of one of his new recordings, and thought him funny and full of good anecdotes. We talked about Bix Beiderbecke, whom he said he had played with and found 'very withdrawn'. Adler and Reilly were utterly different in character. The former at this time had recently announced his intention to have a vasectomy, but as a precaution he was going to save a phial of his semen and put it into cold storage. Auberon Waugh had said, 'And I can't sleep at nights until I find that phial and destroy it.'

WEDNESDAY 16 MARCH Mervyn Levy live, flamboyant and amusing as ever. He told a story of an occasion when he was walking down Park Lane with Quentin Crisp, the latter in full war-paint. All at once as they are passing some traffic lights a lorry pulls up. Driver leans out and sneers at Crisp, 'Oo d'you fink you are, the Queen o' the fuckin' fairies?' Crisp turns and says with a flick of the wrist, 'Yes I am, and I command you to disappear.' At which point, says Mervyn, the lights changed to green and he *did* disappear. Very little seems to put Mervyn out, though I observed two bright red spots on his cheeks the size of a shilling, proof of some inner turmoil, after we'd finished talking about Gaudier-Brzeska. Then while I moved back to the script (back on rails, secure again) Mervyn sat slumped, aware he'd ended a bit abruptly and with slightly muffed final answer. On receiving routine thanks from the producer he said it was like coming round after an operation: 'It's all over, your balls are off.'

At Waterloo Station, another old acquaintance, Ivor Jones, sometime *enfant terrible* of the BMA, who had been to a Special Representative Meeting at BMA House: the event, and the reason for it, had completely passed me by — what on earth are they on about now? What had it been like, I asked Jones. 'Very tame,' he said with a sly look. 'Not like the old days, Ivor,' I said, mainly to flatter him, I suppose. He was certainly a notable medical demagogue in his day, and now he's in single-handed practice in Wiltshire — a peaceful ending, no doubt, to the career of a man who has walked with Prime Ministers. And can it be true he is married to my former secretary, with the Betty Boop eyes, one Miss Pring? Perhaps I should have told him of a conversation with today's producer who had remarked to me once, 'I don't know much about the BMA, but would I be right in thinking they're a bunch of self-important, self-aggrandising farts?' I had to admit he was more or less right but it didn't say much for all those years when I had been professionally responsible for improving their image.

FRIDAY 18 MARCH   Talking of improving your image: at Dollond & Aitchison, where today's eye test was done, they sell spectacle frames with names like Barrister, Troubleshooter, Bravo, Firesmoke, Brunel and Sabre, all of which presumably suit, or flatter, somebody's idea of himself, though I can't quite get the psychological implications of Kestrel, Heron, and other bird names: symbols of aspiration in general, maybe. All these I noted down, observed with suspicion by the girl at the desk. 'Ladies' ' frames are more demure. I observed Secret, Sophie, and Candy, glamour names of the fifties though they now sound more like whores. This evening took daughter Lucy, who's twelve, to a preview of Braham Murray's rock-opera version of *Merchant of Venice*, called for some reason *Fireangel*. Lucy enjoyed it. As for me, life is too short for rock operas: I still haven't heard half of Verdi's. I concede that some of the singers were more or less in tune and kept to the beat (triple forte), except the luckless girl who played the Portia character, who couldn't get a note without sliding obliquely up to it. Meanwhile the Antonio, called Angelo here, yelled his songs at her, frequently ascending into the falsetto and sounding incredibly angry. No wonder, with that strain on the diaphragm. Thoroughly messy set, with too many people in it. Feeble score, no tunes. I see one of the waiters was called Mark Tyme, who also played a valet – or is this a pseudonym for Walter Plinge? Some of the power of the play showed through, none of the poetry.

TUESDAY 22 MARCH   The impresario-actor Ray Cooney, responsible for *Fireangel* and a man of uncomplicated tastes, took us into a dressing room in Her Majesty's Theatre with a loud *Bandwagon* 'Ay-theng-yow': then gave an interview which was more or less self-condemnatory about what he conceived to be the necessary ingredients for a successful stage musical. I can't imagine there'll be much of a run for his show, especially now they've decided to do away with radio-mikes and have all those people careering about with hand-mikes as though in a TV studio. All that technology wasted on so worthless a cause.

Working on *Kaleidoscope* I have observed a common fallacy among bad writers, that eyes alone can express emotion: 'She stared at him, incomprehension written in her eyes' ... and 'wonder mingled with doubt [was] mirrored in her eyes ... ' In the work of such people eyes can also glitter greedily and flash angrily, which is a lot of work for a pair of irises to have to do.

There are other writers with equally sloppy ideas about the involuntary expression of emotion. A prize-winning woman novelist whose new novel we reviewed a few weeks afterwards had written in it of someone exuding 'the sour odour of defeat'. What was this? Would I recognise it if I smelt it? Was it like the smell of feet, and could you remedy it with Odoreaters or Lifebuoy? What smells did it resemble? But of course this was a bogus piece of observation, probably copied from Graham Greene.

Again, in that book, a character was discovered 'stroking his groin'. This scarcely seemed to deserve the intended censure, since I have always understood the groin to be, as the *Shorter Oxford* defines it, the fold or depression on either side of the body between the abdomen and the upper thigh. Nothing wrong with stroking that. Of course this writer clearly meant that the character in question, a nasty piece of work, was stroking his penis. Then I noted in the work of another writer someone talking about the 'bulb' of his penis and made a note that it was time to protest about the peculiar ideas some writers have about human anatomy.

In fact, the more one looked, the more bizarre seemed to be the current misconceptions of what the human body would do under stress. From the same book as those bogus descriptions of people's eyes came phrases so anatomically strange that I copied them out in disbelief: 'A bewildered frown slowly creased his forehead and hung there in the tanned, leathery skin'; 'Giordino flashed a toothy smile'; 'He had the face of a canvas-weary prize-fighter . . . '

Actually, they were all of a piece with that writer's generally slovenly style of expression: 'He was a slender man of medium height with a distinguished face'; 'She looked at him with a secret, womanly smile'; ' "You're straddling an interesting concept," Kemper said. "But one fraught with problems." ' The concept straddled by the book in question was interesting enough and guaranteed massive sales through its title alone: *Raise the Titanic!* Its ludicrously melodramatic plot involved the supposed presence of valuable minerals in the liner's wreck, sinister Bolshevik spies with silky manners and polysyllabic turns of speech ('My compliments to you, gentlemen'), and numerous ballsy Americans. The heroine was at one point brutally stripped before an audience of leering Russian marines, which I imagine the author, Clive Cussler, must have enjoyed writing. Meanwhile the hero, a certain Dirk Pitt ('cool, piercing eyes'), may have been conceived with an actor like the young Charlton Heston in mind. In the event, when the film version appeared in 1980, the part was played by someone else but was described as a disaster on an appropriately titanic scale, sinking Lord Grade's production company beneath a huge debt.

FRIDAY 29 APRIL   Interviewed Richard Gordon: that cheery, medical student persona doubtless conceals a rather hard nut. A funny man, though I'm not too fond of those serious novels, in which he seems a little too obviously determined to go straight. He is the person who, when confronted by Eamonn Andrews bearing an elaborately bound volume and told 'Richard Gordon, this is your lafe', cried 'Oh, balls,' and made a hasty escape. He used to work for the *British Medical Journal* but the waspish Hugh Clegg hated him and put him in charge of obituaries. In the circumstances I doubt if Clegg was one of those old comrades who'd been waiting in the wings on that television occasion.

SUNDAY 15 MAY Yesterday I bought the issue of *The Radio Times*, with now vanished definite article, for 25 January 1935. It cost me £1.50 – face price 2d – from a shop in Cambridge Circus and engrossing reading it is. The advertisements alone, with their well-bred boastfulness, are worth the price: 'DON'T LET 'FLU GET YOU: Famous 2d Remedy Meets National Emergency' . . . 'WE'VE DECIDED ON A PLUS-A-GRAM' . . . 'THE CADBURY COCOCUBS' . . . 'WHISKERS' WONDERFUL GRAMOPHONE' . . . 'IF YOU HAVE A COUGH YOU HAVEN'T TRIED (At All Chemists) MUSTEROLE BRAND MUSTARD OINTMENT: Read the plain straightforward Musterole Guarantee – Ease in five minutes, and usually complete relief in five hours.' And the regular features: 'BOTH SIDES OF THE MICROPHONE', 'WHAT THE OTHER LISTENER THINKS', 'PEOPLE YOU HEAR', 'STROLLING COMMENTARIES'. Oh how sweetly innocent it all seems. *The Radio Times* even had a medical column, rigidly anonymous of course, called *From Physician to Patient*, a title suggesting a Harley Street address, or at least reputation. On 25–1–35 he was on about 'MORE DISEASES OF THE LUNGS', Acute Bronchitis, Pleurisy, Empyema. It reads like a medical textbook. The programmes are all so well-bred: The Wireless Military Band, Mantovani and his Tipica Orchestra (photo of Mantovani shows him aged apparently about fifteen) with eleven pieces on the programme, all named and all composers credited. Every night except Sunday, dance music, sometimes relayed from the Dorchester (Jack Jackson), or the Casani Club (directed by Charles Kunz). On Wednesday 30 January there was a television programme, London National only, lasting 45 minutes and starting at 11 p.m., a programme of songs by Maria Sandra and Gustave Ferrari, and dances by Cleo Nordi: By the Baird Process, said the *RT* announcement, so you couldn't have seen much of the footwork.

THURSDAY 9 JUNE Drove back across England from Wales,

diagonally, on Tuesday, seeing at first hand grass-roots response to this somewhat trumped-up day of national rejoicing. 'It's ER Jubilee', I saw someone had wittily written on a wall somewhere. But people did rise to it. *Times* reports crowds of one million in London to cheer, though the sight of all those chinless wonders lining the balcony of Buckingham Palace on TV was enough to wobble the loyalty of the most convinced supporter of the status quo. The carnival atmosphere was quite infectious, especially in Llanidloes, with its absurd kazoo band in pink and white uniforms tootling *Men of Harlech* in unison down Oak Street. Same kind of thing in countless townships through Shropshire, Worcestershire, Oxfordshire, with their busloads of St Trinian's girls, decorated floats, street parties, bunting galore. Tonight, fireworks all over London and a royal procession down the Thames. Alas, it's raining intermittently.

MONDAY 20 JUNE X is leaving the programme, being *enceinte*, and good luck to her. I shall miss her, but not her habit of picking her nose and chewing the result, popping into her mouth the little bleb of dried, or sometimes wet, mucus, brown with tobacco stains. I think I'm going to vomit, describing it. I've even seen her do it at table in the canteen, supplementing her *Moussaka à la Grècque* with a handy pinch of snot. Someone will have to speak seriously to her about diet in pregnancy.

FRIDAY 4 NOVEMBER Whatever became of Nova Pilbeam, I thought, watching Hitchcock's *Young and Innocent*. Young and innocent indeed . . . half the pleasure of watching those films is to see again the England of my youth: rural roads empty, virtually, of cars, and such cars as there are have running-boards and are always black or navy-blue, and sometimes windscreens you can lift up like the visor on a helmet. Cabbies with numbered badges and uniform caps. Smell of horse-shit on the cobbles, horses not an unusual thing but aeroplanes would make you stop and point. Cigarette cards: I stood on the pavement outside our house on Acre Lane and asked passers-by if they had any they could give me. Usually they had. Most people smoked.

The awful prevalence of the cliché. In the stalls of the Savoy I sat watching a play of threadbare invention called *Alice's Boys*, by William Douglas-Home, which was little more than a vehicle for Ralph Richardson. It was to be one of his last appearances on the stage: he was already seventy-six. Unfortunately he was rather deaf and just a little Parkinsonian, and bumbled his way through with insufficient hold on his lines. However, he probably didn't care very much about the play, which had something to do with a cell of MI6 agents in London, one of whom was a traitor – but which one? And who put the knife into the corpse discovered under the bed in the first Act? And who cares who killed Roger Ackroyd?

Now and then, through some indefinable edge about the proceedings, there was evidence that a sardonic intelligence had been at work on this limp text: and that was so. Lindsay Anderson had been called in as play doctor, rather late in the day, and was credited with its direction. But not even he and Ralph Richardson could conceal that the piece, with its stagy confrontations and uninteresting dialogue, was based on second-hand observation and a misty sort of view of what the espionage business at that period was actually like.

Yet one of the things that counts is an honest belief in what you are doing. Absent from *Alice's Boys*, this quality was clearly present in a novel, that week, with the almost absurdly romantic title *The Sword and the Flame*. It was yet another retelling of the Arthurian legend, by Catherine Christian, who flung herself passionately into the story. So much so, I was nearly persuaded that it might have been like this – Merlin a wandering bard to whom people attributed second sight, Arthur a sort of Roman *colon* or *dux belli* left behind when the Empire shrivelled up and the Saxons, Jutes, Picts and others began their raids. It was a pity bold Sir Bedivere, telling the story and supposedly Arthur's

218

half-brother, was faintly boring, a sort of C. Aubrey Smith cavalry colonel, whose voice would turn gruff when strong emotion
threatened.

It was true the book was full of the clichés of romantic
literature: its heroine, 'with a small face' and a serious look,
a hero who doesn't quite get it when somebody loves him and
any number of 'tow-headed youngsters' gambolling about the
towers and gardens of a Camelot which sounded much too
elaborate, not to say comfortable, for the Dark Ages. Perhaps
in deference to the times Miss Christian had made Medraut (i.e.,
Mordred) homosexual, with a following of like-minded cronies
like Aglavain, with shrill voice. Arthur himself seems a bit of a
fool, trusting Medraut when everyone else can see what a swine
he is, not noticing that Lancelot and Guinevere are conspiring
lovers, although their affair is the talk of the cloisters. We're
told he's a brilliant strategist, but this seems to amount only to
'surprise, and use of cavalry', which wouldn't have been quite
enough.

And yet, you kept settling comfortably back into this book.
What is it about some second-rate works that keeps you awake,
if it isn't the genuine conviction of the author?

MONDAY 15 MAY Walter de la Mare . . . his work hitherto an
unexplored tract: author of what are turning out to be feather-light
and for me feather-significant verses, the literary equivalent of a
book of sketches by, say, Kate Greenaway, pastiches of old nursery
rhymes. I imagine him the kind of man who couldn't resist turning
these things out by the dozen, the way some people whittle sticks.

There is more to de la Mare than meets the eye but I am
not sure I am enamoured of what meets mine. These little puffs
of rhyming verses, with their archaisms and inversions ('Sudden
a gigantic hand he thrust/Into his bosom cold') and repeated
syllables ('Hithery, hethery, I love best/The wind that blows
from out the west'), a sophisticated attempt to take over territory
hitherto occupied by Anon., XVIII C. What should we make of

a man who consistently wrote about children and childhood and animals (equals children, perhaps) and now and then about going backwards in time to some distant, longed-for Arcadia? At its best it diffuses an eerie and faintly exciting atmosphere a bit like Bartók's nature music, but at worst can be exceedingly twee and cute. His son Richard is writing his biography, and I hope we get more from it than we do from Leonard Clark, whose Bodley Head monograph I had been urged to read: his talk of 'magical', 'beautiful', 'extraordinary' verses ('the craftsmanship is there as well as the shining quality and unearthly loveliness') is meaningless – simple-minded words of praise revealing a decidedly simple-minded approach to the verse.

There was a song in my youth that went: 'I like music, sweet or blue/But music makes me do the things I never should do.' It is a peculiar way to enjoy yourself in the way of the amateur musician, voluntarily courting every six weeks or so the possibility of public humiliation. The Wimbledon Symphony Orchestra was performing, in a local church, Handel's *Royal Fireworks Music*, Britten's *Sea Interludes*, the *Flying Dutchman* Overture and Saint-Saëns's 1st Cello Concerto. The church was not a very warm place and its high-Victorian walls retained their tomb-like chill even in rather mild spring weather. But there were no terrible mishaps. However, there was an acoustic problem.

Three months earlier when we had played there, the sound of Mahler 4 was accompanied by loud structural borborygmi as though some huge beast were in labour in the crypt. On this subsequent occasion I mentioned the fact to the jolly young vicar, who explained that the church's antique heating system, now mainly defunct, included a gallery placed at inaccessible height in the eaves with a propeller arrangement for fanning the air along, and this had a worn and rusty bearing. Hence the impromptu *obligato*.

This explanation was conveyed to the soloist, Douglas Cummings, there to play the Saint-Saëns A minor concerto, and he listened to it in wonderment. When I congratulated him on his performance he said he'd sat there playing and thinking of all the awful things he'd done in Paris, whence he had just returned. But I am sure no one but Cummings was aware his thoughts were elsewhere – to the point, evidently, of closing his mind to the groaning noises still audible from the remote Victorian gallery.

John Alldis, the conductor, was in an ill humour afterwards: our guest principal oboist was the principal object of his annoyance. It was hard to play in tune with her and there was an absurd altercation over her cor anglais, on which she played a flat note somewhere in the middle register. It's a bad note, she said, you can't do anything with it. Well, I can't help that, replied John Alldis testily. A solo is a solo . . . especially when it's in the middle of the *Flying Dutchman* Overture. It was impossible to imagine this exchange taking place anywhere else but in an amateur orchestra.

A day or two later – an event practically at the very opposite end of the musical spectrum: an interview with Dave Brubeck. I visited him in a flash hotel in Swiss Cottage. But he was dressed for California – in faultless white trousers, white socks and sneakers, scarlet shirt, pale grey suede jacket. I knew what to expect from his photographs, but was not quite prepared for this piercing-eyed, long-haired, hawk-nosed, patriarchal figure – appropriately so, since the other members of his quartet are now his three sons.

Brubeck told me I was completely wrong to describe him as of academic background: he hadn't been able to read music until well on in years, and he was gratified to tell me a black musicologist had said he owed more to African music than anyone else he had heard. Even so, he had studied with Milhaud, and his piano solo on the LP we were reviewing was very French-impressionist.

THURSDAY 25 MAY On the way out of Broadcasting House late in the evening I saw a frail-looking, slight individual with sandy moustache and gold-rimmed spectacles sitting on the banquette in

BH lobby. Casting hesitation aside, I went over and said, 'Excuse me, are you S. J. Perelman?' 'Yes,' he said. Me: 'Forgive me for confronting you in this way, but I've been an admirer of your work for so long I couldn't let the opportunity go by of talking to you.' Perelman mumbled embarrassed thanks. He was waiting to be called for an interview by Brian Matthews Show but the BH doormen said they knew nothing about it and hadn't heard of the programme. Perelman finally ushered down to B14, blinking owlishly but obviously extremely vexed.

Two great Victorians: John Unrau's book on Ruskin made few concessions to those ignorant of technicalities of architecture, and it made it difficult to read his companion to Ruskin's writing about the subject. Now and then a whiff of excitement escaped from its pages, with moments like Ruskin's remark, 'the capitals of the iron shafts in any railway station . . . are things to make a man wish – for shame of his species – that he had been born a dog or a bee'.

To go with this – Quentin Bell's short book on Ruskin, and this was notable for perfectly preposterous punctuation: whether because of some crack-brained theory or just idleness one could not tell. This deficiency did not help clarify his analysis of Ruskin's ideas, nor his peculiar sexual psychology. Ruskin liked little girls, proposed marriage to two of them, and failed to consummate marriage with the mysterious Euphemia, later Lady Millais. We never found out why, though I suppose no one knows, and never will. Quentin Bell did have some inside information, however: 'We know that Ruskin was addicted, since youth, to auto-erotic practices,' he murmurs discreetly.

But perhaps there is something about the great Victorian figures which attracts eccentric writers. Michael Hastings's biography of Sir Richard Burton was one of the oddest books of 1978. Indeed, some kind of brainstorm must have made him write, 'A black bolt from heaven which always assumed, in Arab eyes, a grave and awesome omen,' and 'The original *dare* in Byron's nature, his angered idealism, the torn heart of rapture would be blended down to pap fodder for the new-found genteel art of recreational reading,' and 'Dick couldn't have given a fart in a bustle factory whether her mother's feelings were becalmed,' and 'The room had a stuffed dark prune drabbet crepuscular about it' (Drabbet – a drab twilled linen, 1851), and 'There was not one black girl who'd hesitate her arms' . . . and so on and so on.

Somewhere in the book he described his subject as 'a selfish caddish odd sod', which could be true, well, roughly, but the real Burton was obscured by Hastings's technicolour prose. In the bibliography, a funny place for such explanations, he alluded to his view that 'the goal of biographer and novelist do intertwine . . . biographer and novelist often link up to share the identical goal of verisimilitude. And all biography remains a form of fiction.'

Nevertheless an autobiography was the all-out winner of the Worst Book of 1978 title: Madeleine Masson's *I Never Kissed Paris Goodbye*. The adjectives I wrote down to describe it were – snobbish, vain, silly, trivial, uninformed, naive, malicious, vindictive and boring. Some misanthrope had presumably convinced her she had a story to tell, and her adventures at the fall of France had more than passing interest – though they only take up a score of pages at the very end.

But the rest was so terrible it made you wonder if it were all a practical joke. 'He was on the hunt, a male animal a-quiver with lust,' 'A virile young male with an urgent sex-urge and great potency', and 'Her ideas about British habits were mimsey, to say the least'. What ceiling had fallen in at Hamish Hamilton that they should pass a book that contained this *aperçu*: 'At St Helena I looked out over the great bastions of heaving water that had kept Napoleon trapped in the house at Longwood, against whose walls he finally bashed out what remained of his life.' Evidently her agent had been justifiably cautious: 'Denise was not certain that my works would achieve immortality.' She was not afraid to acknowledge her obligations: 'Dear Lewis Rose-Macleod, my first editor, to whom I am deeply indebted for teaching me the rules of

223

the trade, told me once that the function of the true journalist was a sponge-like ability to absorb conversation, in order to expunge it as quickly as possible.' So the opposite of sponge is expunge: without Madeleine Masson, I would never have known that. And the crowning annoyance: news came when I was within 30 pages of the finishing line that the item was being dropped.

MONDAY 29 MAY *A bat in the bedroom.* We are in Wales. Phobic about flying creatures, I have always dreaded this . . . a skittering behind the drawn curtain at twenty past one in the morning, a slim, nervous shape veering about the room – us cowering in terror beneath the bedclothes. If I'm going to have my manhood tested, I told B., I'd rather have to fight twenty yobs than walk across the room, draw the curtains, open the window and let the thing out. At length a stratagem was devised, at once audacious and absurd: drawing a blanket with me as I went, I moved across the floor like a bell-tent on legs . . . then moved back to bed – only to have to do the whole thing again in order to shut Lucy's door, whence a sliver of light was attracting the creature. Some time during all this manoeuvring it vanished, a twittering black circumflex, into the dusk. Twenty minutes later the dawn chorus went into action.

Have found admirable man to tend the garden here, one Ted Lewis. I told him he had the same name as a famous band-leader. Ted: 'There used to be an *Alf* Lewis round here . . . ' Then he recounted a tale of that same Alf being questioned by visiting parson who asked him, 'What's the cost of living like round here?' Alf: 'About a shilling a pint.' Further local story I was told today: two local lovers, and the girl became pregnant, but her parents wouldn't let them get married. However, they did insist the boy support the baby, and so he did. As time went on, the little girl used to go round to collect the weekly money until one day her mother told her to go round and say, Daddy, I'm sixteen years old today. Oh yes, said the man, then tell her I'm no longer your father. The child went back with the message, then came back again with the reply:

224

'Mum says you never were.' Sounds like an urban myth to me.

FRIDAY 16 JUNE Commentary for a slide-show by the Centre for Alternative Technology at Machynlleth leads me to wonder if the spearhead of the ecology movement has retreated to mid-Wales. The man who produced this particular piece of work won't reignite the public's interest, alas: his script was exceedingly wild and naive and went far beyond the sort of responsibilities the Centre ought to have taken on. I mean, who wants their views on creative employment, and what is the force of their insistence that everybody ought to build his own house, so managing without a crippling mortgage? What has this to do with windmills and wheelbarrows, solar heat and bicycles? Later I learned that Robin Clarke, sometime editor of *Discovery* and ABSW Chairman, is now sheep farming in Wales, writing the occasional piece for magazines like *The Ecologist* and *New Scientist*. The commune, or whatever it was that he originally joined, foundered in a sort of grand adulterous muddle, adding a much-needed element of farce to the environmentalist movement.

SATURDAY 17 JUNE This morning a breakfast conversation with George Vaughan, eighty in September. Well, I'll try this marmalade. Me: We like that, it tastes of oranges . . . (Pause) . . . We used to have Cooper's Oxford, out of a sense of loyalty, I suppose . . . (Pause) . . . Now we prefer that . . . (Longer pause) . . . Did I ever show you this (gets up, fetches picture book of Victorian and Edwardian London). Dad: Hup, hup (the familiar, glottal A.G.V. chuckle) . . . H'm . . . (turns over exactly two pages, hands it back). Getting out of the Downs Road, is a helluva business. I had a helluva job getting out last time, aiming to go down Lower Downs Road, and on down to Merton Road (warms to his subject) and out by the Emma Hamilton. Finally I had to put *my car* (always said with weighty emphasis) out in the middle of the road and hold up all the traffic until someone let me go. (Silence descends again.) Later, I recounted David's story of eating more pills than lunch in New York the other week.

A.G.V.: I've got all kinds of pills: these for gout, they're very good, then these for arthritis, then these for etc., etc. Well, I suppose when I'm eighty I shall be just as heavy going. Did he find his father heavy going, bound by his own preoccupations? Probably not: the old boy never reached sixty – dead from mustard gas.

FRIDAY 23 JUNE   After lunch I went to see Eddie Hanson, my former Physics master – who nearly forty years ago at school humiliated me, by ordering me to go down to Form I to ask any boy at random how to divide by a hundred – because I hadn't known, having panicked and my innumerate brain having gone numb. He is now an elderly man with a trim grey beard and rather long white hair, ill-fitting denims and Beatle jacket, around his neck a red choker . . . the total effect neat but unattractive. He has turned into not a bad old stick, but several times he praised his own abilities as a teacher (wrong) and exhibited a few other signs of old fogeydom, lamenting loss of standards, and so on. He hadn't much to say about Garrett. I remarked that Garrett made a great thing of the Renaissance Whole Man – taking a broad interest in the sciences and the arts. Eddie said, with his toothy Lancastrian, George Formby grin, I always think he made a great thing of anything he wasn't himself, like his bogus interest in rugger and his pseudo-patriotism. Took five pages of notes on this man, who collects clocks.

SATURDAY 24 JUNE   Sat in East Tower at Shepherds Bush reading *Horizon* commentary and kidding myself I could understand Alec Nisbet's film on membranes called *Bags of Life*. I said it reminded me of a former Company Commander of mine who used to say to us recruits of 'B' Coy, 2nd Battalion, Queen's Royal Regiment, 'Bash on, B, bags of bull!' and this was considered at the time and in the circumstances very jolly and amusing, witty even. Laughter thresholds were generally lowish at the time, I recall. I had a letter from Samuel Hynes suggesting lunch, and could he bring his friend Barbara Hardy, who is writing a novel about a thirties

226

poet and says Raynes Park comes into it. If this is so it becomes more than ever necessary to put down the truth as I understand it about Garrett, Raynes Park, and the entire experience forty years ago.

MONDAY 26 JUNE   Winthrop Labs handed me seven sheets on The Irritable Bowel, with its talk about explosive diarrhoea, flatus, borborygmi, etc. and the usual medical rubbish about 'Mrs Bloggs' and 'Little Willie', these being the names doctors use to refer to mythic but typically dumb-ass patients. Spoke to Samuel Hynes this morning. When I said I had started 'trying to put together a book' on Raynes Park and Garrett he said, with great enthusiasm, 'That's wonderful!' About the most encouraging thing that has happened to date. We have a tentative lunch date when I return from Italia.

WEDNESDAY 28 JUNE   Milan – the first trip abroad for *Kaleido-scope*. I am sitting here looking out at the back of the Scala Theatre, encrusted with ornate architectural detail, me smelling faintly of Italian soap. At the Scala Theatre I have seen *Forza del Destino*. A flunkey showed us to a box perched on the fourth tier immediately above the orchestra, with a horribly oblique view of the stage, most of stage-left being totally invisible. The audience was not, as I'd been told to expect, rowdy and ill-behaved but respectful, quiet and generous with applause: there were several moments when loud clapping after a solo aria was silenced by angry hissing – actually not angry, but firm. Our seats gave a good view of the wings opposite, and of the string section and half the woodwind, luckily including the clarinet section. Incredible how casually these men and women approach a task which fills me with panic. I doubt if the Covent Garden or ENO orchestra, though, would have been quite so *jemenfoutiste* about the job in hand. A bass clarinet player with nothing to do throughout the opera, save for an important solo or two in the last act, sauntered in with the others after the last interval, and sat looking pro-foundly bored, crossing and recrossing his legs, fiddling with his music, exchanging small talk with a neighbouring second violin while the man was actually playing, and now and then wagging his head or an arm to the music. During the *rataplan-rataplan* chorus in Act IV the entire bass section, to a man, took two paces forward and stared round at the stage, as though they had never seen it before. One of the first fiddles got up and walked away somewhere in the middle of the opera; he didn't come back. Perhaps he was ill. The first desk *violini primi* chatted away casually during a *tremolando* passage, and God knows what was going on out of sight in the brass. The conductor, one Edoardo Muller, appeared unconcerned by these goings-on, and it all sounded all right. The chorus was tremendously good, swirling around the stage in the festive scenes, moving together to great effect in the battle, and singing splendidly.

THURSDAY 29 JUNE Sherrill Milnes, making his Scala début, is here to sing Luna in *Il Trovatore*. He told me this morning an individual came to his dressing room with the announcement, '*Sono da claque.*' Milnes thought it was his name: Sono who? But it was an invitation to hand over a small sum (leave it to you, squire) to see to it the boys don't get you hissed. Some of that hissing last night, he suggested, was to *stop* applause the claque considered unjustified, or maybe not paid for. He also thought it unlikely the orchestra would have been messing about the way they did if Mehta or Abbado had been conducting. Is it a full-time job being in the claque? Presumably not. It's probably a malevolent Italian version of the Nureyev fan club, or those fools who chant slogans at the Proms.

SATURDAY 1 JULY *Trovatore* marvellous, sets of enormous, brooding size and wonderful handling of crowds (Visconti production), music played with fantastic *brio* and involvement. Sherrill Milnes (my friend) was superb right from his opening phrase: '*Tace la notte!*' Next to me three small Italian boys were rapt, with occasional awed whispers of '*il trovatore!*' whenever Ermanno Mauro, a portly tenor, came on. To my right, in the stalls, a mountainous woman in black spread all over her seat: as the lights dimmed, I observed her popping into her tiny mouth a sticky sweetie. Afterwards, dining in Biffi's when in swarmed the Zubin Mehta crowd with S. Milnes, who acknowledged us cordially and came over to exchange words a couple of times. Mehta had refused to be interviewed, giving rather curt shrug: BBC radio means nothing to him. Milnes's politeness showed him up. Spent the morning moving with painful slowness round Scala Bicentenary Exhibition. With us was helpful man called Luigi Ferrari whose desire to be of service is alas negated by his terrible English. We conversed in a weird mixture of English, French and operatic Italian and the idea of recording a walk round the exhibition was decisively frustrated.

SUNDAY 2 JULY   Today to Milan Cathedral, apparently the southernmost Gothic cathedral in Europe . . . clambering all over the roof galleries with all this incredibly fussy architectural detail, and acres of it too, like Mervyn Peake's Gormenghast. After lunch took time off to eat an ice cream, in a glass the size of a football, five different kinds, with cream, apricot, maraschino cherries, pineapple and fancy wafers: bloody gluttony I call it. I hated myself for even ordering the thing, let alone getting to the end of it. Should cure one of ice cream for ever. I justified it by claiming to myself it is one of the things tourists are supposed to do: unlikely you'd ever see locals doing it.

MONDAY 3 JULY   Last day here. We ate in the cheapest place yet, called Trattoria Toscana da Michele, seated near a Romanian anaesthetist, plus wife, who works in Germany, a tall, grey-haired, slim, hard-looking man with quite good, clipped English, who was more curious about us than we were about him. I suppose we do cut a rather peculiar figure: we are not tourists, not quite English businessmen. But it shouldn't be too difficult to identify us as media hounds. Tonight we repair to Teatro Lirico for production by Giorgio Strehler of *La Tempesta* by one Gulielmo Shakespeare, starting at nine o'clock and can't possibly be over until one in the morning. To Rome tomorrow.

TUESDAY 4 JULY   Milan, says my producer-companion Brian Barfield, is a complacent and self-satisfied city compared with Rome: there is more raw life here, certainly when you compare the elegance of the Galleria Vittorio Emmanuele and Piazza della Scala with the uproar and crumbling masonry of this interesting quarter. We are in the centre of the repro furniture and French-polishing trade but across the street is a barber and a sixteenth-century tower plus, next door, a pharmacy, a tobacconist, a bar and liquor store and God knows what else. In other words ordinary life goes on around the corner from the Piazza Navona, thronged with tourists and street-traders including a fire-eater, reeking of meths, and a sad little line-up of drop-outs sleeping or smoking in a huddle against the wall. This evening we dine with the legendary Georgina Masson of *Companion Guide to Rome*: our treat, her choice of restaurant. What will she be like? I picture a twittery, slightly fey little old lady with little purses and bags pinned to her clothing.

WEDNESDAY 5 JULY   Well, well. Georgina was a broad-hipped, beefy cavalry-wife with an emphatic style of speech enlivened by frequent *crescendi al fortissimo*. What she has to say is amazingly erudite and she spills her erudition freely. I don't think she stopped talking all evening except to be refuelled now and then with a fresh question. She is leaving Rome in a few days to live in London, retaining some *pied-à-terre* here, driven out, she says, because of the Italian banks. She says they won't hand over any currency due to you from another country: payment of fees in Swiss francs or DM is delayed for weeks or even months and she never knows if she's solvent or broke. She took us – we paid – to a small, cheap, rather good Sardinian restaurant which seemed to have been built in the middle of a traffic island. We ate our saltimbocca and bean salad with motor-cars swooping round us like dive-bombing Stukas. Then she drove us in her matchbox-size Fiat to the Campidoglio and we walked round it and along the Palatine Hill in the luminous light . . . in the dark the soft sound of lovers' laughter . . . the stone glowing faintly golden behind Marcus Aurelius' statue: it seemed to be moving towards us with a sort of benevolent grace and sagacity. What a place. She dropped us in what she airily said was a spot two minutes from the right bridge but which was thirty minutes' walk away through some quite sinister streets. Georgina hadn't flagged. For the first time since I got here I slept like a dead man, awoke at seven-thirty to the sound of two Roman cats in lustful duet.

Later. Spent almost the whole day with Georgina Masson, and what a trial. She goes relentlessly on, square jaw thrust out like a bulldog, shoulders hunched as if ready to charge in and shoulder you to the ground. We scrambled all over the Basilica S. Clemente but didn't finish (more tomorrow, O God) because she had so much to say, then struggled over to the Colosseum and then to the Campidoglio, Georgina walking very slowly and puffing noticeably: she is sixty-seven years old and smokes heavily. Then back to her flat for Lapsang Souchong and fancy biscuits (hungry as hell, took three) and then, just as we were managing to make departure seem an imminent necessity, out came the drinks trolley and another round of stories, some of which we'd already heard, the whole performance aborted at last by good old B.B. determinedly rising to his feet with, Well, Georgina, thank you so *much* for the *tremendously* hard work you've put in today, etc. Taking the hint she went out and telephoned for a cab, said she was going over to the American Academy for some cigarettes and then was going to do absolutely *nothing* for the rest of the day but sit outside and read a detective story. Hard to believe. I felt as if I had fallen under a steamroller. She banged on finally about the Protestant Cemetery: apparently it has been the victim of some fearful cosmetic treatment at the hands of an undertaker by the odd name of Morbidelli. G.M. is ready to savage him, is writing letters and making a huge fuss, with the aid of that same American Academy — but no help worth the name, she complains, from the snobbish British Ambassador, whom she calls a name-dropping social climber. She's not above a bit of name-dropping herself. I wouldn't care to be on the opposing side in a public argument. Another day with her lies ahead.

THURSDAY 6 JULY Christ, what a relentless woman. Tramped over the Church of S. Clemente and Protestant Cemetery, a brisk lunch up on the heights, next a quick grappa at that Sardinian traffic island and then off to the Ostia Antica, where she walked us off our feet again, to collapse at last into a taxi, leaving her to play the dogged Englishwoman on her own, complaining about Italian men, striding out across the Roman traffic with one arm stiffly upraised like a demented traffic warden, arguing shrilly with taxi drivers and enthusing over the prospects that arise on every hand. I found her extremely hard to interview, that was the other thing, nearly impossible to get on terms with someone so pugnacious and U, with her references to Molly Salisbury ('Best gardener in England! Or one of 'em!') and Lady Reed, John Julius and so on. But then, perhaps she is lonely and afraid under all this bluster: last year, she revealed, she had two operations ('minor ones') for cancer. God knows what she can have been like before that: unstoppable, I should think. She knows what she doesn't like: 'arty-farty parties', whatever those are, and anyone who stages any sort of demo. Home tomorrow.

MONDAY 11 SEPTEMBER Met Alan Jay Lerner at *Kaleidoscope*: found him dull and oddly lugubrious considering what he has done, regretting the decline of the big-scale stage musical and I suspect uneasily aware that only *My Fair Lady* was any good . . . I mean, think of *Camelot*! Think of *Gigi*, worse still! I should like to have taken him to task for the grammatical solecisms in *My Fair Lady* which sound so terrible in the mouth of the eminent philologist Higgins is supposed to be: 'By rights he should be taken out and hung/For the cold-blooded murder of the English tongue.' Lerner became almost lachrymose when quoting his own lines about Camelot (Don't let it be forgot [*sic*], That once there

232

was a spot, For one brief shining moment/That was known as Camelot, etc.) and the fortuitous significance they acquired on the death of Kennedy. Lerner has one eye, or only one that works. Perhaps that accounts for his askance view of his trade. Reading Nicholas Monsarrat, yet another best-selling mediocrity. Quote: 'Then chance, the most precious clove-spice in the whole pomander of life, came to his aid, and set him on the high road, perhaps for ever.' There's a thought for today.

TUESDAY 12 SEPTEMBER   And *here* is a good moment from M. M. Kaye's epic *The Far Pavilions* that we're doing: 'She was also sweet and innocent and young (two years younger than Ash) and, in addition to a charming, wilful face that was set off to admiration by a wealth of pale gold ringlets, was the fortunate possessor of a small straight nose that wrinkled deliciously when she laughed, a pair of large cornflower-blue eyes that sparkled with interest and eagerness for life, and a kissable mouth made more inviting by the fact that a dimple hovered near each corner . . . ' And where did she keep all those odds and ends? This book is the fiction bombshell of the season, so Allen Lane confidently expect, and the US paperback rights have gone for a rumoured £57,000-odd.

SATURDAY 23 SEPTEMBER   Günter Grass's book *The Flounder* is giving me reader's cramp. It is a *Kaleidoscope* biggie: 500 pages if it's one, and not a decent narrative thread in sight. Anyway what kind of writer is it who allows the blurb to say: 'Five years before his fiftieth birthday, Günter Grass decided that he would write a major novel as a present for himself.' Funny, that: I had made the same decision, and I didn't do it either.

Epilogue

SO THAT'S ENOUGH of reminiscence and raking over the past. It can become an addiction: sometimes I can almost believe that with an effort of concentration I could call to mind nearly everything that has ever happened in my life. Perhaps the earliest pictures would be imprecise and sketchy, if only at first. Lying in a pram in the front garden staring up at big, white fluffy clouds cruising overhead . . . the smell of the mackintosh cover over the woolly blankets . . . my mother picking me up and comforting me when I was frightened by the huge face of some visitor – a man in a light grey hat . . . walking to my grandmother's house and passing a nearby front garden where there were chickens in a hen-house by the front wall . . .

Then the memories would take on a sharper outline. The room tipping under my feet as my head spins in a dizzy spell. She comforting me again. *Mummy, the room's going round and round!* On another day Dr Gilchrist, our family doctor, picking me up: he places a funny rubber mask over my face and tells me to take a deep breath and I swallow a big mouthful of some sweetish, sickly air. Afterwards she tells me: you've had your tonsils out.

Margate holidays: cricket on the beach, a sand-castle competition won by my brother David, the swimming pool on the promenade with real sea water. Highlight of the fortnight: the

234

annual visit to Dreamland and its penny arcades, the dodgem cars and, keenly looked forward to, a voyage in a wooden tub, the four of us all together, through some mysterious underground waterway designed for lovers, the silence broken by the quiet splashing of the electrically impelled current as we pass grottoes in the dim, romantic light where wooden figures are posed: elves, fairies, magicians. Who are they? What are they doing? Then the round wooden craft twists, and we are floating in a dim tunnel again and suddenly we are out in the warm evening air and the crowds are strolling past, eating ice creams, toffee-apples and fresh cockles from paper bags. I can hear fairground music, the snap of air-rifles being fired; my father takes a turn and wins nothing . . .

Sounds stay tenaciously in my memory: some people, said Copland, are more ear-minded than others. Music is what I experience most sharply. A new memory comes back: I have found a steel paper-clip in the school playground and I am marching about pretending it is a trombone because of its shape. How did this idea come to me? Where have I seen a trombone? Was it in a Salvation Army band I saw on a street corner? Then I am playing with my grandfather's violin: I am on the floor, pushing it along the carpet, pretending it is a boat – the bow is a sailor. They pick it up and take it away. I am very young, perhaps four years old. In the room, the gramophone is playing *The Blue Danube*, then the *Radetzki March*. My uncle puts on his record of the Unfinished Symphony, given him by their neighbour Mrs Bull.

Now I think of Mrs Bull's small daughter June. She is my age. Their big double-fronted house in Upper Tulse Hill has a huge garden. June lets me drive her pedal car all round it, down to the bottom, out of sight of the house, where giant laurel bushes and rhododendrons are dripping after heavy rain. Then we are upstairs in a bedroom – perhaps her parents' room – climbing through a secret doorway to a room above the garage. Mr Bull's big black car is down below but the room we are in is out of bounds: there is a desk there. I open a drawer and there are papers. June whispers to me not to look at them. Why not? What are they? I am in a secret, forbidden place with this pretty little girl, with her curly black hair, merry eyes and dimpled chin. More than sixty years later, I dream still about secret rooms in great, rambling houses, rooms reached through narrow tunnels.

Writing this book has been not unlike a dream: conjuring forth pictures of times and people and places that had been buried under a compost of other lived-through events . . . scraping back layers to get at what is below.

Often I think of John Garrett, the secondary influence on my life, headmaster of the suburban school I went to, with its hand-picked staff and infectious commitment to the arts and radical politics of the thirties. I think of Garrett's small, pedantic handwriting, always in bright blue ink . . . his imperious stare and those italicised vowels. His dandy-aesthete wardrobe and his fashionable opinions. I think of him often and on the whole with gratitude for having brought about for me the sort of education I required, though I might not have known I required it.

His pretensions which once seemed so absurd are now easier to understand: the impulse towards betterment, which animated my father's early life but faded with the Second World War, also moved John Garrett. His talents took him further: to Oxford – for him as for so many others a crucially formative experience – and to his friendship with Auden, Day Lewis and the other members of that group . . . to his first headship, at Raynes Park, and then to Bristol Grammar School. There, the upward movement on his own personal graph flattened out. Further advancement, to somewhere more famous – Harrow, perhaps, or St Paul's – was denied him. I once entertained the view that his stroke, at a comparatively early age, was an answer to the frustration of his own life-plan. But I doubt if his *milieu intérieur* worked quite like that, and measured in terms of social prestige and even celebrity Garrett was far from being a failure.

236

*

We are tied to our past by invisible threads. Would my first marriage have come to grief if my father and mother had not parted? I doubt it. But I think of him and try to imagine his thoughts about it all: his restlessness and disappointment at the way things had turned out after the excitement of demobilisation from a victorious army.

I look back on his life and it doesn't seem to me to have been a happy one. His job doubtless offered a bit more than exciting times in the accounts department – although I suspect there was a lot of that kind of thing attached to the secretary-ship of the Linoleum Association. He succeeded at his job, but not in his home life. Bad enough that his first marriage should have ended in disaster: doubly unfortunate, and unfair as well, that his next one should also have failed. Then, not long after his second wife died, he married yet again. His third wife was a motherly, lonely soul who tried to make him happy, spoiled him with big, rich meals of fruit pies and cream, dumplings and roast meat and potatoes mashed with butter, while he grew more and more moody and dissatisfied. Eventually, gouty, overweight and diabetic; hypertensive, hard-up and irritable; at the age of eighty-six he suffered a stroke. His life came to an end in a hospital on the Kent coast. As it happens, the hospital is only a short drive from Margate. Dreamland was not far away.

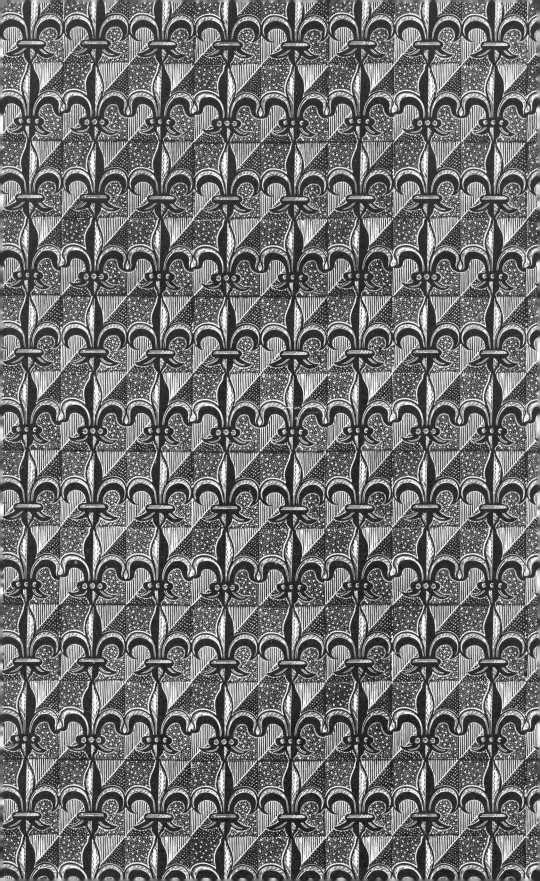